DISCOVERING BASIC

A Problem Solving Approach

Hayden Computer Programming Series

James N. Haag, Consulting Editor
Professor of Computer Science and Physics
University of San Francisco

COMPREHENSIVE STANDARD FORTRAN PROGRAMMING
James N. Haag

COMPREHENSIVE FORTRAN PROGRAMMING
James N. Haag

BASICS OF DIGITAL COMPUTER PROGRAMMING (Rev. 2nd Ed.)
John S. Murphy

BASIC BASIC: An Introduction to Computer Programming in BASIC Language
James S. Coan

ADVANCED BASIC: Applications and Problems
James S. Coan

DISCOVERING BASIC: A Problem Solving Approach
Robert E. Smith

BEGINNING FORTRAN: Simplified, 12-Statement Programming
John Maniotes, Harry B. Higley, and James N. Haag

ASSEMBLY LANGUAGE BASICS: An Annotated Program Book
Irving A. Dodes

PROGRAMMING PROVERBS
Henry F. Ledgard

PROGRAMMING PROVERBS FOR FORTRAN PROGRAMMERS
Henry F. Ledgard

COBOL WITH STYLE: Programming Proverbs
Louis J. Chmura and Henry F. Ledgard

SNOBOL: An Introduction to Programming
Peter R. Newsted

FORTRAN FUNDAMENTALS: A Short Course
Jack Steingraber

DISCOVERING BASIC

A Problem Solving Approach

ROBERT E. SMITH

Staff Consultant, Educational Research

Control Data Corporation

HAYDEN BOOK COMPANY, INC.
Rochelle Park, New Jersey

 Library of Congress Catalog Card Number: 78-134843

Printed in the United States of America

11 12 13 14 15 16 17 18 PRINTING

78 79 80 81 82 83 84 85 86 YEAR

Preface

BASIC (Beginner's All Purpose Symbolic Instruction Code) was developed especially for time-sharing computer users. It was designed for people who had no previous knowledge of computers as well as for those more expert. It was planned for the businessman, the scientist, and the student.

Learning a new computer language is like learning to drive a car. It can be fun and at the same time filled with interesting experiences, or it can be the opposite. In both cases, a great deal depends upon the degree of participation of the learner. The fun and challenge in learning to drive a car quickly evaporate if the learner must memorize many rules and never gets to drive the car. Likewise, the neophyte in computer programming is apt to lose interest if he cannot see progress in terms of computer applications.

The basic premises of this book are built upon these two aspects: learning can be fun and at the same time interesting. It was with this thought in mind that the author decided to take up his pen and attempt to encourage students to develop BASIC skills as they discover how this modern computer language works.

The author used an International Timesharing, Inc. system with a Control Data Corporation 3300 computer at the other end. Your executive commands may be slightly different.

Minneapolis, Minn. ROBERT E. SMITH

Contents

DISCOVERING BASIC

A Problem Solving Approach

Lesson 1
Numbers and Variables

Numbers

Maybe you have heard that computers operate on number representatives. They do. BASIC is excellent in this respect since one can write numbers in a natural way. For example:

157	3.1415	38E5	-256E6
6.2	-77000	.12E-3	-.012E4

The last four may be strange. However, these are quite simple. The letter "E" means "10 raised to a power". Thus:

38E5 is 38 times $(10)^5$ = 38 times 100000 = 3800000
.12E-3 is .12 times $(10)^{-3}$ = .12 times .001 = .00012

Variables

"Variables" are names we select for a dual role: to represent numbers and at the same time, names of the computer cells where these numbers are located. BASIC requires variables to be either: (1) a single letter, (2) a single letter followed by a single digit. For example:

B		3T	
G	These are	6	These are
C1	O.K.	CA2	N.G.
D7		D75	(no good)

A common statement in BASIC is:

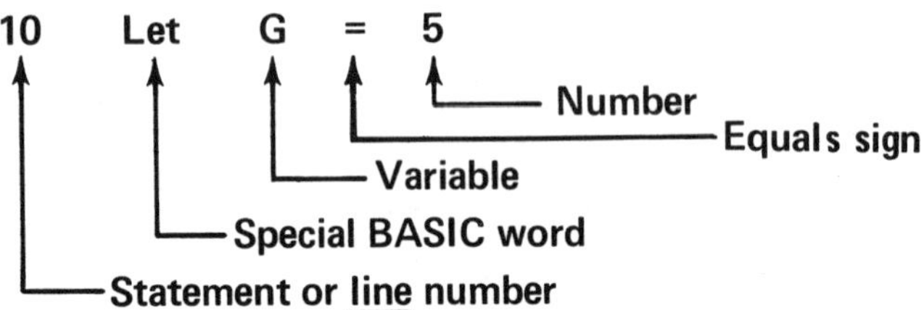

This statement will cause the computer to generate a 5 and put it in a cell whose variable name is "G". Later, we can tell the computer the following:

20 Let G = 17

Now cell G has a 17 placed in it! Therefore cells can hold many different values but only one at a time. It's like your tape recorder - the last one in is it!

Why not compose a little program that uses numbers and variables? First, let's try something hard - multiply 2 by 3!

```
10 LET K = 2
20 LET G = 3
30 LET R = K * G
40 PRINT K, G, R
50 END
```

asterisk (*) means multiply in BASIC

Let's begin with our first problem. First, we enter the system by pushing the "ORIG" button. And dialing the correct number. Back comes a request for identification. This we enter. Then:

Computer Messages:	**You TYPE the Following:**
What System?	BASIC
New or Old?	NEW
New File Name?	AA
READY	10 Let K = 2
	20 Let G = 3
	30 Let R = K * G
	40 Print K, G, R
	50 END
	SAVE
READY	RUN

If you make an error while typing the program above simply:

Retype the line with its number.

To delete a line, simply retype the line number.

To insert a line, use a number between the two numbers where insertion is to occur.

If an error is noticed while typing a line, one can use a backward arrow (←) for each incorrect character. Then type correct ones.

Now change the previous program to:

```
10 LET K = 2
20 LET G = 3
30 LET R = K + G
40 PRINT K, G, R
50 END
```

What is the difference? Yes, addition is +. How about subtraction? Yes, it is –. And divide is the slash,/.

Is it necessary to retype the whole program above? No. Simply type the following:

Computer Messages:	**You TYPE the Following:**
	OLD
Old File Name?	AA
READY	30 LET R = K + G
	SAVE
READY	RUN

If someone else had preceded you on the teletype you might have to first load your program (AA) before the above typing. For example:

	LOAD
From?	AA
Old File?	YES
READY	30 LET R = K + G
	SAVE
READY	RUN

Rerun the same program using minus and slash in line 30.

Lesson 2
Order of Calculations

Have you ever been asked to do a problem such as the following? Try it.

Find: 5 + 10/5 * 2 – 6

Are you somewhat confused? Let's have the computer do this problem. First, write a short BASIC program as:

```
10 LET X = 5 + 10/5 * 2 – 6
20 PRINT X
30 END
```

Now enter the program as follows:

Computer Messages:	You TYPE the Following:
What System	BASIC
New or Old	NEW
New File Name	AA
READY	10 LET X = 5 + 10/5 * 2 – 6
	20 PRINT X
	30 END
	RUN

The answer is: 3! The computer calculates:

Divide first, since divide	= 5 + 10/5 * 2 – 6
precedes the multiply.	= 5 + 2 * 2 – 6
Then multiply. Then	= 5 + 4 – 6
add and then subtract.	= 3

To represent an exponent in BASIC, we use the upper pointing arrow (↑ or some use **). Thus,

2^3 is written 2 ↑ 3.

Let us try another example such as the previous one. Find:

$$5 + 10/5 * 2^3 - 6$$

Our BASIC "program" is as follows:

```
10 LET X = 5 + 10/5 * 2 ↑ 3 - 6
20 PRINT X
30 END
```

Now, the answer is 15! The computer calculates:

<u>First</u> finds exponent value	=	5 + 10/5 * 8 – 6
<u>Next,</u> divide	=	5 + 2 * 8 – 6
<u>Next,</u> multiply	=	5 + 16 – 6
<u>Last,</u> add and subtract	=	15

The order is: <u>negation</u>, <u>exponents</u>, <u>divide</u> or <u>multiply</u> (whichever comes first) and then <u>add</u> and <u>subtract</u>. However, we can change this order by using <u>parentheses.</u> Thus:

$5 + 10/5 * (2^3 - 6) = 9$ Try it !
$5 + 10/(5 * 2^3) - 6 = -0.75$ Try it!
$(5 + 10)/5 * 2^3 - 6 = 18$ Try it !
$(5 + 10)/5 * (2^3 - 6) = 6$ Try it !
$5 + (+ 10^2/5) * (2^3 - 6) = 45$ Try it !

Lesson 3
Built-In Functions

BASIC contains some special "built-in" programs (called "functions") which enable you to do special calculations. These are:

SIN(X)	sine	ABS(X)	abs. value
COS(X)	cosine	LOG(X)	logarithm
TAN(X)	tangent	SQR(X)	square root
ATN(X)	arc tan	RND(X)	random no.
EXP(X)	e to x power	INT(X)	integer part of x

All that is required, is to tell the computer the value of X (the argument) and where to put the result. For example:

```
10   LET X = 976525      This program will find square
20   LET Y = SQR(X)      root of 976525 and put
30   PRINT Y             result in Y Try it!
40   END
```

Of course, you do not have to use "X" all the time to hold the value. Any legal variable is permitted. Also, one can put the value directly in the parentheses. For example:

```
20   LET Y = SQR(976525)                    Try it!
```

Likewise, the argument can be an expression. For example: find sq. root of $3X^2+5$ where X=75.8

```
10   LET X = 75.8
20   LET Y = SQR(3*x↑2+5)                   Try it!
30   PRINT Y
40   END
```

If you have had some of the other functions, they work the same way. To find the natural logarithm of 3, try either of the following:

```
10 LET R=3
20 LET W=LOG(R)   |   20 LET W=LOG(3)
30 PRINT W       or   30 PRINT W
40 END            |   40 END
```

To turn this into a common logarithm (base 10), we can multiply by .434294482 ($\log_{10} e$). For example, common log of 100 is 2. Try the following:

```
10 LET Z=100
20 LET Y=.434294482*LOG(Z)
30 PRINT Y
40 END                          Did you get 2?
```

The random number function might be interesting. Why not try it? For example:

```
10 LET B=RND(X) |
20 PRINT B      or   20 PRINT RND(X)
30 END          |    30 END
```

The "X" (argument) has no significance with RND since the computer simply generates a random number between 0 and 1. Many systems do not require any variable to appear inside the parentheses.

If you have had the trigonometric functions, try a few. Arguments must be in radians. Thus, to find sine of 30 degrees, try:

```
10 LET X=30*3.14159/180 ──┐
20 LET Y=SIN(X)           ↓
30 PRINT Y            30 degrees=30π/180 radians
40 END
```

Lesson 4
Program Looping

So far, we have been calculating one result. In other words, we have been using our computer as a simple "calculating machine". Let's change our tactics.

We want to tell the computer to do something, then make a change and do the thing over again, etc. For example, let's make the computer count from 1 through 25. Try the following program!

```
10  LET N=1
20  PRINT N  ←————————  do something
30  LET N=N+1  ←——————  change something
40  IF N<26 THEN 20  ←——  test no. of loops
50  END
```

The new aspects above are lines 30 and 40. Line 30 increases the old value in N by 1. Line 40 is an "IF" statement. It tells the computer to:

Jump to line 20 if N is less than 26.

NOTE < is the symbol for "is less than".
  > is the symbol for "is more than".
  = is the symbol for "is equal to".

Try counting 10, 20,........ thru 100.

```
10  LET N=10
20  PRINT N
30  LET N=N+10
40  IF N<110 THEN 20
50  END
```

How about 10, 9.5, 9, ... thru .5

```
10 LET J=10
20 PRINT J
30 LET J=J-.5
40 IF J>0 THEN 20
50 END
```

Be relaxed! Don't get the idea there's only one way to do this looping. There are many. For example, try: $\sqrt{100}$, $\sqrt{90}$, $\sqrt{80}$ . . . . thru $\sqrt{10}$.

```
10 LET X=110
20 LET X=X-10
30 IF X=0 THEN 70
40 LET Y=SQR(X)
50 PRINT Y
60 GO TO 20 <----------
70 END
```

Here we use a simple "go to" statement in order to jump back to line 20

Now of course, you can also try it by:

```
10 LET X=100
20 LET Y=SQR(X)
30 PRINT Y
40 LET X=X-10
50 IF X>0 THEN 20
60 END
```

How about these two on your own?

1^3, 3^3, 5^3, 7^3, ... thru 11^3.

1/2, 2/3, 3/4, 4/5, ... thru 9/10.

Lesson 5
Flow Charting

Here is a topic that many time sharers attempt to pass over - or at least neglect. The author's advice is to make it part of your programming. If it does nothing more than document your work for someone else, it is worth your time. In addition, it will be a significant aid to you in the more intricate applications.

Flow charting can be a real bore if you permit it to be. First of all, keep your flow charts broad in scope. Do not attempt to put details into them. Leave that for your BASIC program.

Let us agree, in this course, to use only four symbols. These are:

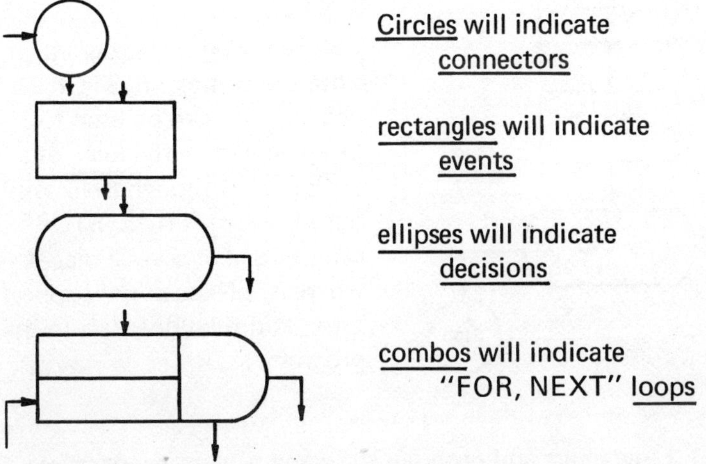

Only the first three will be used at this time.

We begin with an example. Have the computer print a table of square roots with output similar to the following:

```
 1        1
 2        1.41421356
 3        1.73205081
 4        2
 .
 .
25        5
```

Flow Chart

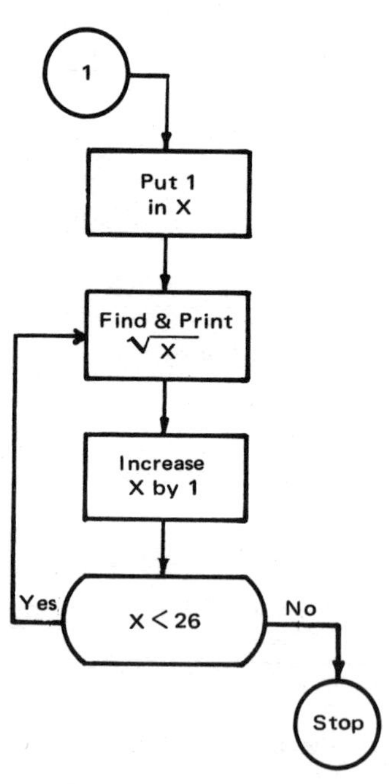

Program

```
10 LET X = 1
20 LET Y = SQR(X)
25 PRINT X, Y
30 LET X = X + 1
40 IF X<26 THEN 20
50 STOP
60 END
```

Before trying this program, note the command, STOP, above. This can be used to bring an end to the logic of a problem. Although END will have the same effect; STOP can be used at several places, whereas, END can only appear once, and then only last in the program.

Flow chart and program the same type of problem as above, except find logarithms.

Lesson 6
Printing a Heading

Assume one wishes to print the heading:

DAYS DAILY AMOUNT TOTAL SAVED

BASIC provides for 5 zones of 15 places each per line. A comma is a signal to "move to the next zone". Thus, the following statement would print the results in A,B,C respectively in zones 1,2,3.

10 PRINT A,B,C

To print heading or label messages, one need only inclose the message in quotes. To print the above heading, one uses:

20 PRINT "DAYS", "DAILY AMOUNT", "TOTAL SAVED"

To skip a line below the heading, one can simply write PRINT without anything following it. Therefore to print the above heading, skip a line, and then print the values 2,3,4 (respectively in A,B,C), one can write:

```
10 LET A=2
20 LET B=3
30 LET C=4
40 PRINT "DAYS", "DAILY AMOUNT", "TOTAL SAVED"
50 PRINT
60 PRINT A, B, C
70 END
```

Try it!

Some systems carry 6 significant digits for non integers and 9 digits for integers. The ITS system (International Time Sharing, Inc.) carries 9 digits for non integer as well as integer.

Generally, the results start one place in from the left zone position. Consequently, for some headings - using quotes - the heading may be slightly askew. Nevertheless, this is not of too great a concern - even a heading that is slightly askew is better than none.

Keep in mind, that by including spaces as part of the heading, it is possible to shift headers to the right. For example:

DAYS	TOTAL
25	335544.31
26	671088.63
27	1342177.27

To move header TOTAL above to the right 2 places, we can write:

30 PRINT "DAYS", "△△TOTAL"

put 2 spaces here ⟶ ↑

To move headers to the left is more difficult. To do so usually requires FORMAT which is another method of printing that we will not examine. For this course, we will be content with "quote" headings even if they are sometimes not perfectly centered.

Lesson 7
An Excellent Way To Save Money

Assume one is able to save money as follows: 1 cent the first day, 2 cents the second day, 4 cents the third day, ... etc; each day doubling the preceding amount saved. Print a table showing the DAYS, DAILY AMOUNT, and TOTAL SAVED if this plan can be followed for 29 days.

Flow Chart

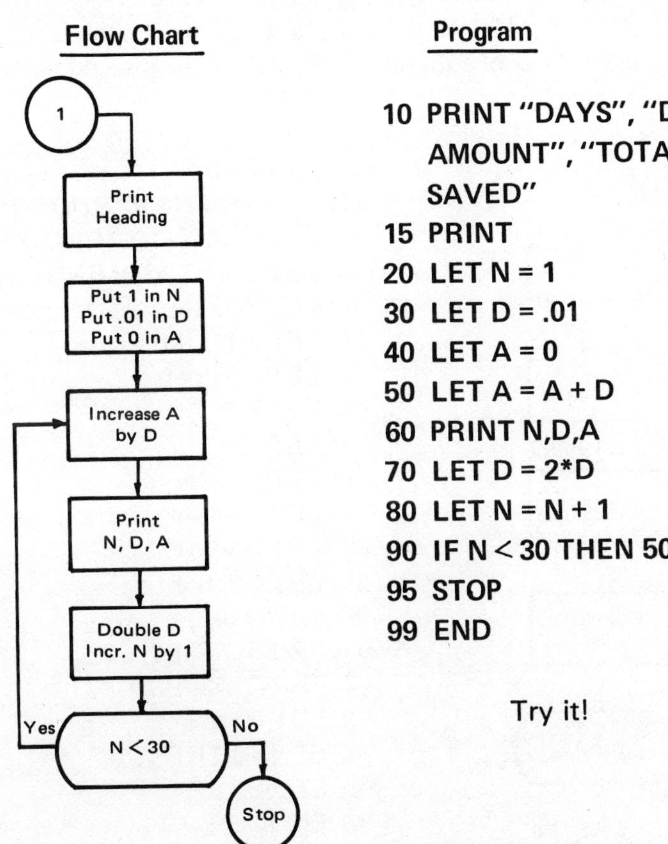

Program

```
10 PRINT "DAYS", "DAILY
   AMOUNT", "TOTAL
   SAVED"
15 PRINT
20 LET N = 1
30 LET D = .01
40 LET A = 0
50 LET A = A + D
60 PRINT N,D,A
70 LET D = 2*D
80 LET N = N + 1
90 IF N < 30 THEN 50
95 STOP
99 END
```

Try it!

Random Magic Squares

A programmer is able to build magic squares by using integer values for J, K, L and arranging these integers as follows:

J + L	L-(J+K)	K + L
K+L-J	L	J+L-K
L - K	J+K+L	L - J

He uses: INT(100*RND(X)) to get 5 sets of integers for J, K, L. By using 100*RND(X) he gets values between 0 and 100. Then the use of function, INT, selects the integral parts of these values.

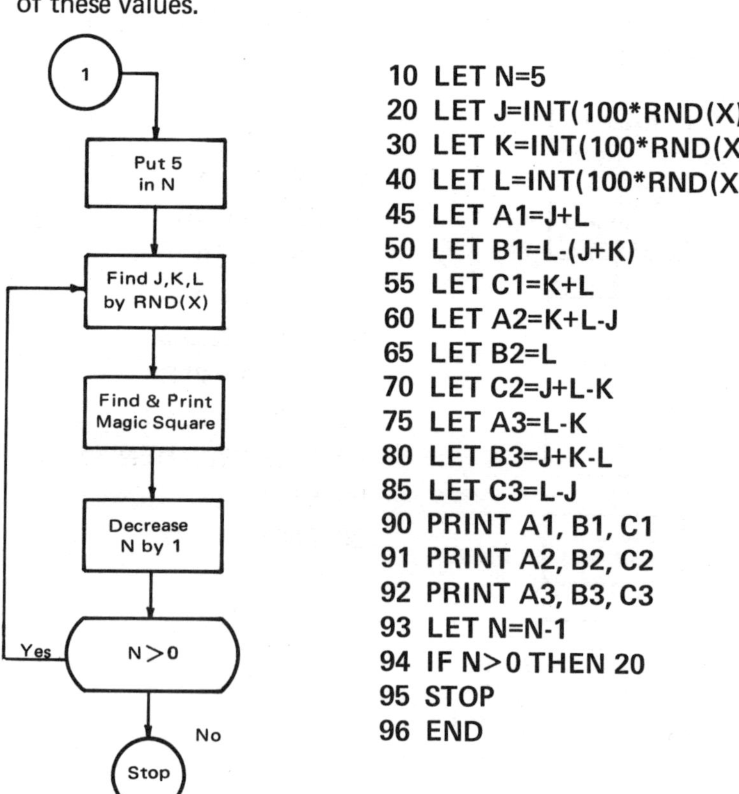


```
10 LET N=5
20 LET J=INT(100*RND(X))
30 LET K=INT(100*RND(X))
40 LET L=INT(100*RND(X))
45 LET A1=J+L
50 LET B1=L-(J+K)
55 LET C1=K+L
60 LET A2=K+L-J
65 LET B2=L
70 LET C2=J+L-K
75 LET A3=L-K
80 LET B3=J+K-L
85 LET C3=L-J
90 PRINT A1, B1, C1
91 PRINT A2, B2, C2
92 PRINT A3, B3, C3
93 LET N=N-1
94 IF N>0 THEN 20
95 STOP
96 END
```

Lesson 8
A Piece of Pi

An exotic value in the world of numbers is the irrational value pi (3.14159265358979323849...). Surprisingly, several sums approach this value when the number of terms increase. For example:

$$\text{pi} = 4\left[1-1/3+1/5-1/7+1/9\ \ldots\ \text{etc.}\right]$$

Write a BASIC program to find and print the above value for 10000, 20000 . . . . 100000 terms.

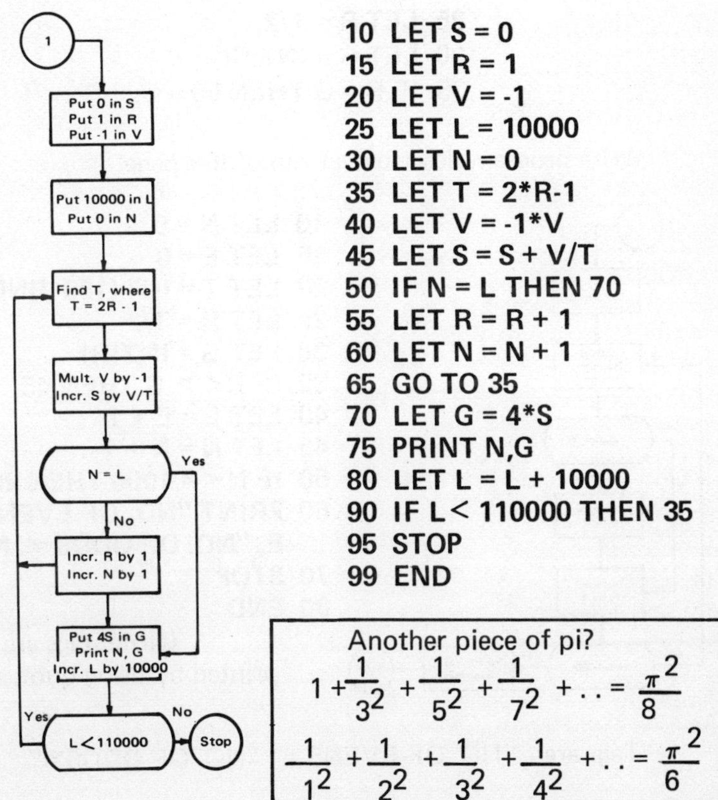


```
10 LET S = 0
15 LET R = 1
20 LET V = -1
25 LET L = 10000
30 LET N = 0
35 LET T = 2*R-1
40 LET V = -1*V
45 LET S = S + V/T
50 IF N = L THEN 70
55 LET R = R + 1
60 LET N = N + 1
65 GO TO 35
70 LET G = 4*S
75 PRINT N,G
80 LET L = L + 10000
90 IF L< 110000 THEN 35
95 STOP
99 END
```

Another piece of pi?

$$1+\frac{1}{3^2}+\frac{1}{5^2}+\frac{1}{7^2}+\ldots=\frac{\pi^2}{8}$$

$$\frac{1}{1^2}+\frac{1}{2^2}+\frac{1}{3^2}+\frac{1}{4^2}+\ldots=\frac{\pi^2}{6}$$

Write a BASIC program to find 1000 random integers between 0 and 100. Determine how many of these are odd and how many are even.

An integer is even if it can be exactly divided by 2. How can one determine a division is exact?

One method is to use the BASIC function, INT(X), which selects the integer part of an argument. Therefore, after a divide, one can use INT to determine if the quotient is an integer. If so, the division is exact. Example: Determine if T is even?

```
25 LET R = T/2
30 LET G = INT (R)
35 IF R = G THEN 50
```

Write program described at top of this page.

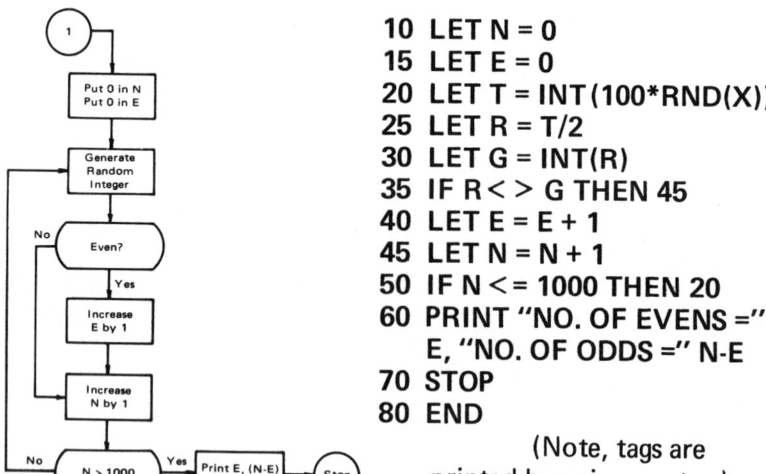


```
10 LET N = 0
15 LET E = 0
20 LET T = INT(100*RND(X))
25 LET R = T/2
30 LET G = INT(R)
35 IF R<> G THEN 45
40 LET E = E + 1
45 LET N = N + 1
50 IF N <= 1000 THEN 20
60 PRINT "NO. OF EVENS ="
   E, "NO. OF ODDS =" N-E
70 STOP
80 END
```

(Note, tags are printed by using quotes.)

Tags are: "NO. OF EVENS =" "NO. OF ODDS ="

Lesson 9
Time Out for Brief Review

The previous problem contained several "goodies". First, the use of INT(X) to determine if a division is exact. Is this clear? How about another example? Assume a random integer between 0 and 1000 is generated. Then divide the integer by 7. If exact, print the number preceded by the message "multiple of 7=". If not exact, simply print the message "not exact".

Let's try this without a flow chart.

```
10 LET Y = INT (1000 * RND(X))
20 LET W = Y/7
30 LET P = INT (W)
40 IF P = W THEN 70
50 PRINT "NOT EXACT"
60 STOP
70 PRINT "MULTIPLE OF 7 = " Y
80 STOP                    (Note use of more than
90 END                     one STOP in program)
```

Another "gem" from Lesson 8 was the use of relational symbols: " < > ". This means less than or greater than. In other words: "not equal". We had not used more than one symbol before. However, BASIC permits six combinations:

=	equal	< > = not equal
<	less than	> = not less than
>	greater than	< = not greater than

A third "ruby" in Lesson 8 was the printing of "tags". By "tags", we mean the cute little messages one can tack on to his results if he wishes to do so. All that is required is to inclose the tag in quotes. If a result follows, it will appear immediately to the right of the message. For example:

```
10 LET N = 1234
20 PRINT "YOU CAN'T EVEN COUNT" N
```

Can you imagine what this will print? Try it !

How about a "trailing tag". For example:

```
10 LET N = 1234
20 PRINT N " ΔΔ  DON'T ASK ME FOR MORE"
```

these are two spaces so that message will not crowd against value in N

So far you have had it pretty soft. Flow charts <u>and</u> programs have been provided. Things are going to become somewhat tougher. In many problems to follow, you will only get a flow chart. In these cases, the author suggests that <u>after</u> your program works satisfactorily, you get a <u>listing</u> (by typing LIST) and <u>paste</u> this on the card beside the flow chart. Or you can hand print (very neatly) your program in the space beside the flow chart. In either case, you will have complete documentation for later use.

Lesson 10
Five Scheming Monkeys

Five monkeys collected a huge mound of coconuts. One night when all were asleep, one awakened and crept quietly to the pile. He ate 1 coconut and then divided the remainder of the pile into 5 equal smaller piles. He then hid one pile, put the other 4 piles back in the original place, and went back to sleep. The 2nd, 3rd, 4th and 5th monkeys did exactly the same, in turn. In the morning all 5 gathered around the diminished mound – each pretending not to notice the decreased size – and for the sixth time one of the coconuts was eaten and the remainder divided into 5 equal smaller piles. How many coconuts were in the original mound?

Since each of the six divisions gave 5 equal parts after 1 had been eaten, the first possible number of coconuts is 6 (1 over 5). The next possible number is 11 (1 over 10), then 16 (1 over 15), etc. Why not have the computer start with 6 and see if it is possible to make six equal divisions after "eating" 1 coconut before each divide? If 6 is not the number, have the computer try 11, then 16, then 21, etc. up thru 100000. Surely, if there is an answer, it should be one under 100000.

Let us also print our results in a form similar to the following with tags as shown:

No. of coconuts = ddddd
No. of coconuts = ddddd
No. of coconuts = ddddd

(Since we are trying all possible numbers up to 100000, there are likely to be several answers.)

Scheming Monkeys (Continued)

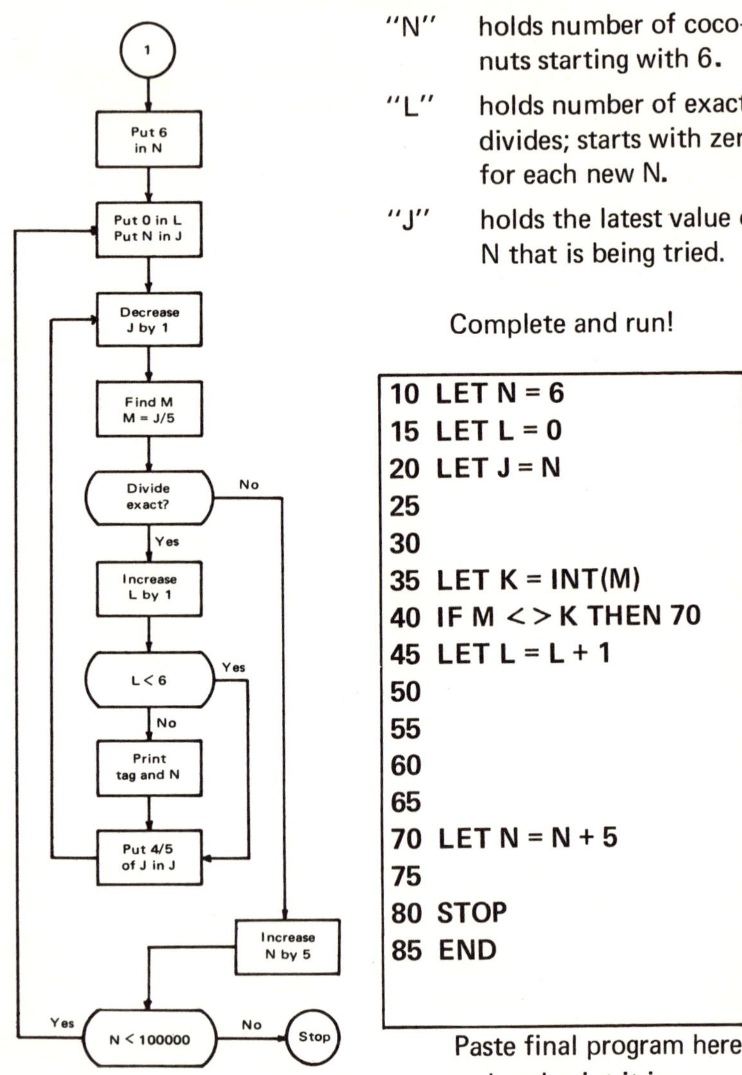

"N" holds number of coconuts starting with 6.

"L" holds number of exact divides; starts with zero for each new N.

"J" holds the latest value of N that is being tried.

Complete and run!

```
10  LET N = 6
15  LET L = 0
20  LET J = N
25
30
35  LET K = INT(M)
40  IF M <> K THEN 70
45  LET L = L + 1
50
55
60
65
70  LET N = N + 5
75
80  STOP
85  END
```

Paste final program here or hand print it in.

Review Test 1

Every once in awhile we stop and take a "sounding" of our progress. This is one. Answer the following questions by placing the correct numbers in the blank lines.

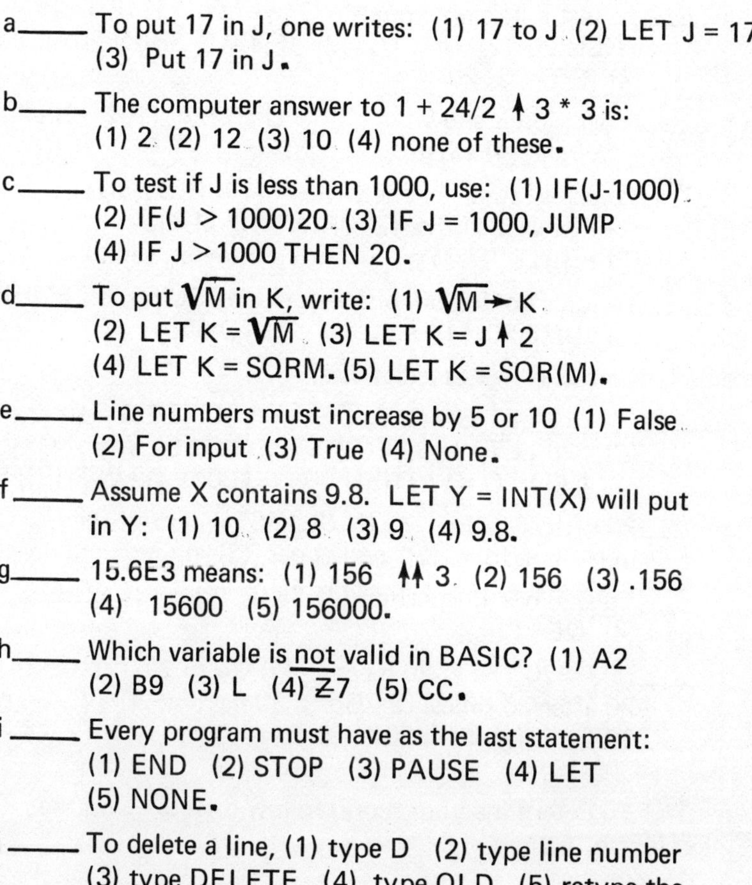

a_____ To put 17 in J, one writes: (1) 17 to J (2) LET J = 17 (3) Put 17 in J.

b_____ The computer answer to 1 + 24/2 ↑ 3 * 3 is: (1) 2 (2) 12 (3) 10 (4) none of these.

c_____ To test if J is less than 1000, use: (1) IF(J-1000) (2) IF(J > 1000)20 (3) IF J = 1000, JUMP (4) IF J >1000 THEN 20.

d_____ To put √M in K, write: (1) √M → K (2) LET K = √M (3) LET K = J ↑ 2 (4) LET K = SQRM. (5) LET K = SQR(M).

e_____ Line numbers must increase by 5 or 10 (1) False (2) For input (3) True (4) None.

f_____ Assume X contains 9.8. LET Y = INT(X) will put in Y: (1) 10 (2) 8 (3) 9 (4) 9.8.

g_____ 15.6E3 means: (1) 156 ↑↑ 3 (2) 156 (3) .156 (4) 15600 (5) 156000.

h_____ Which variable is <u>not</u> valid in BASIC? (1) A2 (2) B9 (3) L (4) Ƶ7 (5) CC.

i_____ Every program must have as the last statement: (1) END (2) STOP (3) PAUSE (4) LET (5) NONE.

j_____ To delete a line, (1) type D (2) type line number (3) type DELETE (4) type OLD (5) retype the line.

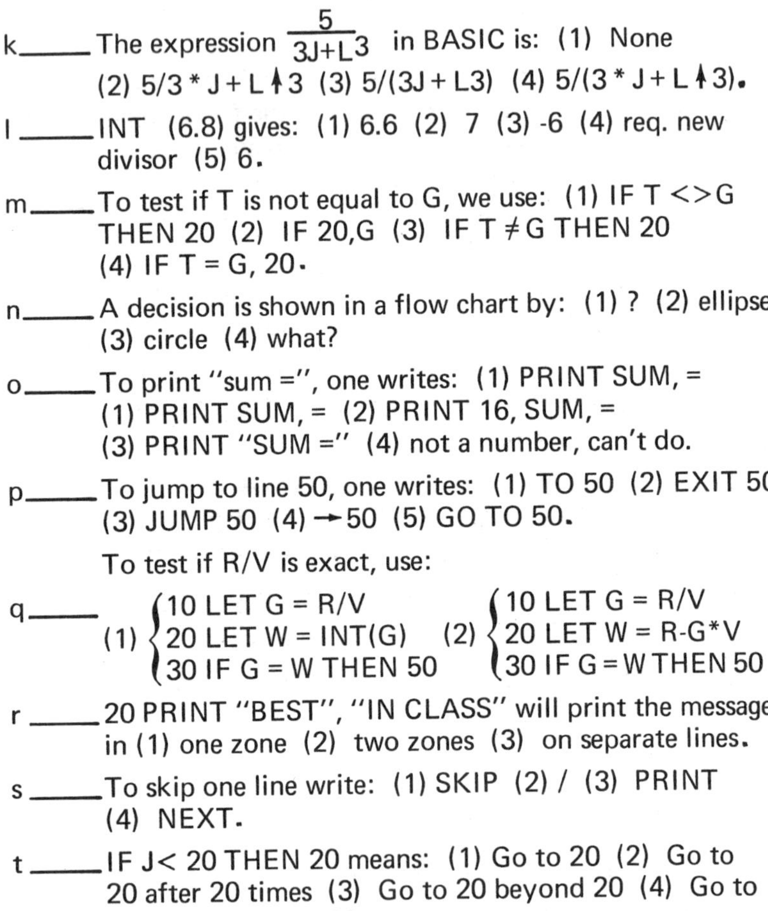

Review 1 (Continued)

k_____ The expression $\frac{5}{3J+L3}$ in BASIC is: (1) None (2) 5/3 * J + L ↑ 3 (3) 5/(3J + L3) (4) 5/(3 * J + L ↑ 3).

l _____ INT (6.8) gives: (1) 6.6 (2) 7 (3) -6 (4) req. new divisor (5) 6.

m_____ To test if T is not equal to G, we use: (1) IF T <>G THEN 20 (2) IF 20,G (3) IF T ≠ G THEN 20 (4) IF T = G, 20.

n_____ A decision is shown in a flow chart by: (1) ? (2) ellipse (3) circle (4) what?

o_____ To print "sum =", one writes: (1) PRINT SUM, = (1) PRINT SUM, = (2) PRINT 16, SUM, = (3) PRINT "SUM =" (4) not a number, can't do.

p_____ To jump to line 50, one writes: (1) TO 50 (2) EXIT 50 (3) JUMP 50 (4) → 50 (5) GO TO 50.

To test if R/V is exact, use:

q_____

(1)
```
10 LET G = R/V
20 LET W = INT(G)
30 IF G = W THEN 50
```

(2)
```
10 LET G = R/V
20 LET W = R-G*V
30 IF G = W THEN 50
```

r _____ 20 PRINT "BEST", "IN CLASS" will print the message in (1) one zone (2) two zones (3) on separate lines.

s _____ To skip one line write: (1) SKIP (2) / (3) PRINT (4) NEXT.

t _____ IF J< 20 THEN 20 means: (1) Go to 20 (2) Go to 20 after 20 times (3) Go to 20 beyond 20 (4) Go to 20 if J is less than 20.

To determine your score, follow directions on the next lesson.

Lesson 11
Scoring Review Test 1

Write your answers to the previous 20 questions in the places below (lines 95-98) putting 5 answers on each line and in order (first 5 on line 95, next 5 on line 96, etc)

Now type in the following program. When you RUN this program, it will tell you how well you did on the first review test.

```
10 LET S =0
12 LET R = 1
15 LET C = 1
20 READ A
25 LET T = R + C
30 IF T < 6 THEN 40
35 LET T = T – 5
40 IF A = T THEN 60
45 LET G = C * R
50 PRINT "YOU MISSED QUESTION NO." G
51 PRINT
55 GO TO 65
60 LET S = S + 1
65 LET C = C + 1
70 IF C < 6 THEN 20
75 LET R = R + 1
80 IF R < 5 THEN 15
85 PRINT
90 PRINT "YOU HAD ΔΔ "S" ΔΔ CORRECT
   ANSWERS"
92 PRINT "IF MORE THAN 15, CONGRATULATIONS"
95 DATA ____,____,____,____,____
96 DATA ____,____,____,____,____
97 DATA ____,____,____,____,____
98 DATA ____,____,____,____,____
99 END
```

Study the previous example. Pay particular attention to the DATA statements (lines 95-98) and the READ statement (line 20) both work together. The computer assigns each data item (following the word, DATA) to the next variable in the READ statement. Thus:

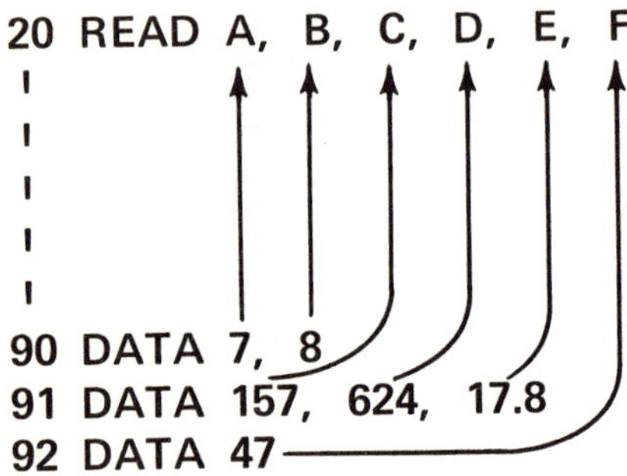

Note: first data item (7) is assigned to first read variable (A); second data item (8) is assigned to second variable (B); etc.

Easy enough — isn't it? One can have as many DATA lines as he desires. When the last data item is gone and the program tries another READ, some systems STOP the program. Other systems continue reading zeros. In such systems an "end of data" signal or flag is usually set. In the ITS system, for example, after READ, one can write

IF END DATA THEN n ← some line no.

This statement is used in this text. If your system does not have this statement, do not use it.

Lesson 12

Let us continue with other examples where data is READ into the computer. One simply lists values opposite each word, DATA, and separates each new value by commas. The computer picks each up, in order, and assigns it to the next variable in the READ statement. Let's try one.

Assume $Y = 3X^3 - X^2 + \sqrt{X}$

Find Y, when X = 3.8, 1, 6.78, and 68.2.

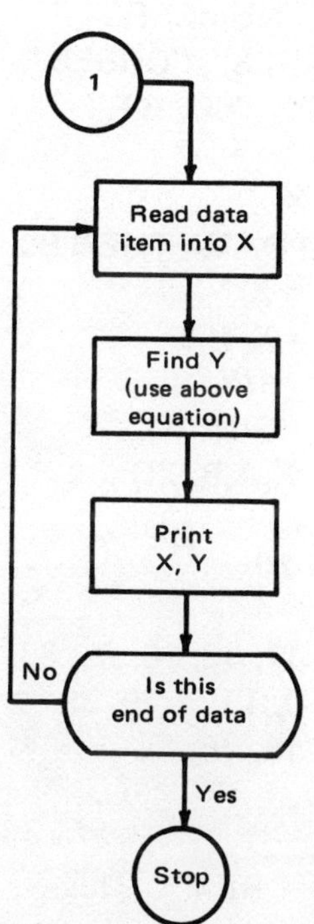


```
10 READ X
20 IF END DATA THEN 60
30 LET Y = 3*X ↑ 3 - X*X +
   SQR(X)
40 PRINT X, Y
50 GO TO 10
60 STOP
70 DATA 3.8, 1, 6.78
75 DATA 68.2
80 END
```

Some systems do not have the command shown in line 20. If yours does not, delete lines 20 and 60. In such systems when data runs out, the program is brought to an "effective stop". Note, all 4 data items above could have been placed in one DATA statement. Any number of DATA statements can be used. Try the above!

Read in 12 numbers of two digits each and print a table (with heading) as shown.

NUMBERS	SQUARES	CUBES	RECIP	SQ. RT.
25	625	15625	.04	5
17	289	4913	.0588	4.12...
etc.	etc.	etc.	etc.	etc.

You may use other values than those opposite DATA below.

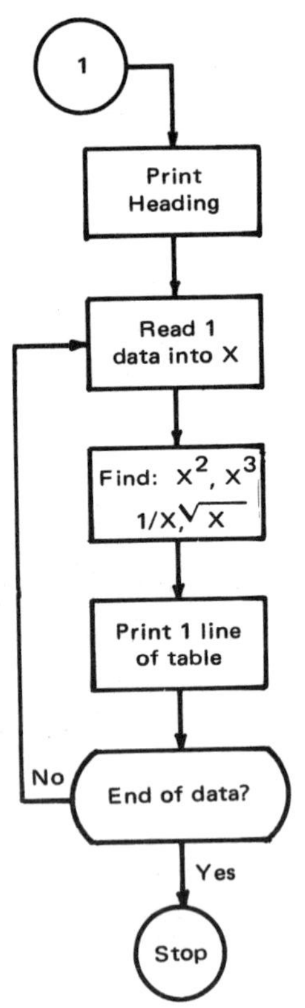


```
10 REM BUILDING A TABLE
15 PRINT "NUMBERS",
   "SQUARES", "CUBES",
   "RECIP", "SQ. RT."
16 PRINT
20 READ X
25 IF END DATA THEN 80
30 LET A = X * X
35 LET B = X ↑ 3
40 LET C = 1/X
50 LET D = SQR(X)
60 PRINT X,A,B,C,D
62 PRINT
65 GO TO 20
80 STOP
90 DATA 17, 32, 16, 25, 88
95 DATA 9, 15, 7, 29, 33
96 DATA 14, 26
99 END
```

Note use of "REM". This simply means "remark". Computer pays no attention to it. Can be used by programmer to identify his programs with names etc.

Lesson 13
Highest Common Factor

Is there a common factor of 629 and 1591? To find out, we can proceed as follows: Divide smaller into larger. If remainder is zero, the divisor is the H.C.F. If remainder is not zero; put the divisor into the dividend and the remainder into the divisor and divide again. Continue until a zero remainder is found. For example:

```
         2
629 | 1591               1
      1258      333 |  629                1
       333              333     296 |  333
rem. ≠ 0                296              296
                rem.≠ 0                   37
                                 rem.≠ 0
```

Therefore, after four divides, the remainder = 0 and thus, the H.C.F = 37

```
           8
   37 | 296
        296
rem. = 0  → 0
```

Remember, the H.C.F. is the divisor when a zero remainder is found.

Let us write a BASIC program to determine the H.C.F. of the following data sets:

2059 and 4189	1935 and 1763
53053 and 689	18103 and 5473
1824 and 6432	148037 and 44011

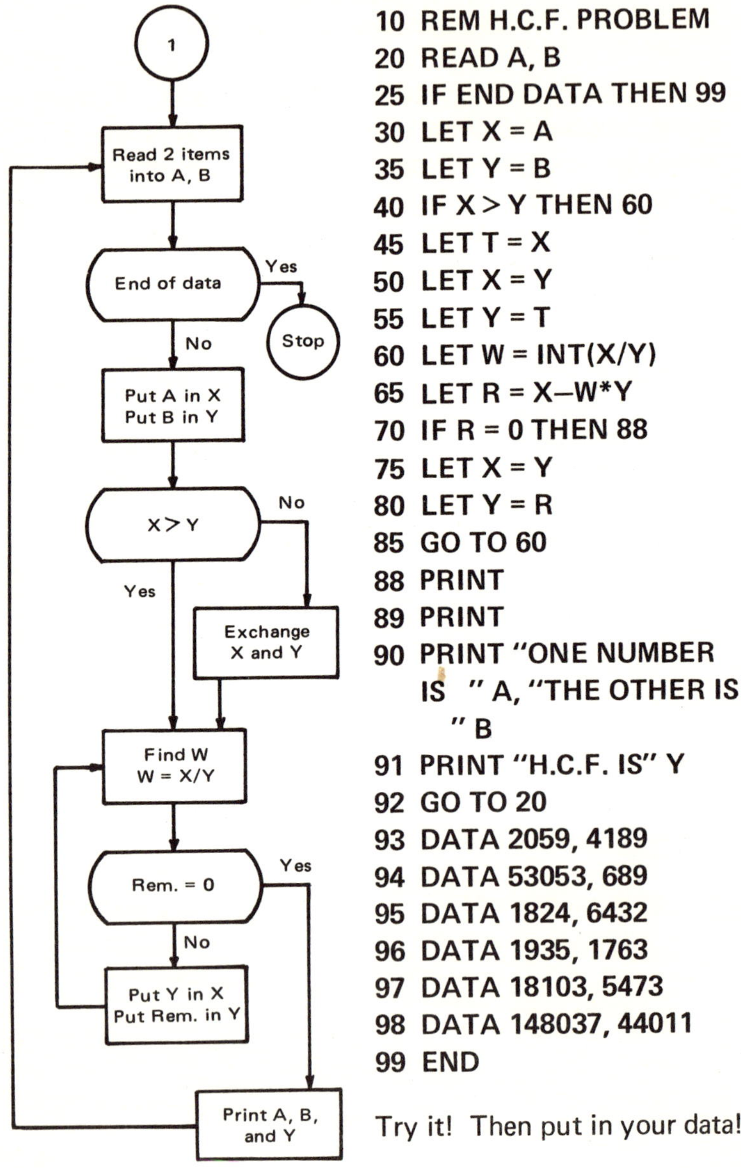


```
10 REM H.C.F. PROBLEM
20 READ A, B
25 IF END DATA THEN 99
30 LET X = A
35 LET Y = B
40 IF X > Y THEN 60
45 LET T = X
50 LET X = Y
55 LET Y = T
60 LET W = INT(X/Y)
65 LET R = X–W*Y
70 IF R = 0 THEN 88
75 LET X = Y
80 LET Y = R
85 GO TO 60
88 PRINT
89 PRINT
90 PRINT "ONE NUMBER
   IS   " A, "THE OTHER IS
     " B
91 PRINT "H.C.F. IS" Y
92 GO TO 20
93 DATA 2059, 4189
94 DATA 53053, 689
95 DATA 1824, 6432
96 DATA 1935, 1763
97 DATA 18103, 5473
98 DATA 148037, 44011
99 END
```

Try it! Then put in your data!

Lesson 14
The Factors of a Positive Integer

There are many applications that depend upon being able to find the factors of a number. For example, how many factors and what is the sum of the factors of 12 – not counting 1 or 12.

First	$\frac{12}{2} = 6$	Since 2 and 6 are different and each are integers, both 2 and 6 are factors.
Next	$\frac{12}{3} = 4$	Again, 3 and 4 are different, each is integral, so 3 and 4 are both factors.
Next	$\frac{12}{4} = 3$	However, we have already counted 3 and 4. Note, the divisor (4) squared is more than 12.

The factors, then, of 12 are: 2,3,4, and 6. There are 4 factors, and their sum is 15. We do not count 1 or 12 since every number is exactly divisible by 1 and itself.

What happens if a perfect square number is factored by this method? For example, 16?

First,	16/2 = 8	Since 2 and 8 are different and 2^2 is not more than 16, 2 and 8 are both counted.
Next	16/3 = 5.33	Since 5.33 is not integral, the divisor 3 is not a factor.
Next	16/4 = 4	Now divisor and quotient are equal. Thus, only 1 new factor (4) is counted.
Next 16/5		Since 5^2 is greater than 16, The process ends.

Use the flow chart below to find sum and number of of factors of: 1134, 1135, 1136, . . . , 1174. Print results under "headers" as shown by example:

NUMBERS	SUM OF FACTORS	NO. OF FACTORS
1134	1770	19

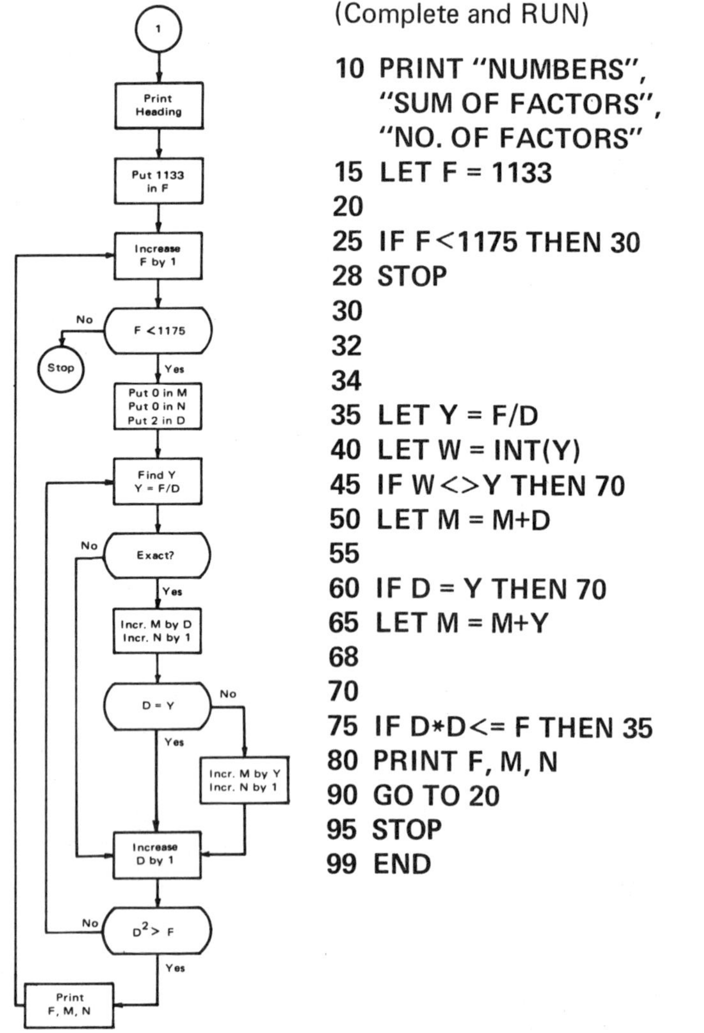

(Complete and RUN)

```
10 PRINT "NUMBERS",
   "SUM OF FACTORS",
   "NO. OF FACTORS"
15 LET F = 1133
20
25 IF F<1175 THEN 30
28 STOP
30
32
34
35 LET Y = F/D
40 LET W = INT(Y)
45 IF W<>Y THEN 70
50 LET M = M+D
55
60 IF D = Y THEN 70
65 LET M = M+Y
68
70
75 IF D*D<= F THEN 35
80 PRINT F, M, N
90 GO TO 20
95 STOP
99 END
```

Lesson 15
Prime Numbers

In the preceding example, those numbers that had no factors are called "prime numbers". These have been studied by countless numbers of people down through the ages. Why not add your name to that list?

The first and only even prime is 2! All others are odd? Can you see why? What is the tenth prime number? Let's see . . .

2, 3, 5, 7, 11, 13, 17, 19, 23, 29
↑ 10th prime

What is the 100th prime? The 1000th? Why don't we find out? Let's review the method first. Suppose one wants to know the "N th" prime. He can proceed as follows:

Put 4 in N. This represents: 2, 3, 5, 7.

From here on, one is only concerned with odd numbers since 2 is the only even prime. Divide each new odd value by odd divisiors, starting with 3, whose squares are not larger. If no divide is exact, a new prime is counted.

For example, all odds 9 thru 23 need only be divided by 3, since 5^2 is greater. Odds 25 thru 47 are only divided by 3 and 5 since 7^2 is greater. Odds 49 thru 79 must be divided by 3, 5, 7; etc.

Each time a new prime is found, the count in N is increased by 1. When the required count is reached the prime is printed along with the count. The following flow chart is provided. Try it!

Print every 100th prime in a table as shown (with tags).

100th prime is 541
200th prime is ,
, ,
, ,
1000th prime is etc.

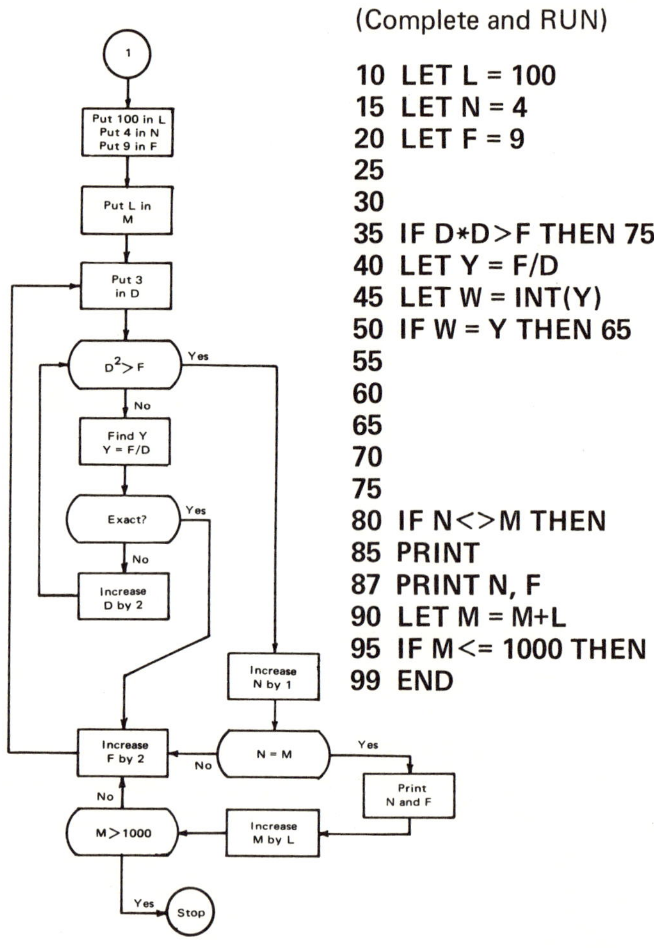

(Complete and RUN)

```
10 LET L = 100
15 LET N = 4
20 LET F = 9
25
30
35 IF D*D>F THEN 75
40 LET Y = F/D
45 LET W = INT(Y)
50 IF W = Y THEN 65
55
60
65
70
75
80 IF N<>M THEN
85 PRINT
87 PRINT N, F
90 LET M = M+L
95 IF M<= 1000 THEN
99 END
```

Lesson 16
Inputs During Execution

Wouldn't it be nice to be able to write a prime number program so that one can tell the computer any number that comes into his mind, at the time, and the program then determines if this number is prime or not? Such a program depends upon being able to input during execution. In BASIC, this is done by the word INPUT followed by names of variables where numbers typed in are to go. When the computer reaches an INPUT command, during the execution, it waits until you type in a value and then it proceeds. More than one INPUT can be used in the same program if desired.

As an example, you are told to "Type in a number". The computer then prints out the number and whether it is even or odd. It then asks for another number, etc. Here it is, try it!.

```
10 PRINT "TYPE A NUMBER"
20 PRINT
30 INPUT A
40 LET B = A/2
50 LET C = INT(B)
60 IF B = C THEN 80
70 PRINT A "ΔΔ IS ODD"
75 GO TO 10
80 PRINT A "ΔΔ IS EVEN"
90 GO TO 10
95 END
```

"Type in a number, I'll tell you if it is prime or not". The flow chart is given, write the program and try it!

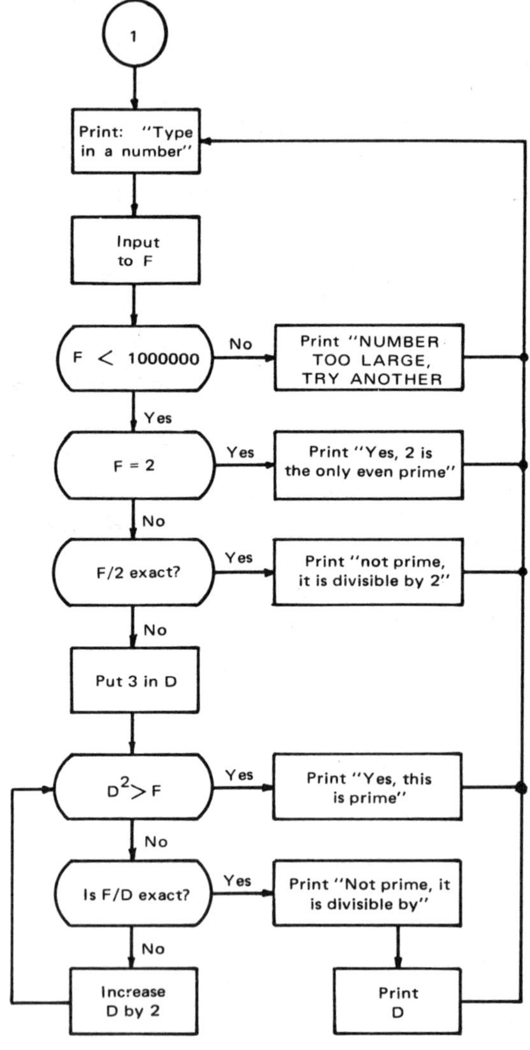

Lesson 17

A famous king became interested in finding which numbers less than 2000 had the largest number of factors. Soon many of his subjects were challenging one another to find numbers that had many factors (exact divisors other than 1 and the number itself).

"I will bestow fortunes on the subjects whose numbers rank 1, 2, and 3," he announced. "The contest ends one week from today and each person can submit but one number and the number of its factors".

"Write a BASIC program that will please the king."

One of the king's subjects came up with the following scheme:

Use F1, F2, F3 to respectively hold the 3 largest "No. of Factors". Also, use N1, N2, N3 to hold the corresponding "Numbers". Use F and N to hold the current "No. of Factors" and "Number" being tested. Lined up, these are

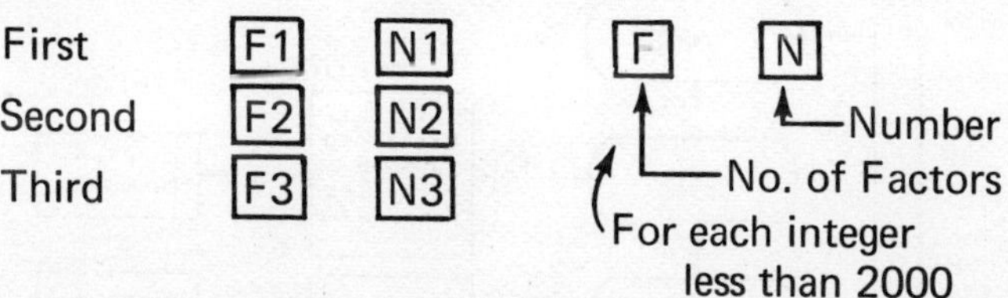

Each "F" is compared first with F3. If not greater, another N is examined. If F is greater than F3, it is compared to F1. If greater, "two shifts" down occur (First to Second, Second to Third), with F and N replacing F1 and N1. If F is between F1 and F2; "one shift" occurs (Second to Third), with F and N replacing F2 and N2. If F is between F2 and F3; F and N replace F3 and N3. The following flow chart shows this scheme.

Three Highest No. of Factors (continued)

Paste or print program here.

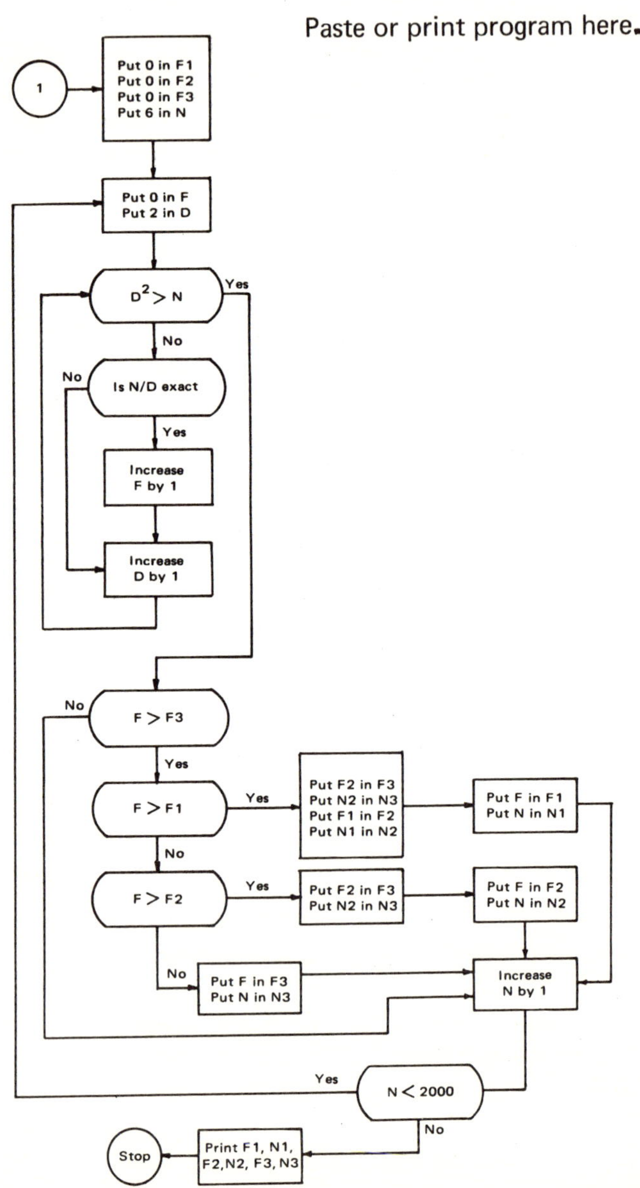

Lesson 18
Finding A Large Product

Many computers will not develop an integer result with more than 9 digits. Let us try a scheme which will develop up to 18 digits in one answer. Our result will be held in 3 cells: A, B, C; where B and C each hold 6 digits.

Let us consider A, B, C as one cell. If C increases beyond 6 digits, B is increased by the amount over 6 digits. Likewise, if B goes over 6 digits, the excess is added to A.

As an example, assume A, B, C hold: 0, 643027 and 864444. We want to add 222222.

A	B	C
0	643027	864444
	1 ←	222222
0	643028	[1]086666

The result is: 0 643028086666. The excess in C was added to B. As another example, assume one wants to multiply A, B, C above by 2. This is equivalent to adding each cell to itself.

A	B	C
0	643027	864444
1 ←	643027	864444
	1 ←	
1	[1]286055	[1]728888

The result is: 1286055728888.

Let us write a BASIC program which will find the product of any 3 integers; where each contains no more than 6 digits.

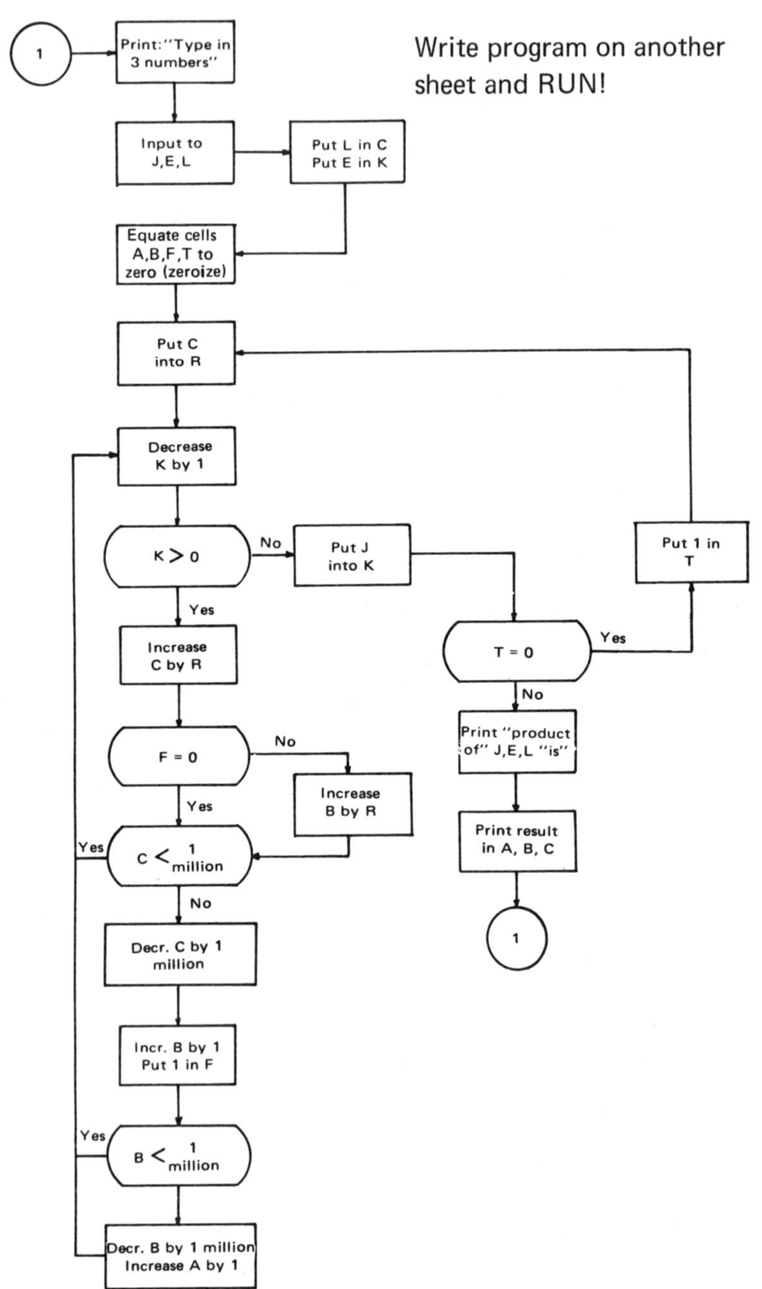

Write program on another sheet and RUN!

Lesson 19
"Friendly" Numbers

Some even number pairs are called "amicable" if the sum of the factors of each are equal to the other number. For example, 220 and 284 are "amicables" since the sum of the factors of 220 is 284 and the sum of the factors of 284 is 220. This is shown below:

Factors of 220 are: 1, 2, 4, 5, 10, 11, 20, 22, 44, 55, 110
The sum = 284 (note, 1 is counted as a factor).

Factors of 284 are: 1, 2, 4, 71, 142
The sum = 220 (note, 1 is counted as a factor).

To find all the pairs of "amicables" up to 10000, let us use a scheme similar to the following:

a. Start with a number, N.
b. Factor it, and find the sum, S, of its factors counting 1 as a factor.
c. If S is more than N, find S1, the sum of the factors of S.
d. If S1 = N, print the amicable pair: N, S.
e. Only even values of N are used, since all amicables are even.

Let us use this scheme on the pair: 220, 284

a. N = 220.
b. Sum of factors of 220 is 284. Thus, S = 284.
c. Since S (284) is more than N (220), find S1 (sum of factors of 284). S1 = 220.
d. S1 (220) = N (220). Therefore, 220 and 284 are amicables and are printed.

Amicables (continued)
(Program runs several minutes)

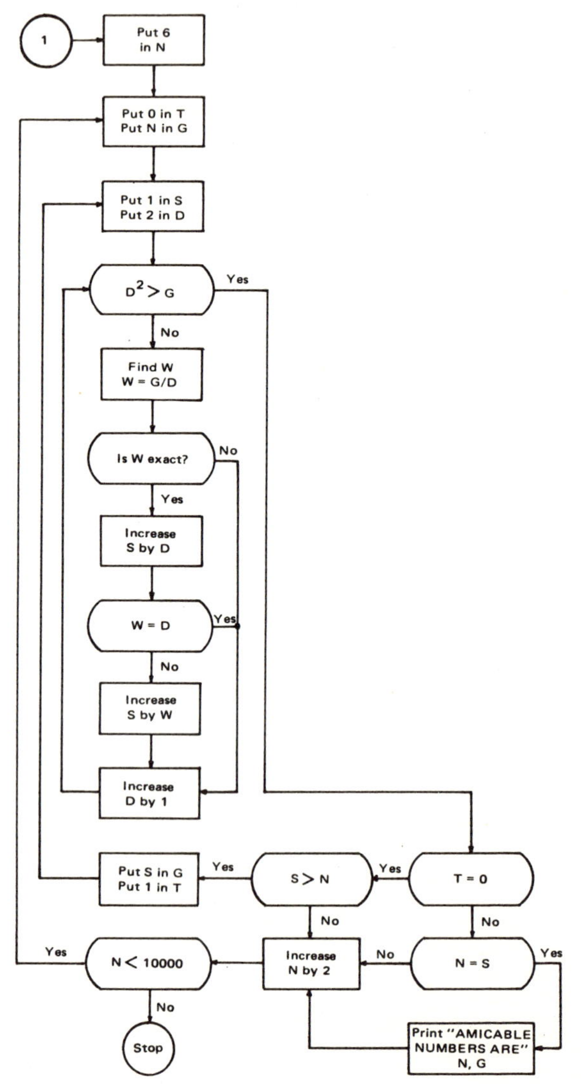

Lesson 20
Review Test 2

Write correct numbers in blanks on the left.

a ____ READ A, B means (1) Put A, B in reader (2) Put first two data items in A and B (3) Read cards A, B.

b ____ REM means (1) remainder (2) revolutions every min. (3) remark (4) remit (5) remote.

c ____ **10 PRINT**
20 PRINT
(1) is not permitted
(2) prints out word, PRINT
(3) requires comma after line 10
(4) skips 2 lines.

d ____ LET F = F-1 (1) puts -1 in F (2) is invalid (3) indicates 0 = -1 (4) subtracts -1 from F (5) replaces F by F-1.

e ____ If M<>N THEN 60 (1) goes to next line if M = N (2) indicated M is similar to N (3) causes M and N to be added (4) is not valid in BASIC.

f ____ **10 PRINT "YES, NO"** prints: (1) YES NO (2) YES, NO (3) YES NO (4) YES followed by NO on the next line.

g ____ **20 INPUT G** will: (1) put G into computer (2) put G in line 20 (3) read data, G (4) delete line 20 (5) put numbers typed into G.

h ____ DATA 6, 7 means: (1) put 6, 7 into DATA (2) put 6, 7 into first two variables after READ (3) go to lines 6, 7 (4) list data items 6, 7.

i ____ DATA 4, A will: (1) put 4 in A (2) put 4A in variables A, B (3) put 4A in DATA (4) invalid.

j ____ (F>N) means: (1) Is F greater than N (2) puts F into N (3) puts more than F into N (4) needs a line number.

Review Test 2 (continued)

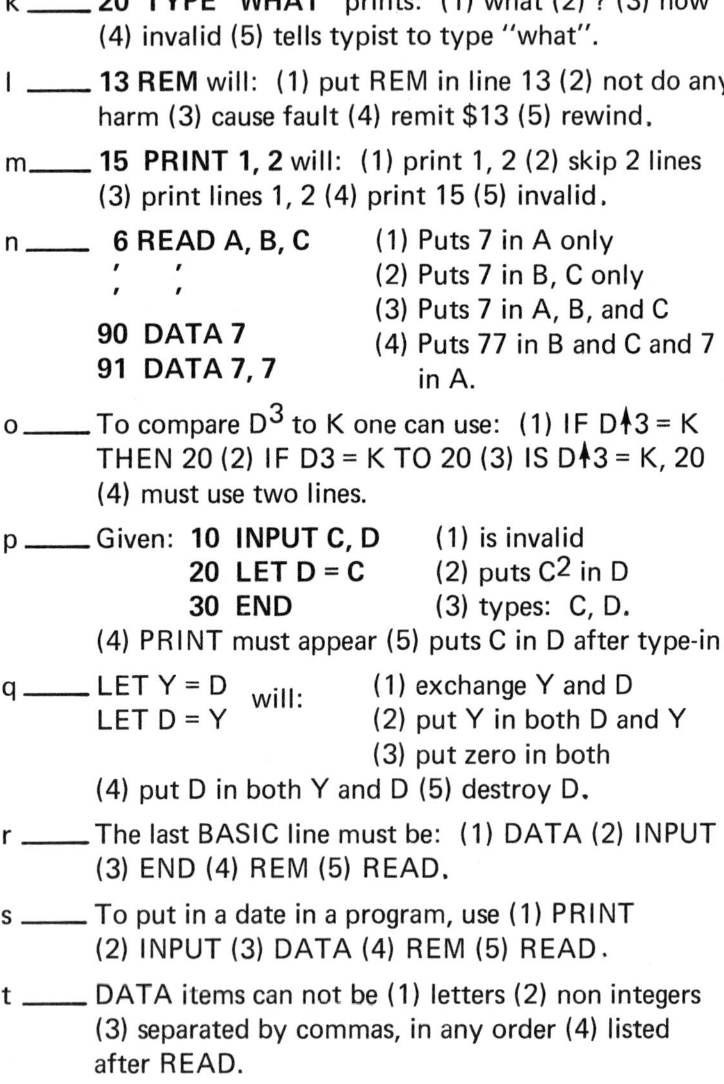

k ____ **20 TYPE "WHAT"** prints: (1) what (2) ? (3) how (4) invalid (5) tells typist to type "what".

l ____ **13 REM** will: (1) put REM in line 13 (2) not do any harm (3) cause fault (4) remit $13 (5) rewind.

m ____ **15 PRINT 1, 2** will: (1) print 1, 2 (2) skip 2 lines (3) print lines 1, 2 (4) print 15 (5) invalid.

n ____

```
6 READ A, B, C
 '     '
 '     '
90 DATA 7
91 DATA 7, 7
```

(1) Puts 7 in A only
(2) Puts 7 in B, C only
(3) Puts 7 in A, B, and C
(4) Puts 77 in B and C and 7 in A.

o ____ To compare D^3 to K one can use: (1) IF D↑3 = K THEN 20 (2) IF D3 = K TO 20 (3) IS D↑3 = K, 20 (4) must use two lines.

p ____ Given:

```
10 INPUT C, D
20 LET D = C
30 END
```

(1) is invalid
(2) puts C^2 in D
(3) types: C, D.
(4) PRINT must appear (5) puts C in D after type-in

q ____

```
LET Y = D
LET D = Y
```

will:
(1) exchange Y and D
(2) put Y in both D and Y
(3) put zero in both
(4) put D in both Y and D (5) destroy D.

r ____ The last BASIC line must be: (1) DATA (2) INPUT (3) END (4) REM (5) READ.

s ____ To put in a date in a program, use (1) PRINT (2) INPUT (3) DATA (4) REM (5) READ.

t ____ DATA items can not be (1) letters (2) non integers (3) separated by commas, in any order (4) listed after READ.

Lesson 21
Scoring Review Test 2

Run the following program. It will tell you how well you did on Test 2.

```
10 PRINT "TYPE IN YOUR ANSWERS, WITH
   CARRIAGE RETURN AFTER EACH"
11 LET N = 0
12 LET S = 0
14 LET R = 1
16 LET N = N+1
17 IF N>20 THEN 60
18 INPUT X
20 LET Y = INT(R*N/5)
24 LET T = R*N - 5*Y+1
25 IF X = T THEN 50
30 PRINT "YOU MISSED QUESTION NO." N
32 PRINT
34 LET G = N/5
36 LET P = INT(G)
38 IF P<>G THEN 16
40 LET R = R+1
42 GO TO 16
50 LET S = S+1
55 GO TO 34
60 PRINT
65 PRINT "YOU HAD△△" S "△△ CORRECT"
70 PRINT "IF MORE THAN 15, CONGRATS"
75 END
```

Lesson 22
Introduction To Subscripts

The previous lesson indicated a need to input 20 answers all at one time, rather than one at a time. Of course, the previous INPUT (line 18) could have listed 20 item names instead of 1. However, this would have required dealing with 20 variables and the program would have been much longer.

A much more elegant technique is to consider a single variable (for example, X) as being subscripted. The mathematical and BASIC representations of the first 5 subscripts of X are:

Mathematics	BASIC
X_1	X(0)
X_2	X(1)
X_3	X(2)
X_4	X(3)
X_5	X(4)

Study and try the following example. Input ten values into X and print them out. Try it!

```
10 LET J = 0
20 INPUT X(J)
30 LET J = J+1
40 IF J<10 THEN 20
50 LET K = 10 - J
60 PRINT X(K)
70 LET J = J - 1
80 IF J>0 THEN 50
90 END
```

Lesson 23
More About Subscripts

BASIC automatically provides for 11 places in its memory cells for any one dimensional array. A "one dimensional array" is a listing of subscripted values in a single line. For example:

Y_0	which in BASIC is	Y(0)
Y_1	" " " "	Y(1)
Y_2	" " " "	Y(2)
,	" " " "	,
,	" " " "	,
Y_{10}	" " " "	Y(10)

One dimensional array

One dimensional arrays are often called: "lists" or "vectors".

If one desires more then 11 places (there are 11 indicated above), he can use the following BASIC dimension statement:

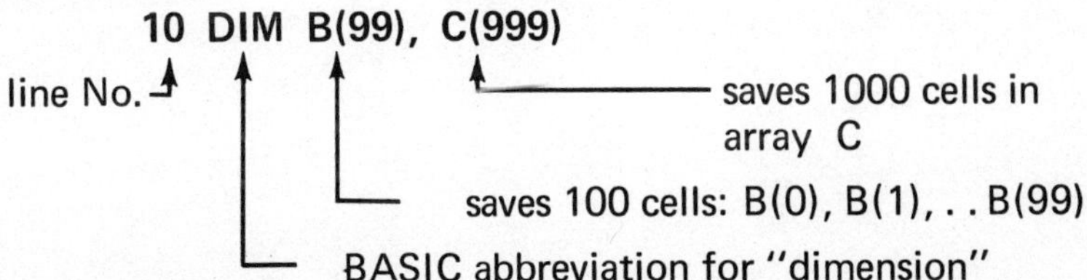

More than one array can be named in the same dimension statement (as shown above) by separating them by commas.

Remember subscripts themselves must be positive and integral. Also do not forget the first BASIC subscript is zero not 1. Let's try an example!

Sorting 20 Numbers

As a first example, let us input 20 numbers into array X and have the computer sort these from high to low (descending order).

Before building a flow chart, let us indicate, by example, an "insertion method" of computer sorting. Assume the following 5 numbers are to be sorted:

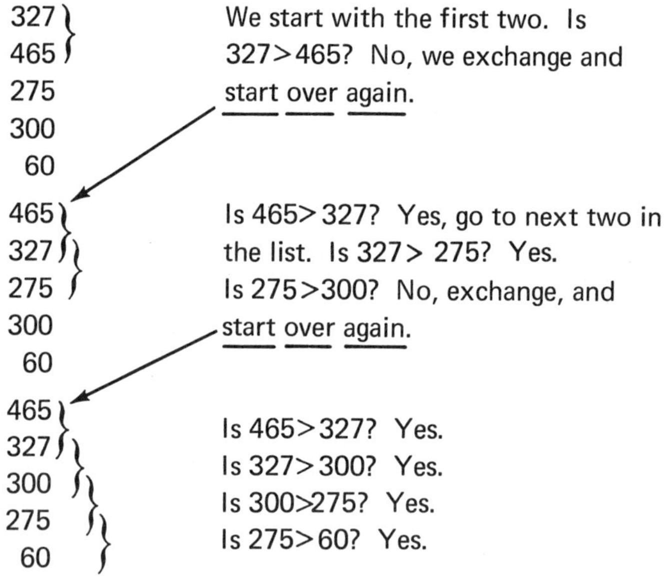

Look easy? It is! Let us program this method; first printing out the unsorted list, followed by the sorted list. We will also write it so that you may easily input more than 20 numbers if you wish.

Sorting Example (continued)

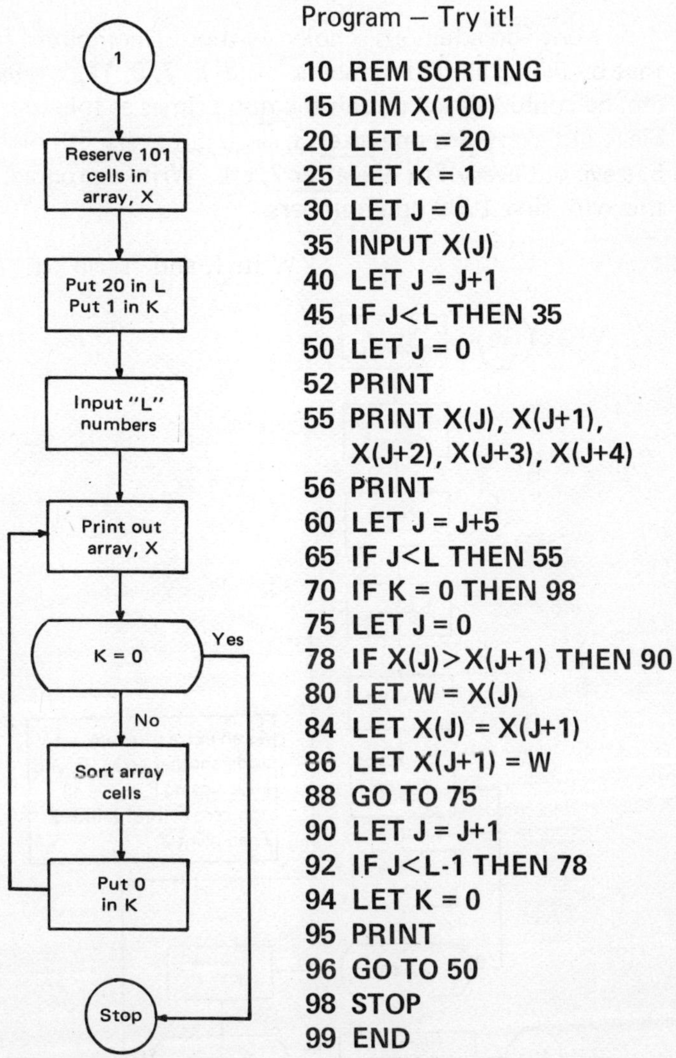

Program — Try it!

```
10 REM SORTING
15 DIM X(100)
20 LET L = 20
25 LET K = 1
30 LET J = 0
35 INPUT X(J)
40 LET J = J+1
45 IF J<L THEN 35
50 LET J = 0
52 PRINT
55 PRINT X(J), X(J+1),
   X(J+2), X(J+3), X(J+4)
56 PRINT
60 LET J = J+5
65 IF J<L THEN 55
70 IF K = 0 THEN 98
75 LET J = 0
78 IF X(J)>X(J+1) THEN 90
80 LET W = X(J)
84 LET X(J) = X(J+1)
86 LET X(J+1) = W
88 GO TO 75
90 LET J = J+1
92 IF J<L-1 THEN 78
94 LET K = 0
95 PRINT
96 GO TO 50
98 STOP
99 END
```

Why is L-1 used instead of L in line 92? Also, note printing 5 per line (line 55).

The Sieve of Eratosthenes

Long ago a famous scholar, without a computer, found that by listing all odd numbers: 1, 3, 5, 7, 9, 11, . . . 999, etc; he could "sieve" out all the non primes as follows: Sieve out every 3rd one after 3; sieve out every 5th one after 5, sieve out every 7th one after 7, etc. Write a program to do this with first 1000 odd numbers.

Write it and "sieve" it!

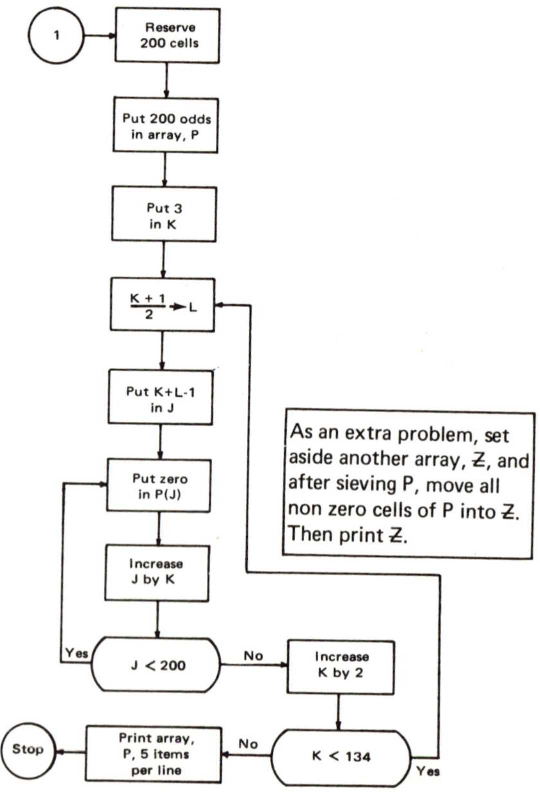

Lesson 24
The Starting Subscript

Arrays in BASIC begin with a zero subscript. In other words, the first cell is referred to as X(0). This means if 100 cells are reserved in array, X, the cell names range from X(0) thru X(99). If 200 cells are reserved in array M, the cell names range from M(0) thru M(199); etc. This is somewhat awkward because it is more natural to consider the first subscript as 1.

However, one can reserve one more than the number needed and then use 1 as the first subscript. Thus, to reserve 100 cells in array, X, let us use the statement:

Now, it is possible to consider the 100 cells as:
X(1), X(2), X(3), ... X(100).

Let us use this scheme to write a BASIC program to develop a compound "amounts table". This table shows the compound amounts of $1 at interest rates: 5, 6, 7, 8 per cent and years: 5, 10, 15, 20, ...50. Let us assume interest is compounded 4 times per year.

The formula we will use is:

$$A = P\,(1+R/T)^{NT}$$

T = Conversion times per year

A = Amount   R = Interst rate   N = No. of years
P = Principal

Compound Interest Table

Write it and Run it!

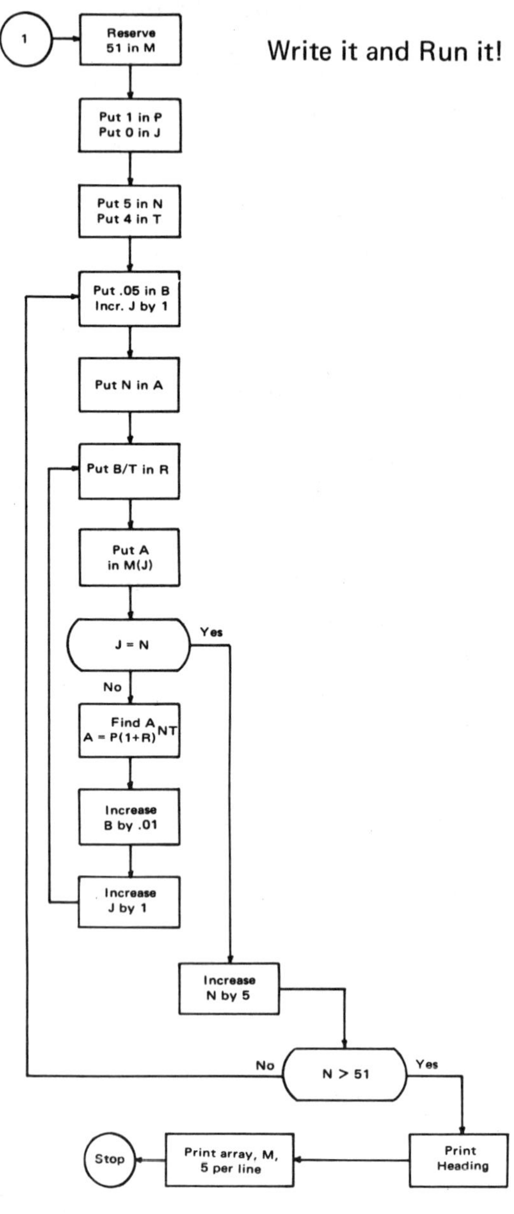

Lesson 25
Two Dimensional Arrays

The previous Interest Table was built upon a philosophy of a one dimensional array. However, it would have been easier to have considered this as two dimensional - with rows and columns. BASIC permits two dimensions. The horizontal cells are rows, the vertical cells are columns. Each cell is in a unique row and column.

Part of the Interest Table, for example, is:

YEARS	5%	6%	7%	8%
5				
10				
15				
.				
.				
50				

This can be considered as a 10 by 5 table or "matrix" - 10 rows and 5 columns. Thus 10 is in row 2, column 1. Its position can be indicated by writing:

M (1,0)

any valid array name → M; 1 → row no. 2; 0 → column no. 1

If one wishes to use two dimensions, he must indicate this in his dimension statement. For example to use 10 rows and 5 columns in array M, above; one writes:

DIM M(9,4)

No. of rows (using subscripts: 0, 1, 2, . . 9) → 9

No. of columns (using subscripts: 0, 1, 2, 3 and 4) → 4

Let us repeat the Interest Table using two dimensions and years: 10, 20, . . . 100 .

Complete it, try it!

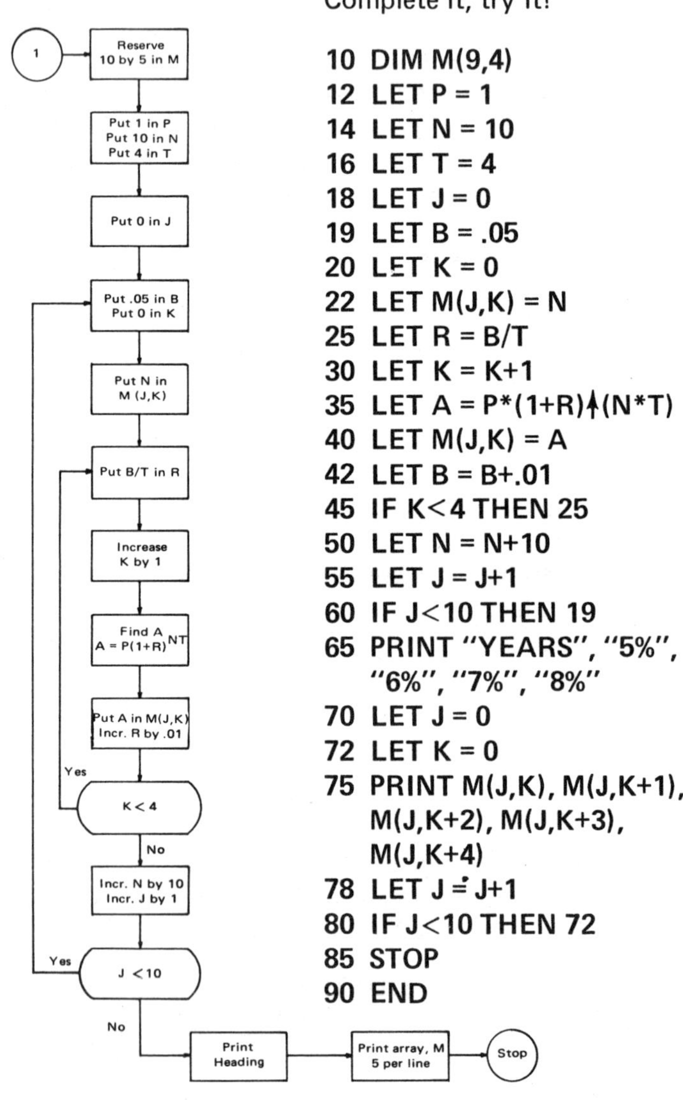


```
10 DIM M(9,4)
12 LET P = 1
14 LET N = 10
16 LET T = 4
18 LET J = 0
19 LET B = .05
20 LET K = 0
22 LET M(J,K) = N
25 LET R = B/T
30 LET K = K+1
35 LET A = P*(1+R)↑(N*T)
40 LET M(J,K) = A
42 LET B = B+.01
45 IF K<4 THEN 25
50 LET N = N+10
55 LET J = J+1
60 IF J<10 THEN 19
65 PRINT "YEARS", "5%",
   "6%", "7%", "8%"
70 LET J = 0
72 LET K = 0
75 PRINT M(J,K), M(J,K+1),
   M(J,K+2), M(J,K+3),
   M(J,K+4)
78 LET J = J+1
80 IF J<10 THEN 72
85 STOP
90 END
```

More Practice on Arrays

21 numbers are printed in 7 rows and 3 columns, such as the following:

5	1	6
2	17	21
4	95	43
11	15	50
33	23	16
42	39	67
3	77	85

A person is asked to pick one of these numbers and then type in only the column (1, 2, or 3), it is in.

These 21 numbers are then moved into an array of one dimension – making sure the column named is between the other two. For example, if column 3 is named, the arrangement is as follows:

old col. 1	old col. 3	old col. 2
5, 2, 4 3	6, 21, 43 . . .85	1, 17, 95, . . . 77

Numbers are printed again, starting with the first number in the one dimensional array and again they are listed in 3 columns. This time they appear as:

5	2	4
11	33	42
3	1	17
,	,	,
,	,	,
etc.	etc.	etc.

For the second time, the person looks for the same number and types in the column where it is.

The numbers are moved to the one dimensional array a second time - with the selected column between the other two.

For a third time the numbers are listed in 3 columns, a column number is indicated, and the numbers are placed in the one dimensional array.

The 11th number of this array is then printed. This is the number the person first selected! Try it!

You Pick It, I'll Find It (Complete and run)

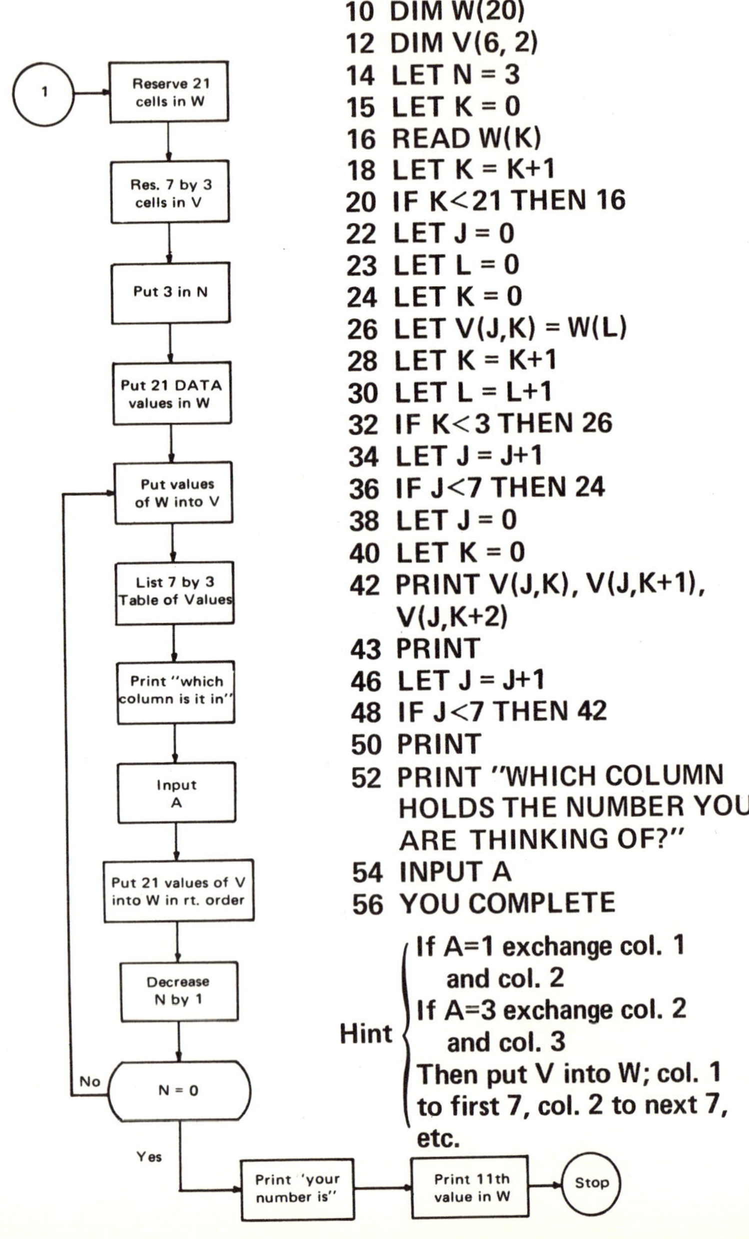


```
10 DIM W(20)
12 DIM V(6, 2)
14 LET N = 3
15 LET K = 0
16 READ W(K)
18 LET K = K+1
20 IF K<21 THEN 16
22 LET J = 0
23 LET L = 0
24 LET K = 0
26 LET V(J,K) = W(L)
28 LET K = K+1
30 LET L = L+1
32 IF K<3 THEN 26
34 LET J = J+1
36 IF J<7 THEN 24
38 LET J = 0
40 LET K = 0
42 PRINT V(J,K), V(J,K+1),
   V(J,K+2)
43 PRINT
46 LET J = J+1
48 IF J<7 THEN 42
50 PRINT
52 PRINT "WHICH COLUMN
   HOLDS THE NUMBER YOU
   ARE THINKING OF?"
54 INPUT A
56 YOU COMPLETE
```

Hint:
- If A=1 exchange col. 1 and col. 2
- If A=3 exchange col. 2 and col. 3
- Then put V into W; col. 1 to first 7, col. 2 to next 7, etc.

Lesson 26
The FOR - - NEXT Instruction

Since looping is almost always involved in applications, BASIC has a special command to make looping more efficient. The following flow chart boxes indicate the main parts of this new command. It is called "FOR - - NEXT"

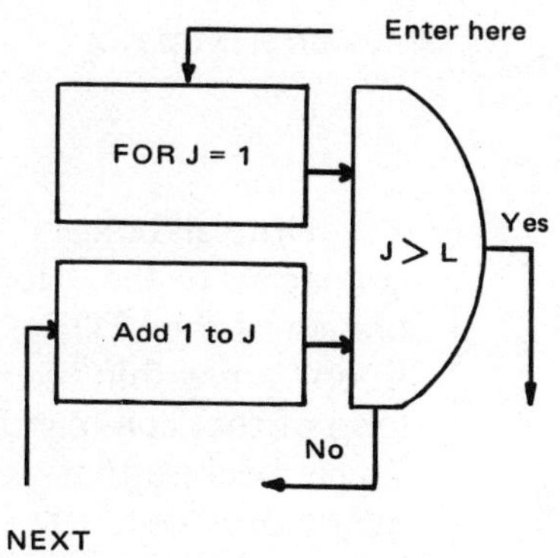

FOR J = 1 TO L

This says: start J = 1, and increase J by 1 until J is greater than L.

As an example assume one wants to print out the numbers: 1, 2, 3, ... 100.

```
10 FOR J = 1 TO 100 STEP 1
20 PRINT J
30 NEXT J
```

Can you see what happens? J (the subscript) is set to 1. Then 1 is printed. NEXT J (at line 30) returns to the FOR command and STEP (1, in this case) is added to J. Another print occurs (this time, = 2), etc. This continues until J>100. At that time a jump occurs to the line numbers that follows line 30.

If one omits STEP above, the computer assumes it is 1. Thus the above example can be:

```
10 FOR J = 1 TO 100
```

The Square of the Hypotenuse . . .

In a right triangle, the square of the hypotenuse equals the sum of the squares of the other two sides. Thus, in a 3, 4, 5 right triangle $5^2 = 3^2 + 4^2$. Find and print the sides of all such triangles if each of the 2 legs is integral, less than 100, and each hypotenuse is a prime number.

(Program is on next page)

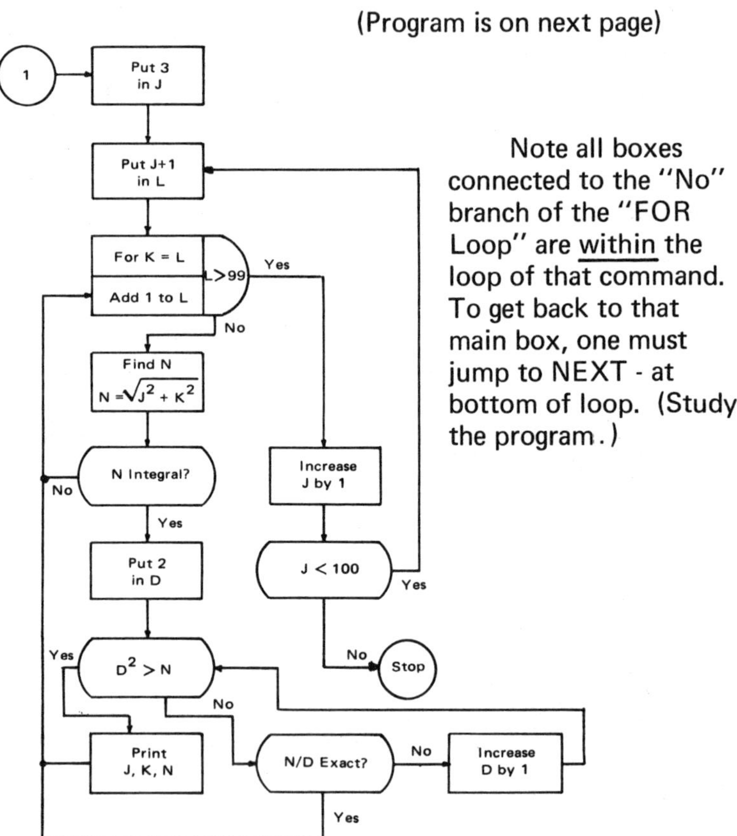

Note all boxes connected to the "No" branch of the "FOR Loop" are within the loop of that command. To get back to that main box, one must jump to NEXT - at bottom of loop. (Study the program.)

Sides of Triangle (continued)

```
 9 PRINT
10 PRINT "SIDE A", "SIDE B", "HYPOTENUSE"
12 LET J = 3
14 LET L = J+1
20 FOR K = L TO 99 STEP 1
24 LET N = SQR (J*J+K*K)
28 LET W = INT(N)
30 IF N<>W THEN 70
35 LET D = 2
40 IF D*D>N THEN 65
45 LET F = N/D
48 LET W = INT(F)
50 IF F = W THEN 70
55 LET D = D+1
60 GO TO 40
65 PRINT
66 PRINT J, K, N
70 NEXT K
75 LET J = J+1
80 IF J<100 THEN 14
85 STOP
90 END
```

Once more, note how one returns to the FOR command. For example, at line 50, IF F = W, one wants to return to the main FOR command so that the "next" K will be used. To do this, one jumps to line 70 (NEXT K).

A Random Test Theory

A theory states that of N random numbers, the largest is the (N/e+1)th approx. 1/e times. For example, in 1000 sets of 50 random numbers per set, the largest should be the 19th (50/e+1) approximately 367 times (1000/e) where e = 2.72. The following problem generates 100 sets of 10 random numbers each; 200 sets of 20 each; 300 sets of 30 each; etc. . . . thru 500 sets of 50 each. It tests this theory and prints out the following:

SETS	NOS. PER SET	NO. HITS	THEORY
100	10		

"Hits" = no. of times the largest no. of a set is the (N/e + 1)th one in the set.

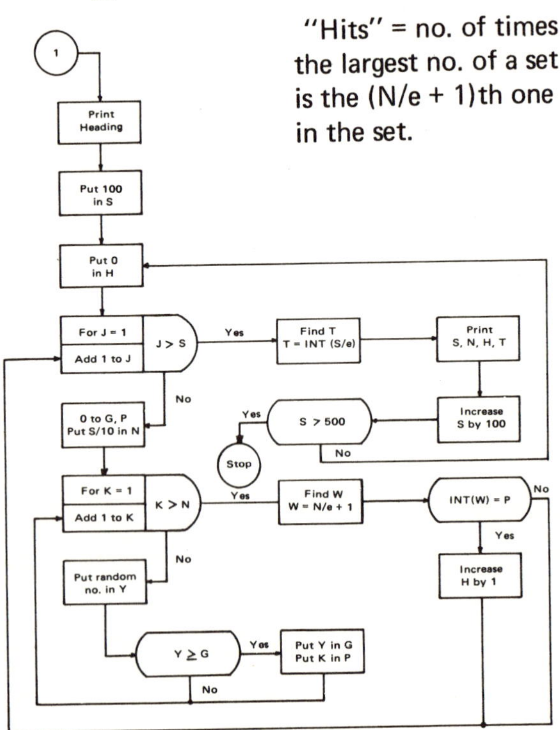

Lesson 27
Nested FOR - - NEXT Loops

The previous problem indicated a loop within a larger loop. Two FOR - - NEXT statements were used. These re-represented "nested loops". Nesting is permitted as long as a inner loop does not try to extend beyond the outer loop. For example:

```
┌┌ FOR    X
││ FOR    W
│└ NEXT   X
└  NEXT   W
```

This is not allowed. The inner loop (W) can not extend beyond the outer loop (X).

Let us simulate the tossing of a coin by generating random numbers of one digit, multiplying each by 5, and determining if the last digit of each product is zero or five. If zero, it is counted as HEADS; if five, it is counted as TAILS.

Write a BASIC program to print number of "heads" and "tails" of 100, 200, 300, . . . 1000 "tosses". Use heading similar to one below.

TOSSES HEADS TAILS

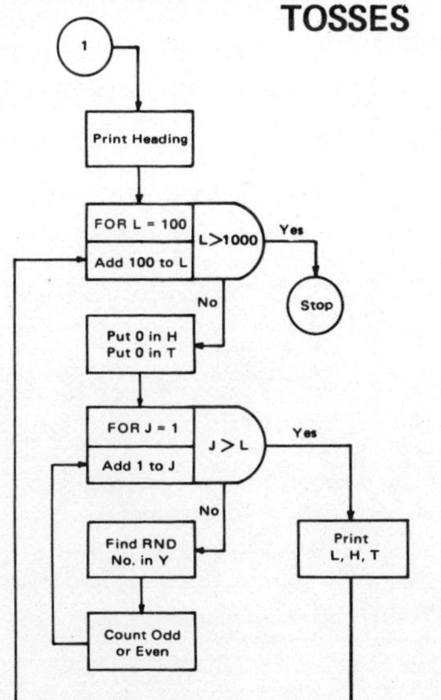

ITS system has a command, RANDOM, which starts the random series generator at a place related to one's CPU time. If your system has a similar command, use it.

Write it and try it!

The Ladies Auxiliary Bazaar

A fund raising scheme sold "chances" that had been generated by random numbers. Each "chance" cost $1 and contained four 1 digit numbers. Rewards were made on the following:

4 numbers alike . . . $100
3 numbers alike $10
2 numbers alike . . . . . $1 (for each pair)

Print a table showing possible Profit or Loss (Loss is a negative) for 1000, 2000, . . . 10000 chances. Use heading similar to the following:

CHANCES 4 ALIKE 3 ALIKE PAIRS PROFIT/LOSS

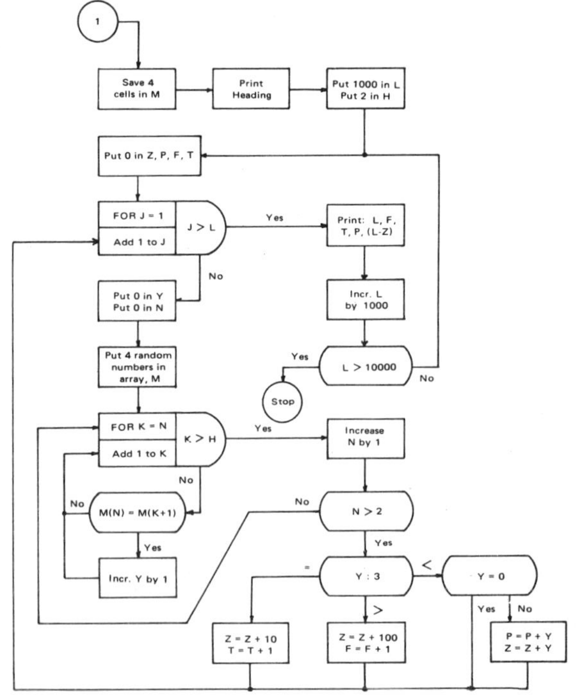

Lesson 28
User Defined Functions

BASIC provides for certain "standard functions" as: SQR, LOG, etc. However, there are times when the programmer wants to "define" a function so that it can be used many times in the same program.

As an example, assume one wants to print a table of tangents, with a heading similar to:

Angle, X   Tan X   Tan(X+90)   Tan(X+180)   Tan(X+270)

Let us also assume angles: 0, 5, 10, 15, thru 90 degrees are to be used. This program will require finding the tangent four times for each angle X. Of course, one can do this by looping thru the same calculation four times or he can define a new function (in this case, the tangent) and compute each new angle by this function. To do this, one must define his function as follows:

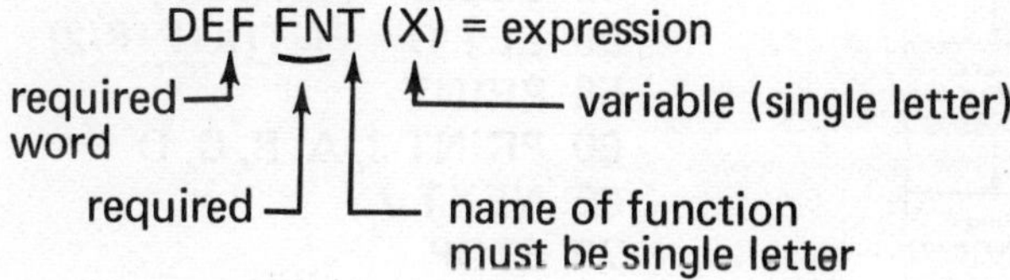

Name of the defined function must be 3 letters: the first two of which are FN. From then on in the program, one can refer to these 3 letters to find the same value as the expression (on right above).

For example, to define tangent and use it, we can write:

```
            10 DEF FNT(X) = SIN(X)/COS(X)
later --->  50 LET Y = FNT(X+90)
later --->  80 LET Z = FNT(X+180)
```

Let us use this technique in writing this program.

Study it, run it!

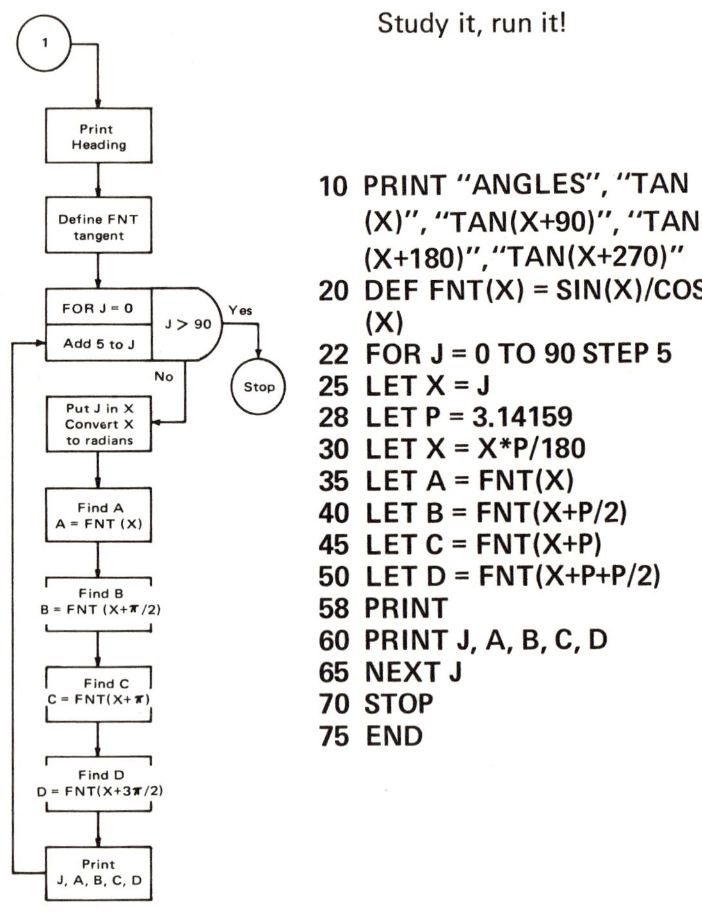


```
10 PRINT "ANGLES", "TAN
   (X)", "TAN(X+90)", "TAN
   (X+180)","TAN(X+270)"
20 DEF FNT(X) = SIN(X)/COS
   (X)
22 FOR J = 0 TO 90 STEP 5
25 LET X = J
28 LET P = 3.14159
30 LET X = X*P/180
35 LET A = FNT(X)
40 LET B = FNT(X+P/2)
45 LET C = FNT(X+P)
50 LET D = FNT(X+P+P/2)
58 PRINT
60 PRINT J, A, B, C, D
65 NEXT J
70 STOP
75 END
```

Note: Line 20 defines the function "T" by

DEF FNT(X) = SIN(X)/COS(X)

From then on (see lines 35, 40, 45, 50) a reference to "FNT(X)" gives:

SIN(X)/COS(X)

The two roots of a quadratic equation $AX^2 + BX + C = 0$ can be found by the rule:

$$2 \text{ Roots} = \frac{-B \pm \sqrt{D}}{2A} \quad \text{where } D = B^2 - 4AC$$

Write a program to find and print the 2 roots for any given inputs: A, B, C. If D is negative, print "negative discriminant". Use "FND" to define $B^2 - 4AC$.

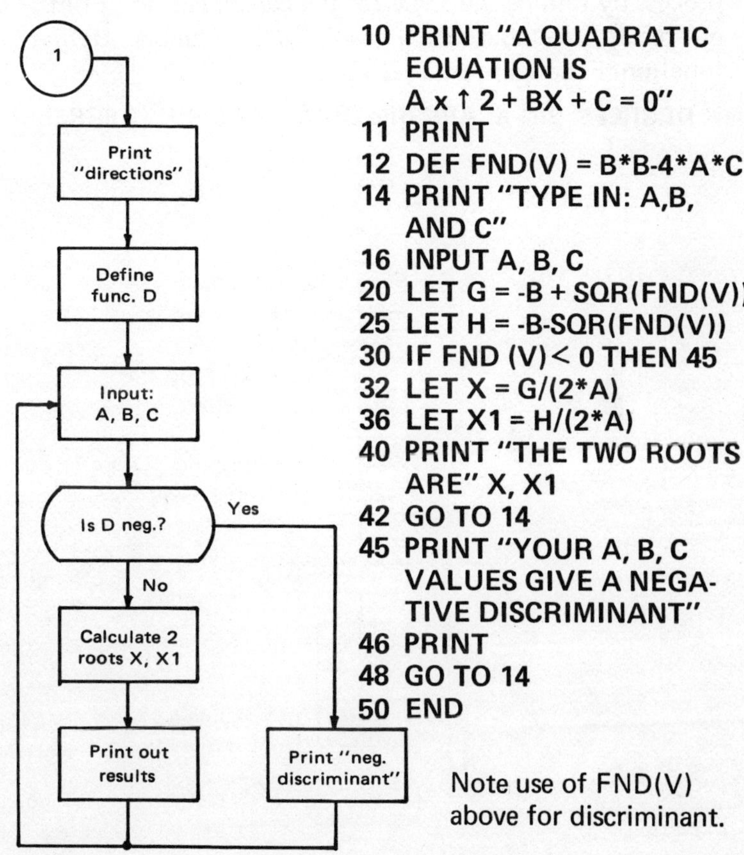


```
10 PRINT "A QUADRATIC
   EQUATION IS
   A x ↑ 2 + BX + C = 0"
11 PRINT
12 DEF FND(V) = B*B-4*A*C
14 PRINT "TYPE IN: A,B,
   AND C"
16 INPUT A, B, C
20 LET G = -B + SQR(FND(V))
25 LET H = -B-SQR(FND(V))
30 IF FND (V)< 0 THEN 45
32 LET X = G/(2*A)
36 LET X1 = H/(2*A)
40 PRINT "THE TWO ROOTS
   ARE" X, X1
42 GO TO 14
45 PRINT "YOUR A, B, C
   VALUES GIVE A NEGA-
   TIVE DISCRIMINANT"
46 PRINT
48 GO TO 14
50 END
```

Note use of FND(V) above for discriminant.

The arc sin X can be found by:

(1) arc sin X = $\pi/2 - \sqrt{1 - X}$ (F)

(2) where: F = A + BX + CX^2 + DC^3 + EX^4

and A = 1.57078786 D = −.03575663

B = −.21412453 E = .00864884

C = .08466649

For this problem, let us first find sine Y where Y = 5, 7.8, 10.6, 13.4, 16.2.. thru 89 degrees. Then reverse the process by finding the angle for the calculated sin. Print out results in a table with a heading shown below. Define function F equal to rule (2) above.

X DEGREES SIN X ARC SIN (RAD) ARC SIN (DEGREES)

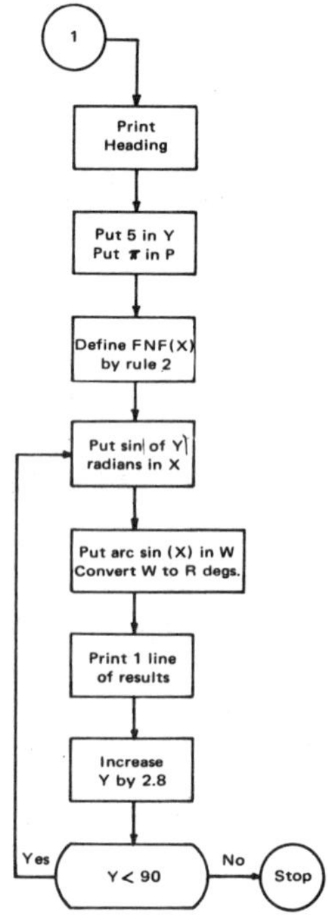

Lesson 29
Subroutines

The "DEF FN" command is limited to single BASIC statements. More often, one wants to be able to repeat a series of statements several times in one program. In such cases one can use the "GOSUB" instruction. The form is:

GOSUB s

"s" is any line number

This has the same effect as a GO TO. The computer goes to where the subroutine starts but when RETURN is encountered (at end of subroutine) the computer comes back to the statement that follows the GOSUB.

As an example, assume one wants to input A, B, and C one at a time, and if not zero add its reciprocal (I/A is reciprocal of A), and print. The program can be written as:

```
10 INPUT A
12 LET X = A
14 GO SUB 50
16 INPUT B
18 LET X = B
20 GO SUB 50
25 INPUT C
28 LET X = C
29 GO SUB 50
30 PAUSE
50 IF X<> 0 THEN 60              }
55 PRINT "ZERO DIVISOR"          }
58 RETURN                        } Subroutine
60 LET Y = X + 1/X               }
62 PRINT X, Y
65 RETURN
70 END
```

Note use of PAUSE in line 30. This is like STOP except one can continue by typing: "GO TO", for example:

GO TO 10

Try it!

What is 66 in base 3? Base 6? Base 8, Base 2? To solve, one continually divides until the quotient is zero, saving successive remainders. Thus, to find base 3 equivalent of 66, one proceeds as follows:

3⌊66 3⌊22 with rem. = 0 3 ⌊7 with rem. = 1 3 ⌊2 with rem. = 1 0 with rem. = 2	Now remainders in <u>reverse</u> order make the result Thus 66 = 2110 in base 3

The following program finds base 3, 6, 8, and 2 equivalents of numbers: 15, 46, 77, 108, . . . 511 and prints results under heading shown. (Octal is base 8, binary is base 2.) Also note use of subroutine.

NUMBERS BASE 3 BASE 6 OCTAL BINARY

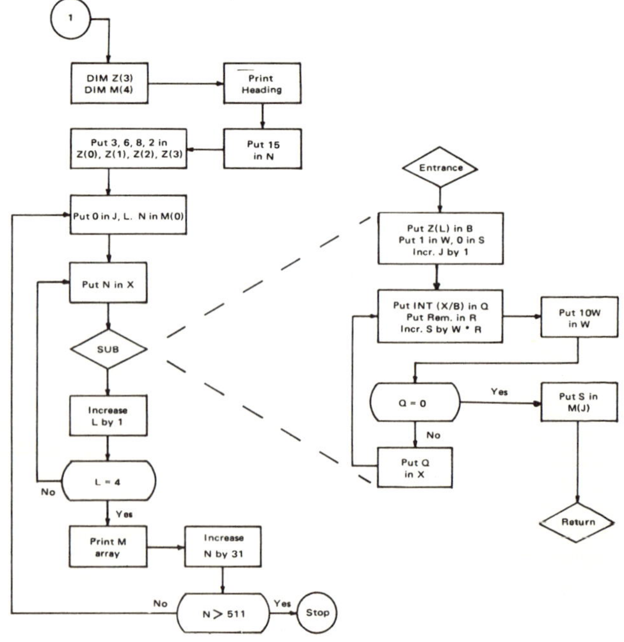

Lesson 30
Two Practice Problems

The 3 consecutive numbers: 72, 73, 74 are unique since each equals the sum of 2 squares. Thus:

$$72 = 6^2+6^2$$
$$73 = 3^2+8^2$$
$$74 = 5^2+7^2$$

Find all similar sets less than 1000. Print out as shown with heading at top and dotted line after each set.

NUMBERS		SQUARE OF		SQUARE OF
72	=	6	plus	6
73	=	3	plus	8
74	=	5	plus	7

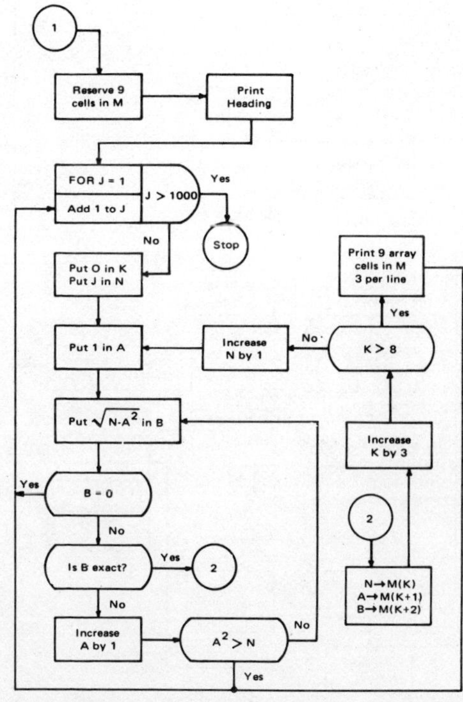

Unit Fractions

Did you know any proper fraction can be expressed as the sum of unit fractions? For example,

$$\frac{17}{21} = \frac{1}{2} + \frac{1}{4} + \frac{1}{17} + \frac{1}{1428}$$

An explanation of how to find these can be found in The Bases of FORTRAN by this author (Control Data Corporation, Minneapolis, Minn. 1967). The program below uses the technique outlined in this reference. Write it and try it!

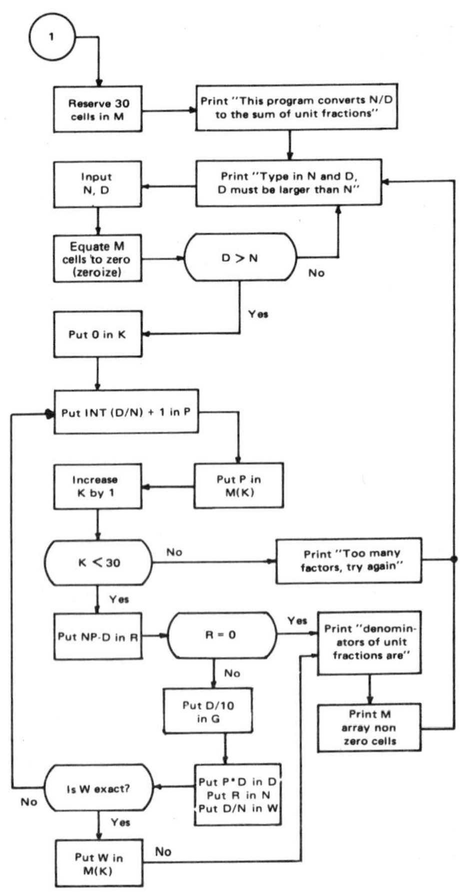

Review Test 3

Place the correct number in blanks at the left.

a_____ Given J_X^2 the subscript is (1) X (2) J (3) 2 (4) J^2 (5) none of these.

b_____ To represent the 3rd element in an array F in BASIC, one uses: (1) F(3) (2) F(2) (3) F(3rd) (4) F(2nd), (5) F(DIM).

c_____ To put aside 31 cells in array, M, one uses: (1) DIM M(30) (2) DIM(30) (3) DIM M(29) (4) DIM M(31).

d_____ A 7 by 4 array in Y can be saved by: (1) DIM (7 by 4) (2) DIM Y(6, 3) (3) DIM(28) (4) DIM Y(4, 7) (5) DIM Y(3, 6).

e_____ To start M at 3 and increase by 3 until M exceeds 26, one can use: (1) FOR M=3 (2) FOR M=3 TO 26 (3) FOR M=3 TO 26 STEP 3 (4) None of these.

f_____ A subscript in BASIC is always an integer or integral expression (1) false (2) true.

g_____ To print 3, 7, 11, ... 59, one can use:

10 FOR J=3 TO 59 STEP 4	(1) Truc
20 PRINT J	(2) Line 20
30 GO TO 10	(3) False

h_____ The flow box shown below means: (1) FOR J = 3 TO 10 (2) FOR J = 5 TO 100 (3) FOR J = 5 TO 10 (4) none of these.

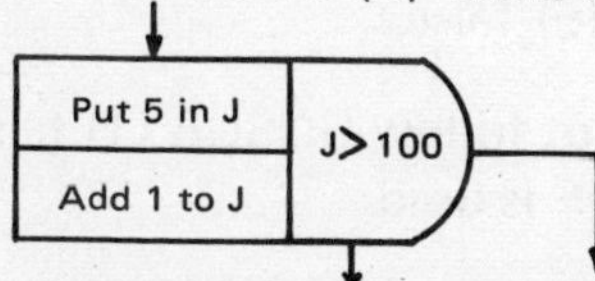

i_____ To loop back to the previous flow box, one uses (1) the top arrow (2) the rightmost arrow (3) none of these (4) bottom arrow.

j —— "NEXT L" will (1) add 1 to L (2) reduce L by 1 (3) zeroize L (4) add "Step" to L (5) print next L.

k —— "DEF" is used to: (1) define F (2) list data (3) define a function (4) remarks (5) defend it.

l —— "GOSUB" is used to: (1) go to END (2) exit (3) substitute (4) go to a subroutine (5) to submit.

m —— "GOSUB T" is: (1) permitted (2) first in the program (3) not allowed (4) go to submarine T.

n —— "NEXT J" can follow "NEXT K" (1) always (2) never (3) yes (4) depends (5) K then J.

o —— PAUSE rather than STOP is: (1) invalid (2) best (3) seldom used (4) faster (5) a temporary halt.

p —— Can one use subscripts in a program if DIM is <u>not</u> used? (1) No (2) None of these (3) only if DEF is present (4) yes.

q —— DIM (3,4,3) is: (1) used to reserve 24 cells (2) needed for subscripts J, K, L (3) permitted (4) width, length, height (5) invalid.

r —— FOR K = 0 TO 0, is: (1) meaningless (2) zero (3) hang up (4) valid (5) invalid.

s —— REM can only appear once in each program (1) depends (2) true (3) only if GOSUB is used (4) only first (5) false.

t —— GOSUB can not follow GOSUB (1) false (2) true (3) only if DEF is used.

Lesson 31
Scoring Review Test 3

Type in the following scoring program, run it and determine your score on Test 3.

```
10 PRINT "TYPE IN 5 ANSWERS PER LINE SEPARTED
                    BY COMMAS AND A"
11 PRINT "CARRIAGE RETURN AT THE END OF EACH
12 PRINT                   LINE."
13 PRINT
14 LET J = 1
15 LET G = 1
18 LET S = 0
20 INPUT N(1), N(2), N(3), N(4), N(5)
22 GOSUB 50
24 LET J = J+1
26 IF J<5 THEN 20
30 PRINT
35 PRINT "YOU HAD" S "CORRECT ANSWERS"
40 PRINT "IF MORE THAN 15, CONGRATS".
45 STOP
50 LET T = 0
52 LET K = J+1
54 LET M = 1
56 FOR L = J TO K
58 IF N(M) <> L THEN 65
60 LET S = S+1
62 GO TO 70
65 PRINT "YOU MISSED QUESTION", G
70 LET M = M+1
72 LET G = G+1
74 IF G>20 THEN 100
75 NEXT L
80 IF T>0 THEN 96
82 LET T = 1
84 LET K = J+2
86 IF K>5 THEN 90
88 GO TO 56
90 LET K = K-1
92 LET T = 2
94 GO TO 56
96 IF T<> 2 THEN 100
97 LET T = 1
98 IF N(M) = 1 THEN 60
99 GO TO 65
100 RETURN
101 END
```

Review Problem
Smallest Number for Given Number of Divisors

The smallest number having but 1 divisor is 1. The smallest number having but 2 divisors is 2. The smallest number having but 3 divisors is 4. The smallest number having but 4 divisors is 6 (1, 2, 3, and 6). Write a program to find smallest numbers having 1, 2, 3, . . . 16 exact divisors. Try it!

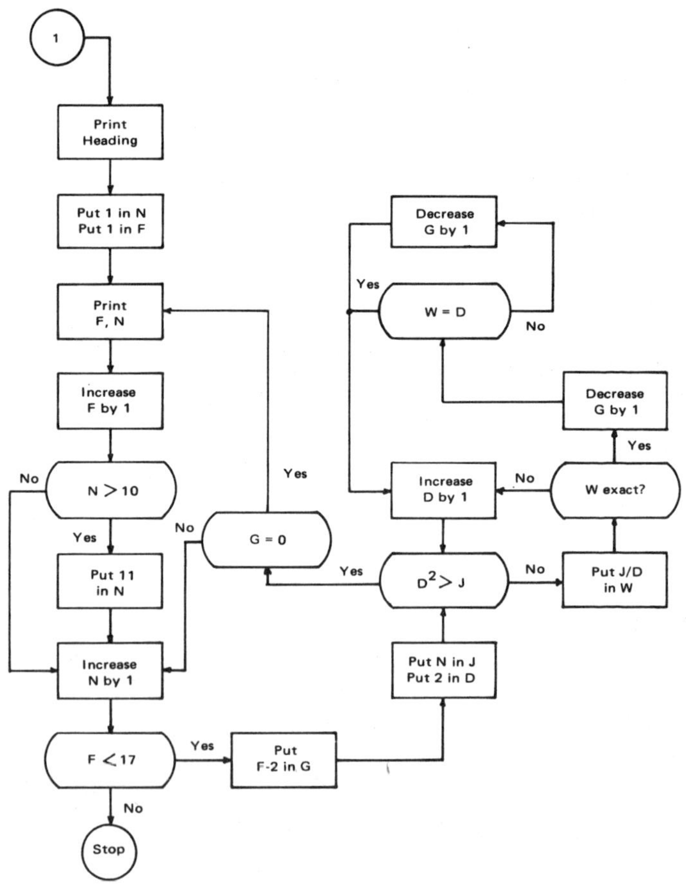

Lesson 32
Introduction to Matrix Operations

We will define a "matrix" as a rectangular array of quantities enclosed in large parentheses. For example:

$$\begin{pmatrix} 2 & 3 & 4 \\ 5 & 6 & 7 \end{pmatrix} \quad \text{and} \quad \begin{pmatrix} 5 & 6 & 7 \\ 4 & 8 & 12 \end{pmatrix}$$

Each number above is an "element". Each matrix can be considered as having rows (horizontal) and columns (vertical). Those above have 2 rows and 3 columns. In BASIC, one could indicate the dimension of these as

M(1, 2)

name of matrix (any single letter) → M

indicates 2 rows: 0 and 1 → 1

indicates 3 columns: 0, 1, and 2 → 2

BASIC provides several "matrix commands" to enable one to perform important "matrix operations". As an example, assume one wishes to add the two matrices above and put the result in matrix C. The sum is:

$$\begin{pmatrix} 2 & 3 & 4 \\ 5 & 6 & 7 \end{pmatrix} + \begin{pmatrix} 5 & 6 & 7 \\ 4 & 8 & 12 \end{pmatrix} = \begin{pmatrix} 7 & 9 & 11 \\ 9 & 14 & 19 \end{pmatrix}$$

Try this and several other matrix adds by the following:

```
10 DIM A(1,2), B(1,2), C(1,2)
20 INPUT A(0,0), A(0,1), A(0,2) \
25 INPUT A(1,0), A(1,1), A(1,2) /  put in A elements
30 INPUT B(0,0), B(0,1), B(0,2) \
35 INPUT B(1,0), B(1,1), B(1,2) /  put in B elements
38 MAT C = A+B                     add 2 matrices
40 MAT PRINT C                     print matrix, C
50 GO TO 20                        return for more input
60 END
```

(Try subtraction in line 38!)

Matrix Operations (Continued)

Matrix commands are preceded by "MAT". Also, but one arithmetic operation per statement is permitted. Other facts about matrices are:

A matrix can be a single column as: This is often called a "column matrix". $\begin{pmatrix} 5 \\ 7 \\ 8 \end{pmatrix}$

If number of rows = number of columns, one often calls it a "square matrix".

If all elements in the leading diagonal are 1 and all other elements are zero, it is a "unit matrix" or " identity matrix". An example square identity matrix is: $\begin{pmatrix} 1 & 0 & 0 \\ 0 & 1 & 0 \\ 0 & 0 & 1 \end{pmatrix}$

To put zeros in all elements of array M, one can write in BASIC: **10 MAT M = ZER.** To put all ones in M: **20 MAT M = CON.** If subscripts are used, dimensions are changed before zeros or ones are inserted. The program below indicates these concepts. Try it!

```
10 DIM U(3,2), V(3,2), W(3,2)
20 LET R = 1
24 FOR J = 0 TO 3
28 FOR K = 0 TO 2
30 LET U(J,K) = R
40 NEXT K
45 NEXT J
50 GO TO (60, 70, 80, 90) R
60 MAT V = U
62 MAT W = U+V
63 PRINT
64 MAT PRINT U, V, W
66 GO TO 95
70 MAT V = ZER
71 PRINT
72 MAT PRINT U, V
74 GO TO 95
80 MAT V = CON
81 PRINT
82 MAT PRINT U, V
86 GO TO 95
90 MAT W = ZER(0,2)
91 MAT V = CON(3)
92 MAT PRINT V, W
95 LET R = R+1
96 IF R<5 THEN 24
98 STOP
99 END
```

Lesson 33

Multiplying a Matrix by a Quantity or Number

To multiply a matrix by a number or expression, one simply encloses the expression in parentheses and multiplies the matrix. Thus to multiply matrix X by a number in R, one writes **MAT Y = (R)*X.** For example to find:

$$\begin{pmatrix} 2 & 2 & 2 \\ 2 & 2 & 2 \end{pmatrix} \begin{pmatrix} 3 & 3 & 3 \\ 3 & 3 & 3 \end{pmatrix} .. \text{ thru} .. \begin{pmatrix} 5 & 5 & 5 \\ 5 & 5 & 5 \end{pmatrix}$$

```
10 DIM X(1,2), Y(1,2)
15 LET T = 2
20 MAT X = CON
30 LET R = 2
40 MAT Y = (R)*X
42 PRINT
43 PRINT
45 MAT PRINT Y
50 LET R = R+1
60 IF R<6 THEN 40
70 LET T = T-1
80 MAT X = DIM(2,1)
83 MAT Y = DIM (2,1)
85 IF T>0 THEN 20
90 STOP
95 END
```

Note, lines 80, 83 above change the dimensions of arrays X and Y from 2 by 3 to 3 by 2, without changing their contents. Of course, the total cells must be the same in both dimensions. Thus 2 by 3 and 3 by 2 are each 6 total cells.

Rerun the above program by changing line 80 to:

```
80 MAT X = DIM (5)
```

A Changing Pattern

Write a BASIC program to print out the pattern:

00100
01110
11111

Then, change the dimension from 3 by 5 to 5 by 3 and print again.

Write and Try it!

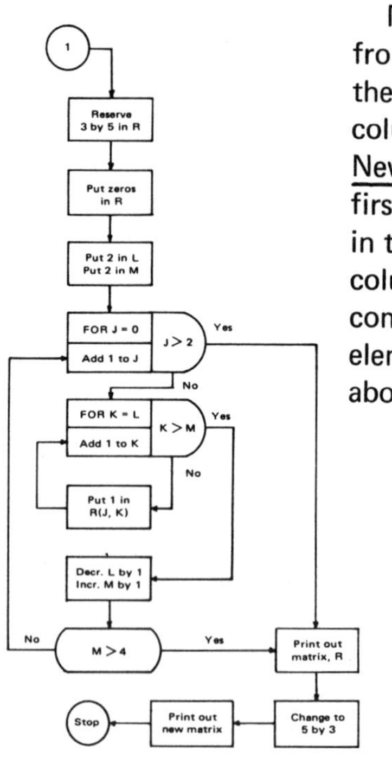

Note: changing dimensions from 3 by 5 to 5 by 3 is <u>not</u> the same as <u>transposing</u> rows to columns and columns to rows. <u>New</u> columns are composed first from <u>old</u> columns. Thus, in the above the <u>new</u> <u>first</u> column (of 5 rows) will be composed from the first 5 elements of columns 1 and 2 above.

Lesson 34
A Matrix Transpose

Sometimes, one wants to be able to "transpose" a matrix. This means to make rows into columns and columns into rows. For example:

$$\begin{pmatrix} 3 & 2 \\ 1 & 6 \\ 4 & 5 \\ 9 & 7 \end{pmatrix} \xrightarrow{\text{Tranposed is:}} \begin{pmatrix} 3 & 1 & 4 & 9 \\ 2 & 6 & 5 & 7 \end{pmatrix}$$

To transpose a matrix S to R one simply writes:

```
10 MAT R = TRN (S)
```

Write a program to print the pattern shown on the right. Transpose, and print again.

```
2 2 2 2 2
0 0 2 0 0
0 0 2 0 0
2 2 2 2 2
```

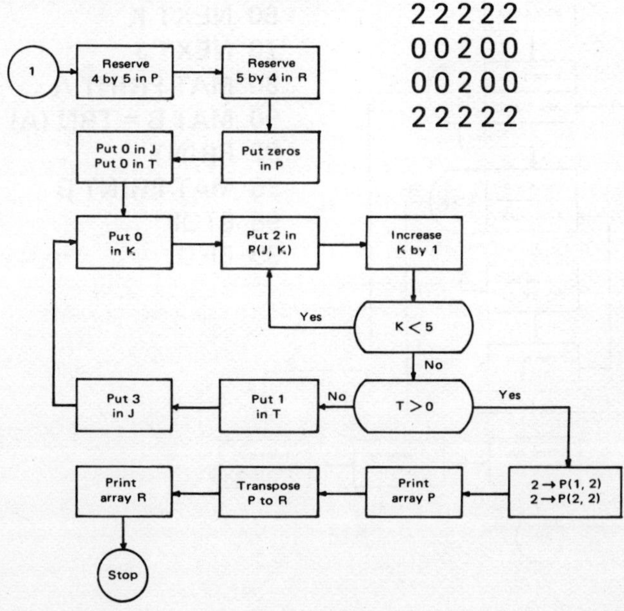

Generate matrix A below. Transpose to matrix B. Print both matrices.

Matrix A

$$\begin{pmatrix} 0\ 5\ 10 \ldots\ldots\ldots 45 \\ 1\ 6\ 11 \ldots\ldots\ldots 46 \\ 2\ 7\ 12 \ldots\ldots\ldots 47 \\ 3\ 8\ 13 \ldots\ldots\ldots 48 \\ 4\ 9\ 14 \ldots\ldots\ldots 49 \end{pmatrix}$$

Matrix B

Since A has 5 rows and 10 columns; B must have 10 rows and 5 columns

Program (Try It!)

```
10 DIM A(4,9), B(9,4)
20 FOR J = 0 TO 4
30 FOR K = 0 TO 9
40 LET N = 5*K+J
50 LET A(J,K) = N
60 NEXT K
70 NEXT J
80 MAT PRINT A
90 MAT B = TRN (A)
92 PRINT
95 MAT PRINT B
96 STOP
99 END
```

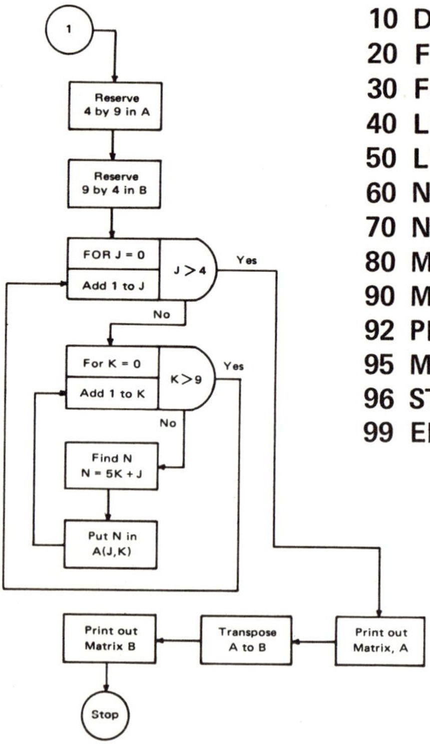

1
Reserve 4 by 9 in A
Reserve 9 by 4 in B
FOR J = 0
Add 1 to J
J > 4
Yes
No
For K = 0
Add 1 to K
K > 9
Yes
No
Find N N = 5K + J
Put N in A(J,K)
Print out Matrix, A
Transpose A to B
Print out Matrix B
Stop

Lesson 35
Product of Two Matrices

To multiply matrices A and B giving C, learn the line JacK and JilL went on a LarK where:

C(J,K) = A(J,L)*B(L,K)

rows of C = rows of A
cols. of C = cols. of B
cols. of A= rows of B

$$\begin{pmatrix} 1 & 2 & 3 \\ 4 & 5 & 6 \\ 7 & 8 & 9 \end{pmatrix} \quad X \quad \begin{pmatrix} 10 & 11 & 12 \\ 13 & 14 & 15 \\ 16 & 17 & 18 \end{pmatrix} \quad =$$

$$\begin{pmatrix} 1(10)+2(13)+3(16) & 1(11)+2(14)+3(17) & 1(12)+2(15)+3(18) \\ 4(10)+5(13)+6(16) & 4(11)+5(14)+6(17) & 4(12)+5(15)+6(18) \\ 7(10)+8(13)+9(16) & 7(11)+8(14)+9(17) & 7(12)+8(15)+9(18) \end{pmatrix}$$

$$= \begin{pmatrix} 84 & 90 & 96 \\ 201 & 216 & 231 \\ 318 & 342 & 366 \end{pmatrix}$$

Write a program to generate A and B and the product C.

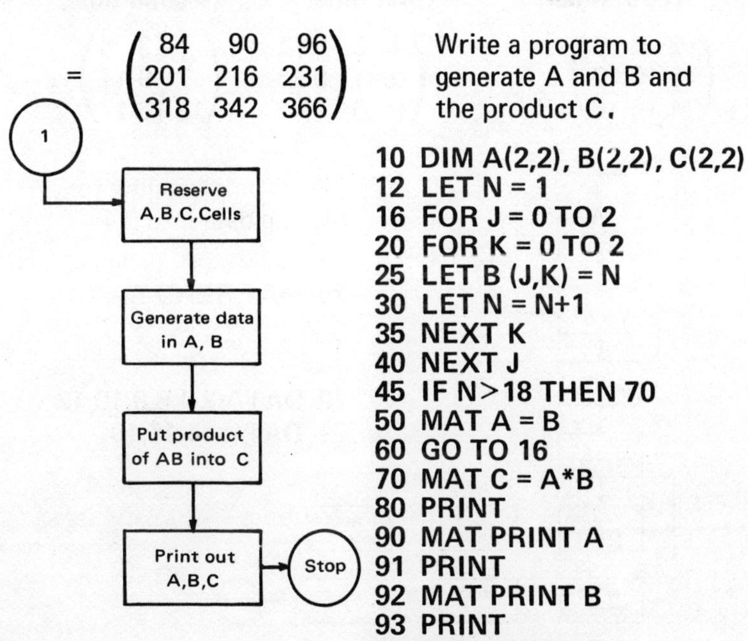


```
10 DIM A(2,2), B(2,2), C(2,2)
12 LET N = 1
16 FOR J = 0 TO 2
20 FOR K = 0 TO 2
25 LET B (J,K) = N
30 LET N = N+1
35 NEXT K
40 NEXT J
45 IF N>18 THEN 70
50 MAT A = B
60 GO TO 16
70 MAT C = A*B
80 PRINT
90 MAT PRINT A
91 PRINT
92 MAT PRINT B
93 PRINT
94 MAT PRINT C
99 END
```

An identity matrix I is the following:

$$\begin{pmatrix} 1 & 0 & 0 \\ 0 & 1 & 0 \\ 0 & 0 & 1 \end{pmatrix}$$

Note: all elements are zero except the "leading diagonal elements" which are each equal to 1.

To create an identity matrix in BASIC one simply writes a statement similar to: **10 MAT M = IDN.** Here, M is made into an identity matrix. The letter, I, often represents an identity matrix. If A is a matrix, (A)(I) = (I)(A) (the commutative law holds). This is generally <u>not</u> true if neither factor is an identity matrix. Thus (A)(B) ≠ (B)(A) .

Write a program to find (A)(B) = C and (B)(A) = C; where B is the matrix shown; A is first equal to I above, then, to that shown.

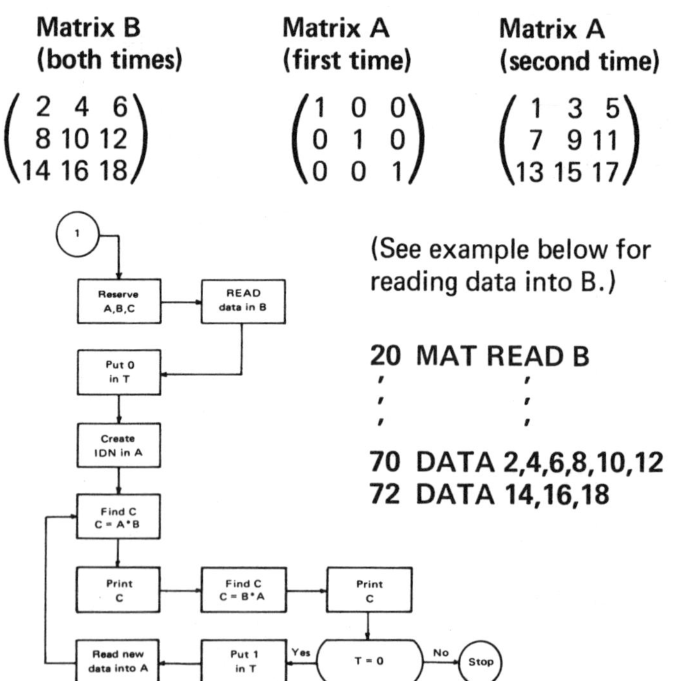

Matrix B (both times)

$$\begin{pmatrix} 2 & 4 & 6 \\ 8 & 10 & 12 \\ 14 & 16 & 18 \end{pmatrix}$$

Matrix A (first time)

$$\begin{pmatrix} 1 & 0 & 0 \\ 0 & 1 & 0 \\ 0 & 0 & 1 \end{pmatrix}$$

Matrix A (second time)

$$\begin{pmatrix} 1 & 3 & 5 \\ 7 & 9 & 11 \\ 13 & 15 & 17 \end{pmatrix}$$

(See example below for reading data into B.)

```
20 MAT READ B
'           '
'           '
'           '
70 DATA 2,4,6,8,10,12
72 DATA 14,16,18
```

Lesson 36
Practice Session

Assume matrix A (see below) is multiplied by matrix B (a column matrix) that changes as indicated. Find and print successive products.

Matrix A **Matrix B**

$$\begin{pmatrix} 1 & 2 & 3 \\ 4 & 5 & 6 \\ 7 & 8 & 9 \end{pmatrix} \times \begin{pmatrix} a \\ b \\ c \end{pmatrix} \qquad \begin{array}{l} a = 0, 1, 2, 3 \\ b = 0, 1, 2, 3 \\ c = 2 \end{array}$$

Where <u>all</u> 16 possible arrangements of a, b, c are stored and printed from array D (16 rows, 3 cols.).

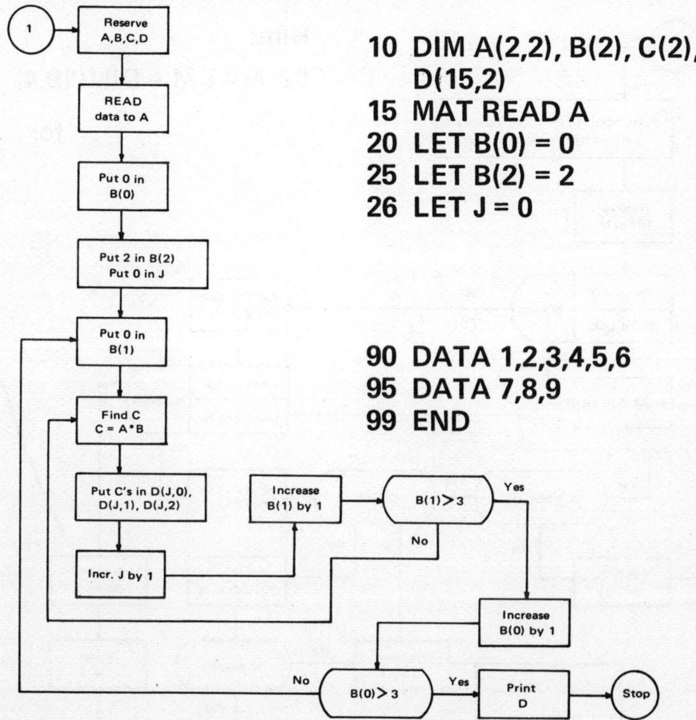


```
10 DIM A(2,2), B(2), C(2),
   D(15,2)
15 MAT READ A
20 LET B(0) = 0
25 LET B(2) = 2
26 LET J = 0



90 DATA 1,2,3,4,5,6
95 DATA 7,8,9
99 END
```

A review problem (after Lesson 31) found least numbers having 1, 2, 3, ... 16 exact divisors. Let us expand this problem by another technique. Reserve 100 cells in M. Fill M with 9999 values. Put 1, 2 in the first two cells. Then examine the even values of N from 4 to 2000, finding the number of exact divisors of each. Each number of divisors is stored at the same location number in M if it is smaller than any previous value at that location. For example, for N = 48, the number of divisors is 10. Thus, 48 is stored at the 10th cell of M if that cell does not contain a smaller value than 48.

After all values of N have been examined, redefine the dimensions of M to one of 20 rows and 5 columns (see hint) and print. Try it!

Hint:

92 MAT M = DIM(19,4)

for

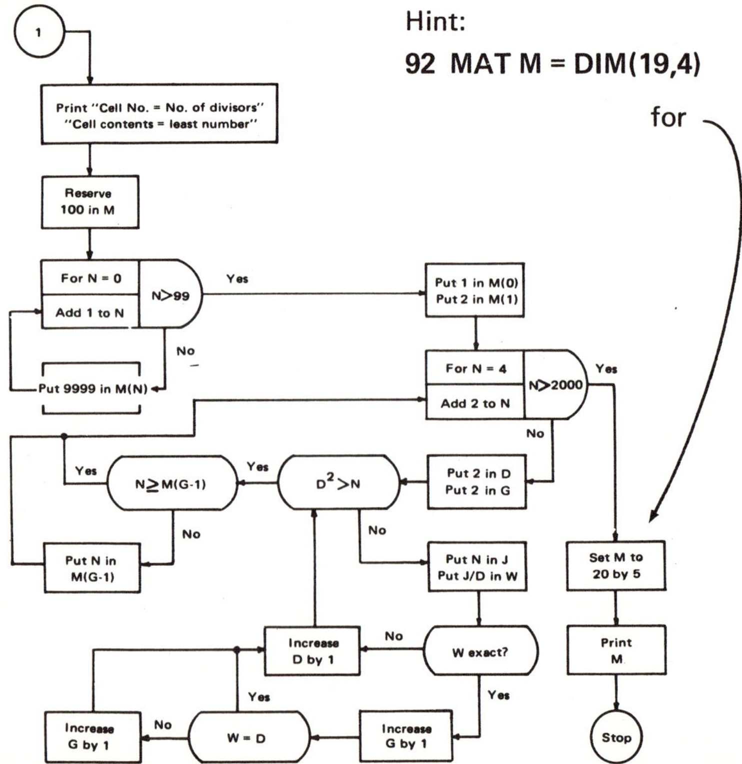

Lesson 37
The Inverse of a Matrix

The inverse of matrix A is another matrix which when multiplied by A gives an identity matrix. Thus, if (A)(B) = I, then B is the inverse of A. For example:

$$\begin{pmatrix} 2 & -2 & 4 \\ 2 & 3 & 2 \\ -1 & 1 & -1 \end{pmatrix} \begin{pmatrix} -1/2 & 1/5 & -8/5 \\ 0 & 1/5 & 2/5 \\ 1/2 & 0 & 1 \end{pmatrix} = \begin{pmatrix} 1 & 0 & 0 \\ 0 & 1 & 0 \\ 0 & 0 & 1 \end{pmatrix}$$

Either of the first two matrices above is the inverse of the other since the product is an identity matrix. BASIC provides the following statement to find an inverse:

MAT A = INV(B)

Here the inverse of matrix B is placed in matrix A. Both A and B must have equal dimensions.

But it is possible to get an inverse whose value is zero or nearly zero (due to round off errors). To avoid mis-using such an inverse, one can write:

MAT A = INV(B, X)

Inverse of B will go to A and its determinant value will go to X.

← Value of inverse will go to X.

Write a program to find the inverses of

$$\begin{pmatrix} a & a+1 & a+2 \\ a+3 & a+4 & a+5 \\ a+6 & a+7 & a+7 \end{pmatrix}$$

where a = 0, 1, 2, ...9
Store values of each inverse at W.

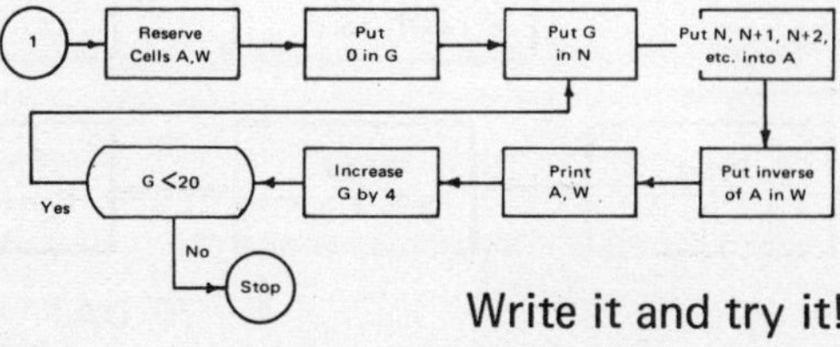

Write it and try it!

Solving Simultaneous Linear Equations

Using matrices, one can solve sets of linear equations. For example:

$$\begin{cases} 3x+2Y-Z = 4 \\ x+\ Y+Z = 6 \\ x-2Y+2Z = 3 \end{cases}$$

Can be written:

Matrix A

$$\begin{pmatrix} 3 & 2 & -1 \\ 1 & 1 & 1 \\ 1 & -2 & 2 \end{pmatrix} \begin{pmatrix} X \\ Y \\ Z \end{pmatrix} = \begin{pmatrix} 4 \\ 6 \\ 3 \end{pmatrix}$$

Multiplying both sides by the inverse of the first matrix will give X, Y, Z.

$$\begin{pmatrix} X \\ Y \\ Z \end{pmatrix} = \begin{pmatrix} \mathrm{INV(A)} \end{pmatrix} \begin{pmatrix} 4 \\ 6 \\ 3 \end{pmatrix}$$

$$\begin{pmatrix} X \\ Y \\ Z \end{pmatrix} = \underbrace{\frac{1}{13} \begin{pmatrix} 4 & -2 & 3 \\ -1 & 7 & -4 \\ -3 & 8 & 1 \end{pmatrix}}_{\text{inverse of A above}} \begin{pmatrix} 4 \\ 6 \\ 3 \end{pmatrix} = \frac{1}{13} \begin{pmatrix} 13 \\ 26 \\ 39 \end{pmatrix} = \begin{pmatrix} 1 \\ 2 \\ 3 \end{pmatrix}$$

Write a BASIC program to solve the above set of equations using the scheme shown.

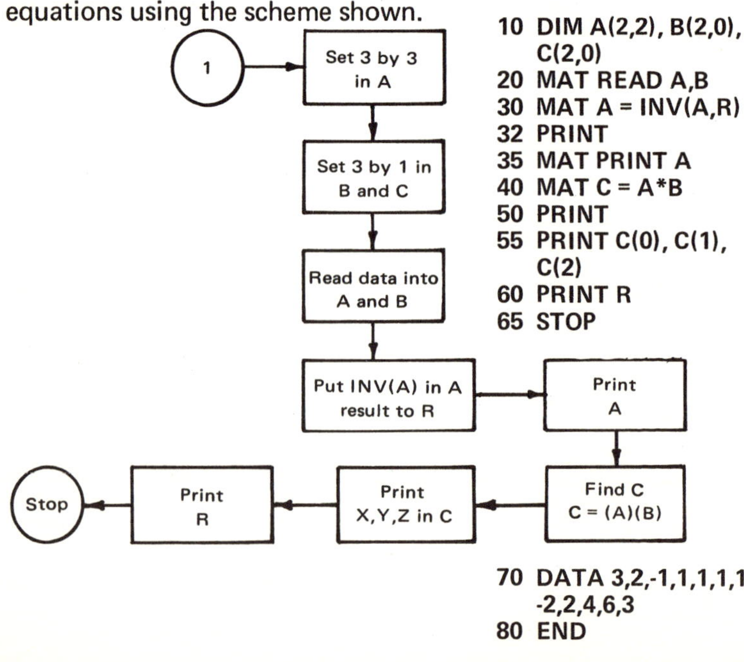


```
10 DIM A(2,2), B(2,0),
     C(2,0)
20 MAT READ A,B
30 MAT A = INV(A,R)
32 PRINT
35 MAT PRINT A
40 MAT C = A*B
50 PRINT
55 PRINT C(0), C(1),
     C(2)
60 PRINT R
65 STOP
70 DATA 3,2,-1,1,1,1,1,
     -2,2,4,6,3
80 END
```

Lesson 38

Review Matrix Applications

Write a program to permit one to enter any set of 3 linear equations, print these, and their solutions. Flow chart and part of program is below.

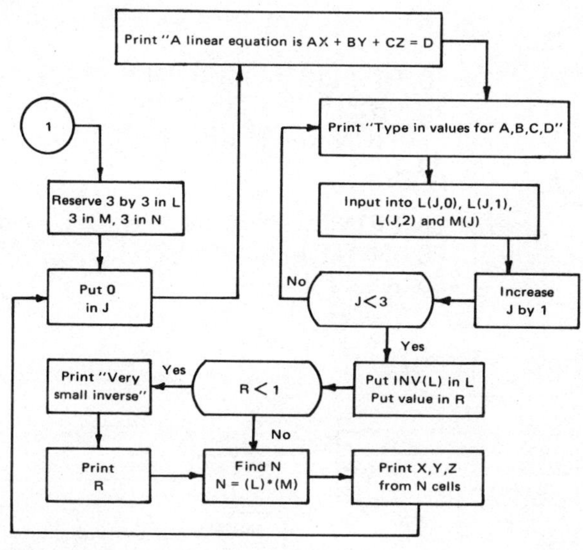


```
10 DIM L(2,2), M(2), N(2)
15 LET J = 0
18 PRINT " A LINEAR EQUATION IS AX+BY+CZ = D"
20 PRINT
28 PRINT "TYPE IN VALUES FOR A,B,C, AND D"
29 INPUT L(J,0), L(J,1), L(J,2), M(J)
30 LET J = J + 1
32 IF J <3 THEN 20
35 MAT L = INV(L,R)
40 IF ABS(R) > 1 THEN 50
45 PRINT
46 PRINT "INVERSE IS SMALL, IT IS:" R
50
```

Let us use the same scheme to solve sets of <u>four</u> linear equations. For example

$$\begin{cases} W+2X+Y-2Z = 0 \\ 2W-X-Y+Z = 1 \\ W+2X+3Y-3Z = 2 \\ 3W-3X-2Y+3Z = 3 \end{cases} \qquad \begin{pmatrix} 1 & 2 & 1 & -2 \\ 2 & -1 & -1 & 1 \\ 1 & 2 & 3 & -3 \\ 3 & -3 & -2 & 3 \end{pmatrix}^{-1} \begin{pmatrix} W \\ X \\ Y \\ Z \end{pmatrix} = \begin{pmatrix} 0 \\ 1 \\ 2 \\ 3 \end{pmatrix}$$

Results here are: W=1, X=2, Y=3, Z=4. Try It!

```
10 DIM L(3,3), M(3), N(3)
15 PRINT "A 4TH ORDER LINEAR EQUA-
   TION IS AW + BX + CY + DZ = E"
20 FOR J = 0 TO 3
24 PRINT
28 PRINT "TYPE IN A, B, C, D, AND E"
30 INPUT L(J,0), L(J,1), L(J,2), L(J,3), M(J)
35 NEXT J
```

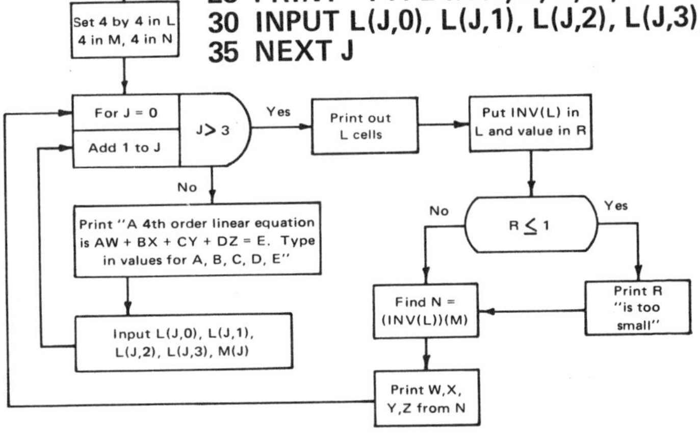


```
40 PRINT
42 MAT PRINT L
45 MAT L = INV(L,R)
50 IF ABS(R) > 1 THEN 60
55 PRINT "INVERSE" R "IS SMALL, IT
   IS" R
60 MAT N = L*M
65 MAT PRINT N
68 GO TO 20
70 END
```

Lesson 39
The "Explosion" Process

A process (using matrices) that determines how many of each part is needed is often called an "explosion matrix". As an example, in home building assume average costs for expenses shown are:

Expenses	Ramblers	Split Levels	Colonials
Material	17,500	16,200	12,400
Labor	6,200	5,500	4,900

Find the expense of materials and labor if a builder plans to build: 6 ramblers, 11 splits, and 15 colonials during the next year.

We can write the above "tableau" as a matrix. The product of this matrix and the matrix formed by the desired number of homes should give the result. Thus:

$$\begin{pmatrix} 17500 & 16200 & 12400 \\ 6200 & 5500 & 4900 \end{pmatrix} \begin{pmatrix} 6 \\ 11 \\ 15 \end{pmatrix} = \begin{pmatrix} \text{materials} \\ \text{labor} \end{pmatrix}$$

Write a program to print cost of materials and labor (using cost assumptions) for R ramblers, S splits, and C colonials; if R = 1, 2, 3, ...10 S = 2R-1, and C = 2R+3. Also find totals of each.

The basic program (on next page) prints results in a table similar to the following. Complete it and try it!

Ramblers	Splits	Colonials	Materials	Labor
1	1	5		
2	3	7		
3	5	9		
,	,	,		
,	,	,		
10	19	23	______	____
	TOTAL COSTS			

House Building (continued)

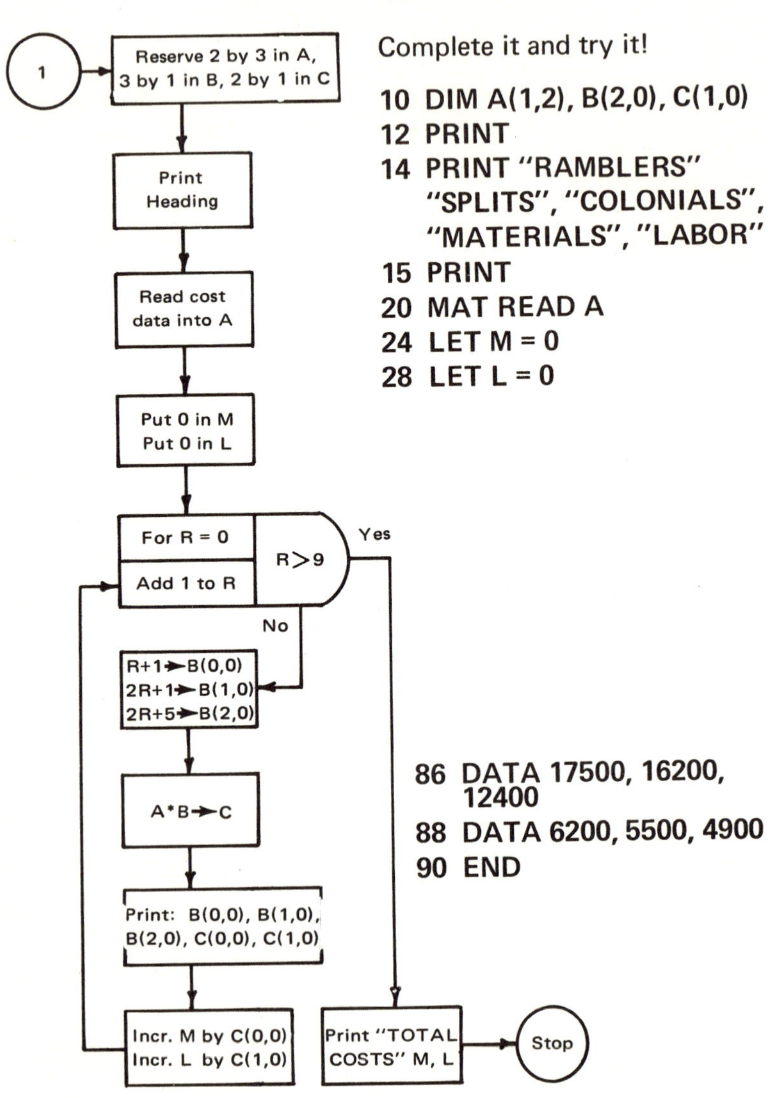

Complete it and try it!

```
10 DIM A(1,2), B(2,0), C(1,0)
12 PRINT
14 PRINT "RAMBLERS"
   "SPLITS", "COLONIALS",
   "MATERIALS", "LABOR"
15 PRINT
20 MAT READ A
24 LET M = 0
28 LET L = 0

86 DATA 17500, 16200,
   12400
88 DATA 6200, 5500, 4900
90 END
```

Two More Explosions

A clothing company uses 3 yards of cloth to make each of 3 types (A, B, C) of women's coats. The following table indicates per cents of dacron, cotton, and wool in the 3 suit categories.

	Coat A	Coat B	Coat C
Dacron	40	45	25
Cotton	10	30	15
Wool	50	25	60

Design a program to print the number of yards of cloth (dacron, cotton, and wool) needed to make 100, 150, 200, 250, 300 coats if the ratios of A to B to C coats is always 1 to 3 to 6.

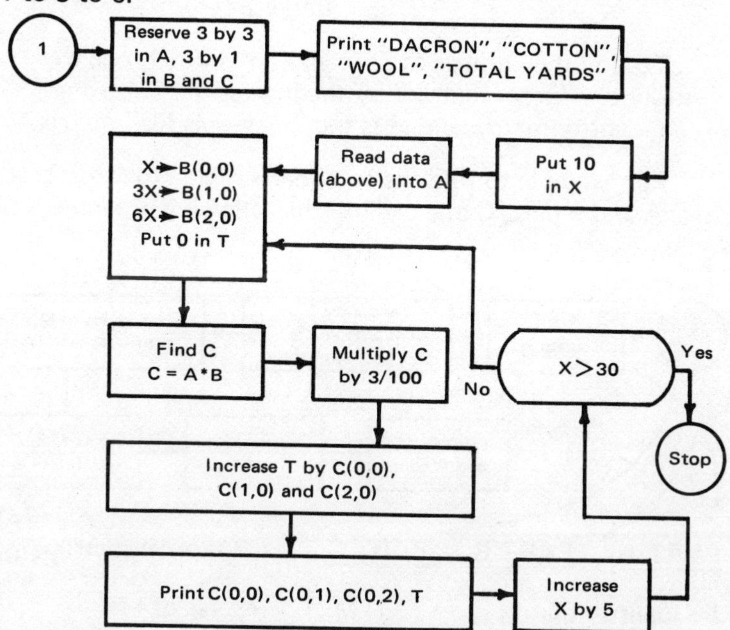

A "Bill of Materials File"

Such a file indicates parts and subparts that are contained in a whole product. For example:

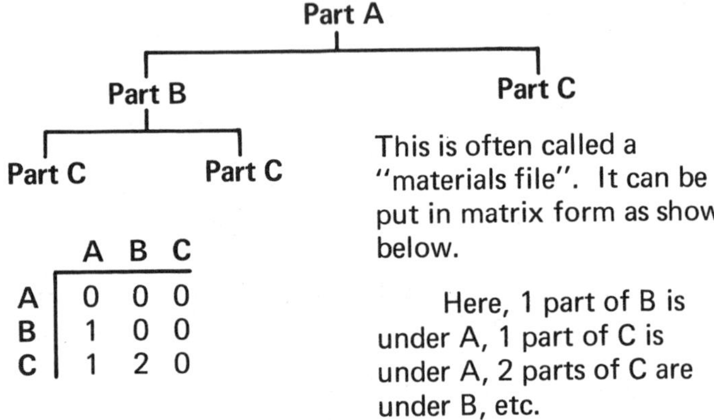

	A	B	C
A	0	0	0
B	1	0	0
C	1	2	0

This is often called a "materials file". It can be put in matrix form as shown below.

Here, 1 part of B is under A, 1 part of C is under A, 2 parts of C are under B, etc.

To find the number of parts in a total order, one can multiply the "order matrix" by the inverse of (I-M) where I is an identity matrix and M is the "materials file" matrix.

For example to find the total parts in an order for 8 parts A and 5 parts C one can use the following program. Write it and try it!

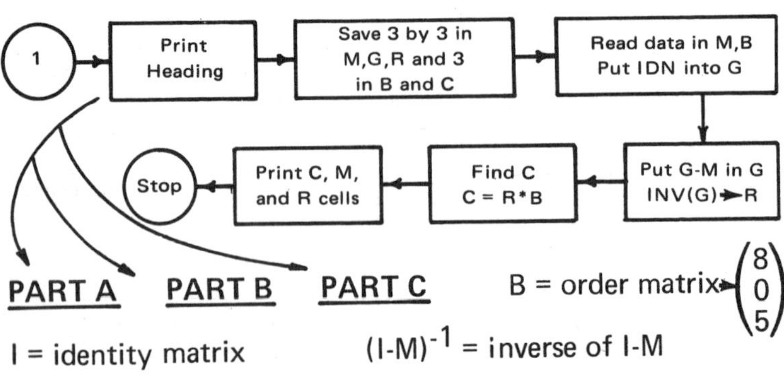

Lesson 40
Review Test 4

Write correct numbers in blanks on the left.

a —— M(1,2) indicates: (1) a matrix M of 2 rows, 3 columns (2) matrix 1 by 2 (3) neither of these.

b —— R(2,7) indicates there are: (1) 2 rows, 7 columns (2) 24 elements (3) 27 units (4) 2 by 7 zeros.

c —— To add matrix A to matrix B, one can write: (1) Add A to B (2) C = A+B (3) MAT C = A+B (4) LET MAT C = A+B (5) MAT C = MAT A+MAT B.

d —— To add matrix A to matrix B and subtract matrix C, one can write: (1) D = A+B-C (2) none of these (3) MAT D = A+B-C.

e —— To put zeros in matrix A, one can write: (1) A = 0 (2) MAT A = 0 (3) put zero in A (4) MAT A = ZER (5) MAT A = NONE.

f —— To put ones in matrix A, one can write: (1) MAT A = CON (2) MAT A = 1 (3) MAT A = ONES (4) MAT A = CONSTANT 1 (5) MAT A = CON(1).

g —— MAT PRINT A, B will: (1) print 2 numbers (2) print A rows and B columns (3) print out cell contents of matrix A followed by matrix B.

h —— To multiply matrix A by 10, one writes: (1) MAT A = (10)*A (2) A = 10*MAT A (3) can't do this (4) MAT A =MAT A*10.

i —— Assume R contains 100. Which of the following are <u>not</u> valid (1) LET X = R, (2) LET R = 10 (3) FOR J = R TO 1000, (4) MAT C = R*X.

j —— To change matrix A from 3 by 2 to 2 by 3; one writes: (1) MAT A = (2,3) (2) MAT A = 2 by 3 (3) MAT A = DIM(2,3) (4) MAT A = DIM(1,2).

k—— MAT R = TRN(R) will: (1) reverse R (2) transfer R (3) transpose R (4) truncate R.

l —— Matrix A is 3 by 2; matrix B is 2 by 7; matrix C is 3 by 8. How about MAT C = A*B ? (1) It is O.K. (2) invalid.

m—— The product of a matrix and its inverse results in: (1) fault (2) zero (3) negative (4) not allowed (5) an identity matrix.

n —— To put the value of the inverse of matrix B at W, one can write: (1) W = INV(B) (2) MAT W = INV(B) (3) A = INV(B,W) (4) MAT W = MAT B (5) MAT A = INV (B,W).

o —— MAT READ A will: (1) put A into a matrix (2) print contents of A (3) put zero into cell A (4) skip a line (5) read data of program (opposite DATA) into matrix A.

p —— INPUT and READ cannot both be used in the same program (1) false (2) true.

q —— MAT PRINT will: (1) skip a line (2) is not allowed (3) print out matrix cells.

r —— MAT R = INV(R) will: (1) give an error (2) change R to R+1 (3) put inverse of R in R (4) cause an error (5) input data to R.

s —— Matrix A is 3 by 2; matrix B is 2 by 4. What must matrix C be to put A*B in C? (1) 3 by 5 (2) 3 by 4 (3) 4 by 2 (4) 4 by 3.

t —— MAT A = TRN(A) is: (1) permitted (2) zero (3) equal to 1 (4) an error (5) none of these.

Lesson 41

Scoring Review Test 4

The following program will tell you how well you did on Test 4. Try it!

```
10 DIM M(6,2), L(4)
12 PRINT "TYPE IN YOUR 20 ANSWERS, 5 PER LINE"
14 PRINT "SEPARATED BY COMMAS"
16 LET K = -1
18 LET J = 0
20 LET N = 0
25 INPUT L(0), L(1), L(2), L(3), L(4)
30 LET K = K+1
32 IF K< 3 THEN 40
34 LET J = J+1
36 IF J>5 THEN 60
38 LET K = 0
40 LET M(J,K) = L(N)
45 LET N = N+1
50 IF N<5 THEN 30
55 GO TO 20
60 LET M(6,0) = L(3)
62 LET M(6,1) = L(4)
64 LET T = 1
66 LET S = 0
68 FOR J = 0 TO 6
70 FOR K = 0 TO 2
72 LET G = (J+1)*(K+1)
74 IF G<6 THEN 78
75 LET G = G-5
76 GO TO 74
78 LET R = G-INT(G/6)
80 IF M(J,K)< > R THEN 86
82 LET S = S+1
84 GO TO 87
86 PRINT "YOU MISSED
   QUESTION NO". T
87 LET T = T+1
88 IF T>20 THEN 94
90 NEXT K
92 NEXT J
94 PRINT
96 PRINT "YOU HAD",
   S, "CORRECT"
97 PRINT "IF MORE
   THAN 15 CONGRATS"
98 STOP
99 END
```

Review Practice Problem 1

Assume world population is 3.5 billion. Also assume each person requires at least 4 sq. ft. of space. How many sq. miles (in thousands) are required to hold the population? Let us make it more general by letting population increase by .5 billion thru 10 billion and assume each person requires: 4 sq. ft., 1 sq. yd., 16 sq. ft., or 1 acre of space.

Let us use the rule:

$$\text{sq. miles, } M = \frac{P(1600)Y^2}{(55)\ (88)} \qquad \text{where:}$$

P = billions of people
Y = sq. yds. per person (2/3, 1, 4/3, 70)

Print a table similar to the following:

No. People (in billions)	Sq. mi. (in 1000's), if space per person is: 4 sq. ft.	1 sq. yd.	16 sq. ft.	1 acre

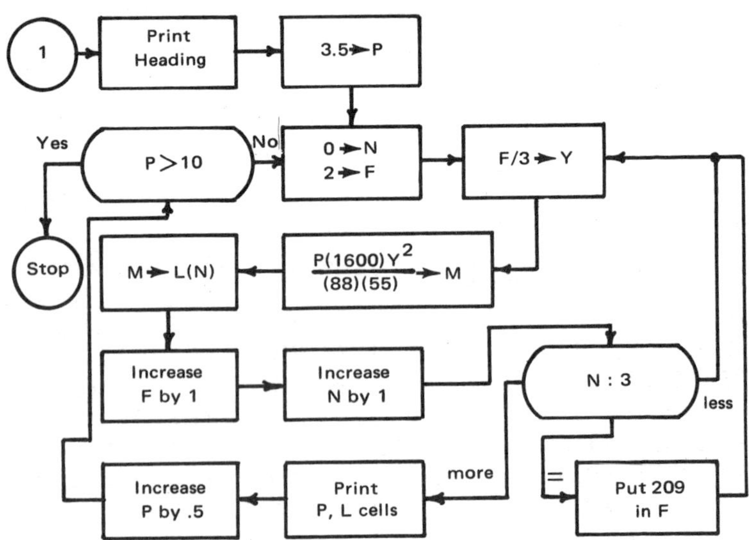

Review Problem 2

Find the squares of all integers through 100 whose tens digit is odd. Print out a table with heading similar to that shown below. How about the units digit of each result?

NUMBER SQ. OF NO. TENS DIGIT UNITS DIGIT

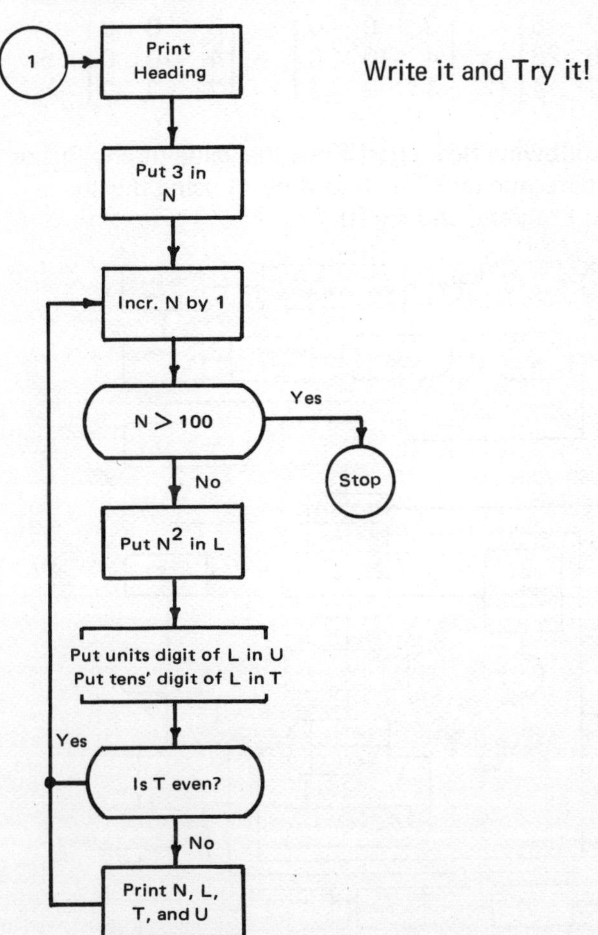

Write it and Try it!

Review Problem 3

A determinant is a square array of numbers whose value can be found by special rules. One rule is to zeroize all elements above the diagonal and the product of the elements left in the diagonal then equals the value of the determinant. For example:

$$\begin{vmatrix} 3 & 12 & 6 \\ 4 & 6 & 28 \\ 1 & 2 & 4 \end{vmatrix} = \begin{vmatrix} 3 & 0 & 0 \\ 4 & -10 & 20 \\ 1 & -2 & 2 \end{vmatrix} = \begin{vmatrix} 3 & 0 & 0 \\ 4 & -10 & 0 \\ 2 & -2 & -2 \end{vmatrix} = 60$$

The following flow chart finds the value of any <u>3rd</u> or <u>4th</u> order determinant (3 by 3 or 4 by 4) using the above technique. Program, and try it!

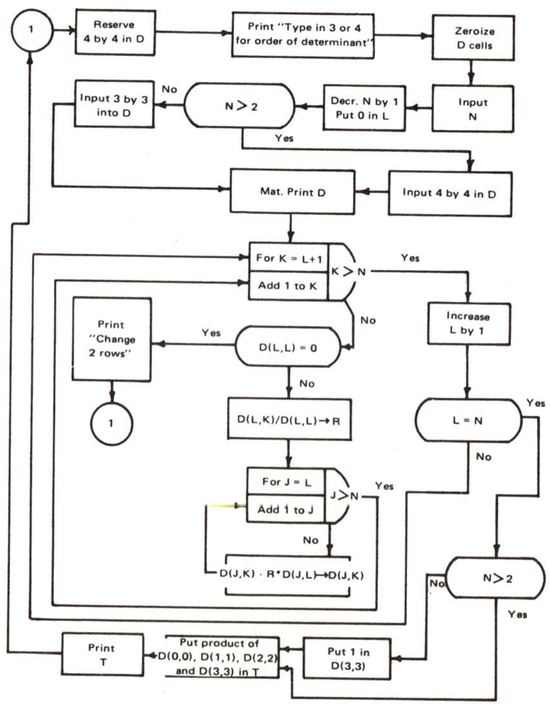

Review Problem 4

The area of a right triangle is equal to twice its perimeter. The sides of the triangle are integers and each less than 100. Find the triangles.

Assume sides are: A, B, C. Then:

$$(1)\quad \frac{(A)(B)}{2} = 2\,(A+B+C)$$

The flow chart follows, write it, try it! Heading is:

SIDE A SIDE B SIDE C AREA PERIMETER

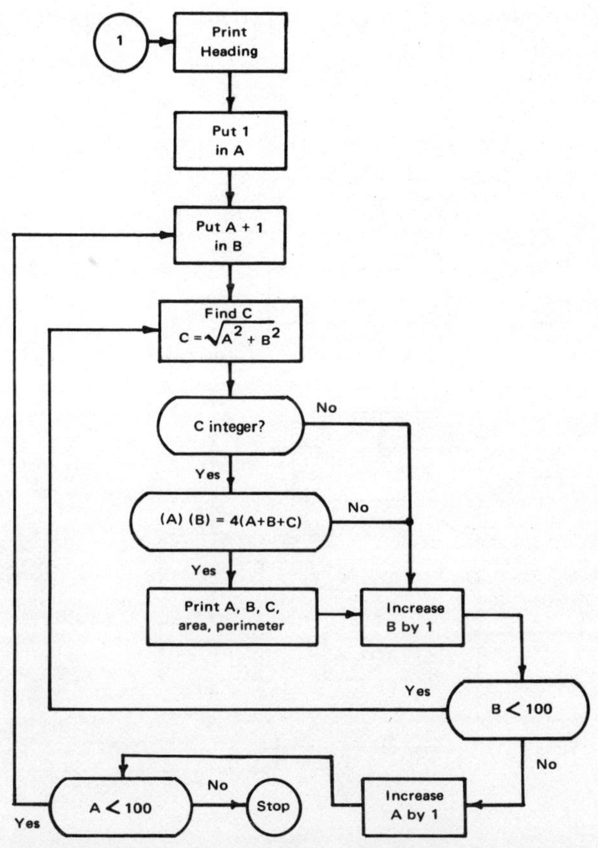

Review Problem 5

Let us calculate cube roots of integers: 2, 4, 6, ... 98 using the rule:

$$A = \frac{1}{3}\left[\frac{N}{A^2} + 2A\right]$$

where A is initially equal to (N+1)/2

However, after initial A is found, each succeeding A is the value of the preceding A. The rule above is applied, for each N, until the absolute difference between N/A^2 and A is zero or close to zero.

The following flow chart is provided. Complete the program and try it!

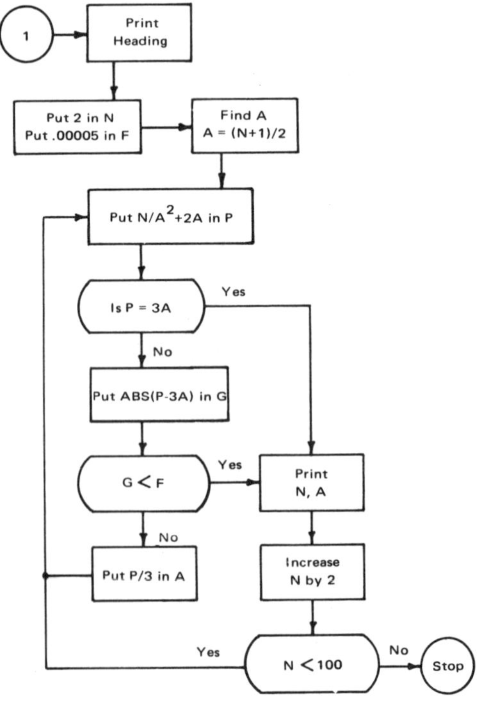

Review Problem 6
A Chi-Square Test

In statistics, one often makes use of a technique such as the following. Assume 720 persons are asked to choose their favorite cars. Observed facts (fo) were:

Choice	Car A	Car B	Car C	Car D	Totals
Yes	50	35	50	105	240
No	30	65	100	165	360
Don't know	10	20	12	78	120
	90	120	162	348	720

These are "observed facts". Now, one can find "Expected facts" (fe) as follows:

Choice	Car A	Car B	Car C	Car D	Totals
Yes	30	40	54	116	240
No	45	60	81	174	360
Don't know	15	20	27	58	120
	90	120	162	348	720

$$\text{Where each expected fact} = \left(\frac{\text{Its col. sum}}{\text{grand sum}}\right)\left(\frac{\text{Its row sum}}{1}\right)$$

One can now use these two tables to find:

$$X^2 = \text{Chi Square} = \sum \frac{(fo\text{-}fe)^2}{fe}$$

Starting with the first columns in the two tables, gives:

$$X^2 = \frac{(50\text{-}30)^2}{30} + \frac{(30\text{-}45)^2}{45} + \frac{(10\text{-}15)^2}{15} \text{. . . . etc.}$$

Our problem is to write a program which will permit one to input any 4 categories (A, B, C, D) for 3 choices (Yes, No, Don't know), print the observed facts, the expected facts, and the value of Chi Sq. Use the following flow chart - try it!

Solution to Chi Square

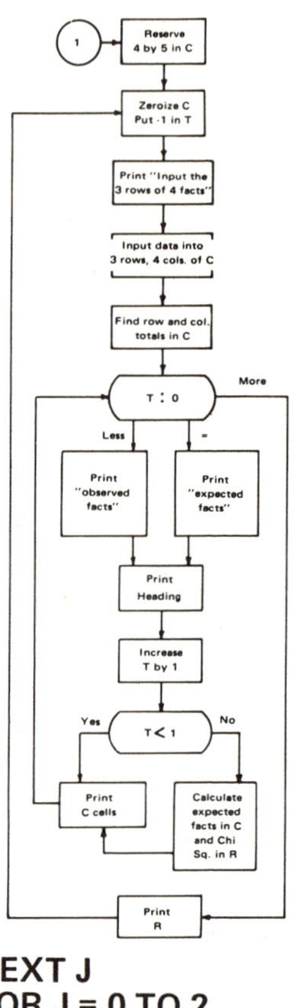


```
10 DIM C(3,4)
11 MAT C = ZER
12 LET T = -1
15 PRINT "INPUT 3 ROWS
   OF 4 NUMBERS EACH"
18 PRINT
20 INPUT C(0,0),... C(0,3)
21 INPUT C(1,0),... C(1,3)
22 INPUT C(2,0),... C(2,3)
25 LET W = 0
26 FOR K = 0 TO 3
27 FOR J = 0 TO 2
28 LET C(3,K) = C(3,K) +
29 NEXT J              C(J,K)
30 NEXT K
32 FOR J = 0 TO 3
34 FOR K = 0 TO 3
36 LET C(J,4) = C(J,4) +
38 NEXT K              C(J,K)
40 NEXT J
41 IF W <> 0 THEN 80
42 IF T> 0 THEN 85
43 IF T< 0 THEN 48
44 PRINT "EXPECTED
   FACTS"
46 GO TO 49
48 PRINT " OBSERVED
   FACTS"
49 PRINT
50 PRINT "A", "B", "C",
   "D", "TOTALS"
52 LET T = T+1
53 IF T< 1 THEN 80
55 LET R = 0
56 FOR J = 0 TO 2
58 FOR K = 0 TO 3
60 LET P = C(3,K)/C(3,4)*
   C(J,4)
61 LET R = R+((P-C(J,K))↑
      2)/P
62 LET C(J,K) = P
63 NEXT K
64 NEXT J
65 FOR J = 0 TO 2
66 LET C(J,4) = 0
68 NEXT J
70 FOR K = 0 TO 4
72 LET C(3,K) = 0
74 NEXT K
75 LET W = 1
78 GO TO 26
80 MAT PRINT C
82 GO TO 42
85 PRINT R
88 GO TO 11
90 END
```

Review Problem 7
A Die Tossing Experiment

Assume a die with faces: 0, 1, 2, 3, 4, 5, is thrown until the total sum of throws first exceeds 12. What is the most likely total? The following table indicates the solution.

Possible sums prior to last throw	Possible total sums, after last throw, that exceed 12
12	13, 14, 15, 16, 17
11	13, 14, 15, 16
10	13, 14, 15
9	13, 14, Most likely sum
8	13 ⟵ is obviously 13.

Write a BASIC program to simulate the tossing of this die until the sum 12 is exceeded 1000, 2000, . . . 10,000 times; each 1000 times showing the total sums. Use heading as shown:

SUM = 13 SUM = 14 SUM = 15 SUM = 16 SUM = 17

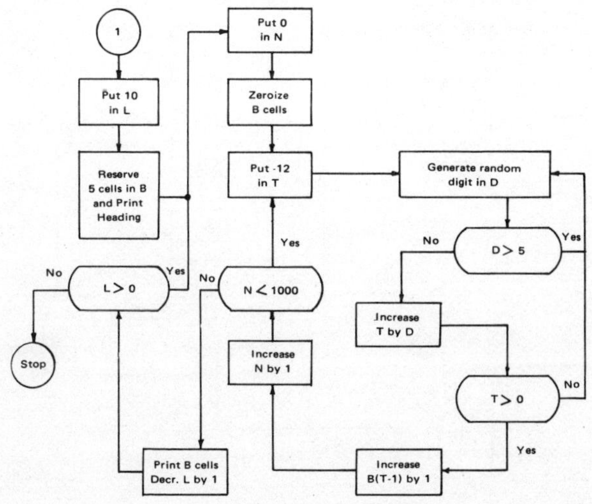

Review Problem 8

A dictator once decided to grant amnesty to 1000 prisoners - each locked in cells numbered 1, 2, 3, . . . 1000. His amnesty included the following: The jailor first unlocked each of the 1000 cells. Then starting with the 2nd cell (number 2), he turned the key in every 2nd cell. Then starting with the 3rd cell he turned the key in every 3rd cell; then starting with the 4th, he turned the key in every 4th cell, etc. Each turn of the key either locked or unlocked the cell door. When he was completely done those with unlocked doors could leave. Who were the lucky ones?

We can have the computer solve this by the following: First put 1 in each of 1000 cells. This represents all cells as being unlocked. Now add 1 to every 2nd cell. Then 1 to every 3rd cell, etc. At the end, those cells containing odd numbers are free! Right? Unlock, lock, unlock, lock . . . . . . is the same as: odd, even, odd, even, ... Try it!

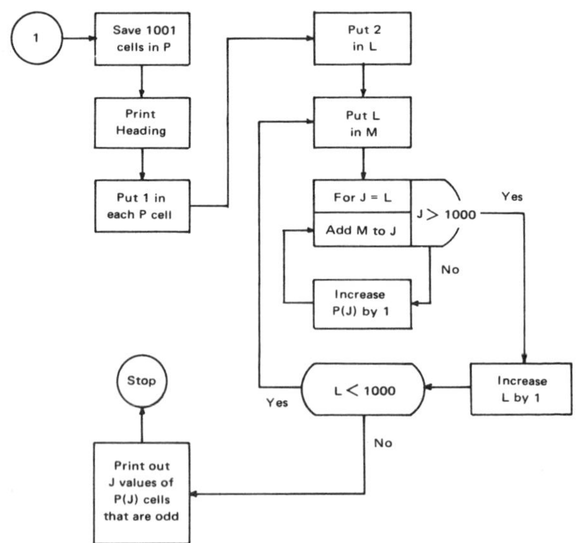

Review Problem 9

A rug dealer sells three grades of carpeting priced at \$13.95, \$16.95, and \$19.95 per sq. yd. All rolls come in either 9 or 12 foot widths. Many customers want to know prices, extra yardage, etc. by using either or both 9 and 12 foot rolls. For example, assume a lady needs carpeting for an 8 ft. by 10 ft. room. She will want to know information such as:

	Left Overs	13.95 Rug	16.95 Rug	19.95 Rug
12 ft. roll	4 by 10	186.00	226.00	266.00
12 ft. roll	2 by 8	148.80	180.80	212.80
9 ft. roll	1 by 10	139.50	169.50	199.50

The flow chart below will give data such as this for any size rug that can be cut from 9 or 12 foot rolls. Write program and try it! You must complete "pricing subroutine".

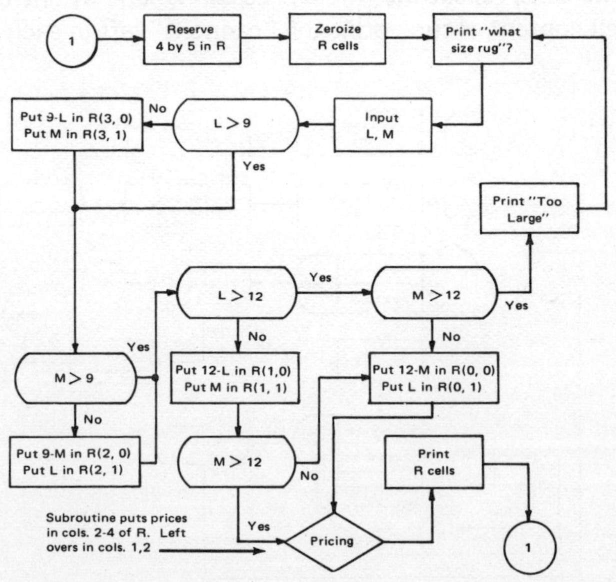

Review Problem 10
The Case of the Frightened King

A king's castle was defended by cannons on each of 100 hills that stretched in a straight line to the South. One day the king issued these orders: "First, take all cannons off the 100th hill; then replace the number of cannon on each hill by the number of hills to its south having an equal or less number of cannon. Continue doing this until no change can occur on any hill. Then let me know how many cannons are on each hill."

To simulate these orders by computer, let us put 99 random integers into the first 99 cells and zero into the last cell of an array. These are the initial cannons. Now, replace each integer by the number of following integers which are equal or less. Each time at least one cell is changed through all 100 cells; repeat the whole process. When not one change in cell content occurs, print the "cannons" left in each cell. Try it!

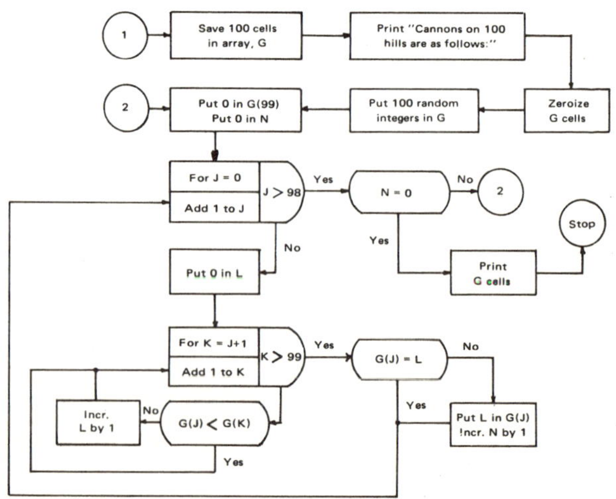

Review Problem 11

"Perfect Numbers" are those that equal the sum of their factors. Euclid's formula: $2^{N-1}(2^N-1)$ gives all the even perfect numbers. No one has yet found an odd one. The formula gives a perfect number only if (2^N-1) is prime. This, in turn, is prime only if N is prime. Yet a prime N rarely gives a prime (2^N-1).

Write a BASIC program to find and print the first 5 perfect numbers. Start with N=2, and print results in a table such as the following:

N	2↑N	2↑(N-1)	2↑N-1	PERFECT NUMBER
2	4	2	3	6

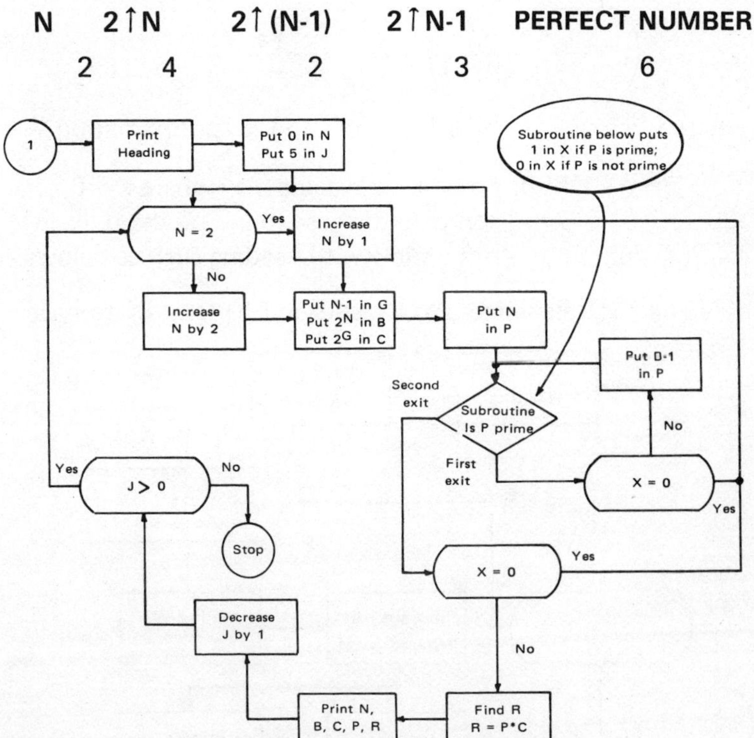

Review Problem 12

In mathematics, there are many uses for the natural base, "e", which has the approximate value of 2.718281828. When this value is raised to different powers, (for example, e^x), it is often called the "exponential function" or "natural function". BASIC provides a built in function for e^x, using EXP(X). These built-in functions are usually calculated by approximation formulae. The one below is an approximation for e^x that is quite accurate if the value of x is less than 1.5

$$e^x = \frac{\left(1 + \frac{3x^2}{28} + \frac{x^4}{1680}\right) + \left(\frac{x}{2} + \frac{x^3}{84}\right)}{\left(1 + \frac{3x^2}{28} + \frac{x^4}{1680}\right) - \left(\frac{x}{2} + \frac{x^3}{84}\right)} + R$$

where R is the remainder (or error), in the approximation.

Write a BASIC program to calculate e^x where x = 0, .15, .30, .45, ... 3 and compare to those found by the built-in EXP(X) function. Print a table with heading such as below:

X Value Calculated e to x Built-in EXP(X) Difference

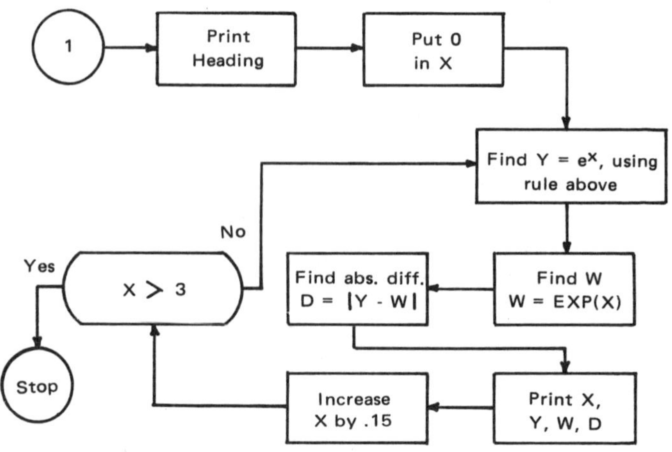

Review Problem 13
A Search For Special Three Digit Integers

If the 3 digit integer, 200, is reversed, the product of the original number and its reverse is a perfect square. Thus: (200)(002) = 400 and 400 is the square of 20. Another similar pair is 300 and 003; 400 and 004; etc. Likewise, the integer, 111, has an equal reverse, which gives a perfect square product. Are there pairs not containing zero digits and where the reverse is not the same as the original? Write a BASIC program to find out. Use the following heading:

NUMBER REVERSE PRODUCT SQUARE ROOT

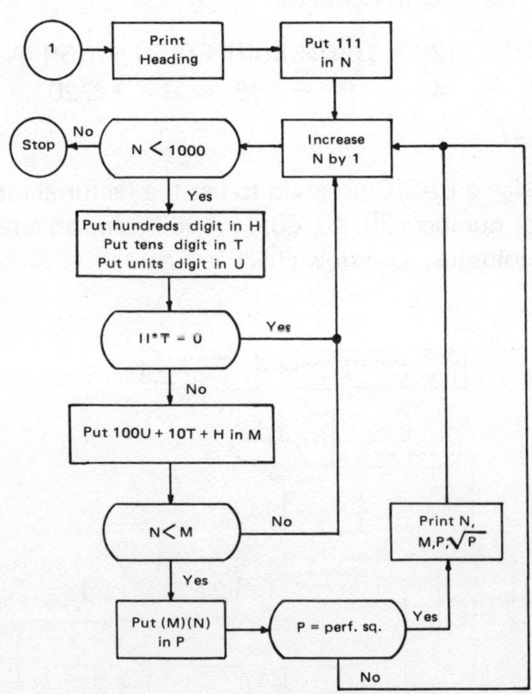

Review Problem 14
Factorial Representation of Integers

As an example, continuously divide 827 by: 2, 3, 4, 5, 6, and 7; saving remainders each time. Thus:

2⌋827	
3⌋413	rem. = 1
4⌋137	rem. = 2
5⌋34	rem. = 1
6⌋6	rem. = 4
7⌋1	rem. = 0
0	rem. = 1

The last divide is when the quotient = 0. Now, the remainders (in order of appearance) are the factorial representation. In this case, 121401

121401 can be considered as:

$$1(1!) + 2(2!) + 1(3!) + 4(4!) + 0(5!) + 1(6!)$$
$$= 1 + 4 + 6 + 96 + 0 + 720$$
$$= 827$$

Design a BASIC program to list the factorial representations of numbers 20, 40, 60, ...1000 using an array of 10 rows, 5 columns. Use flow chart as a guide.

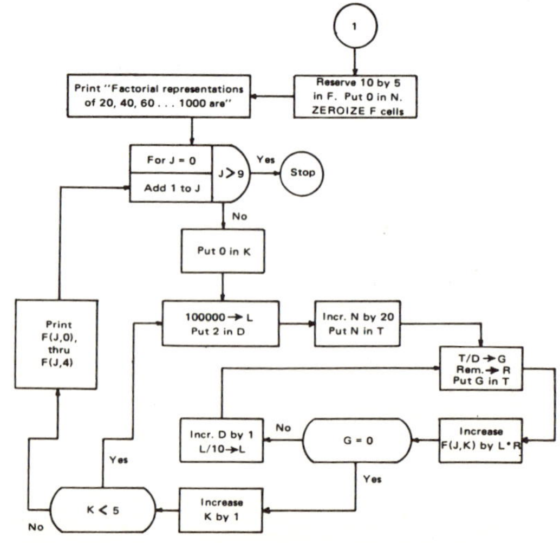

Review Problem 15
Approximating Pi Using Random Numbers

The drawing below shows a quarter circle inside a unit square. The area of the square is 1; whereas, the area of the circle part is $\pi/4$. In the dotted triangle ABC, if the distance C is less than 1, the point C is within the circle part. If distance, AC, equals 1, point C lies on the circle arc and we will consider it as within the circle. However, if the distance AC is more than 1, point C lies outside the circle part.

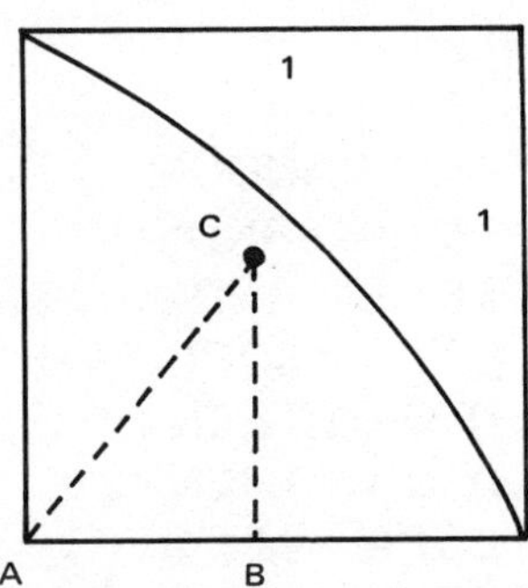

If one knows AB and BC, he can find AC by the rule:

$$AC=\sqrt{(AB)^2 + (BC)^2}$$

Example: If AB = .42, BC = .65

$$AC=\sqrt{(.42)^2 + (.65)^2}$$

AC = .77 approx.

The probability that a point at C will fall inside the circle is the ratio of the area of the quadrant ($\pi/4$) to the area of the square (1). This means point C should fall inside approx. $\pi/4$ times. Let us design a BASIC program to test our random number function and at the same time approximate the value of π. We will do this as below.

(1) In all, find 2000 random pairs between 0 and 1.
(2) Assign each pair respectively to AB, BC (as above).
(3) Calculate AC by the rule (example above).
(4) Add 1 to either: L, E, or M depending on whether AC is less, equal, or more than 1.
(5) After each 200 pairs print: L, E, M, (L+E)/K where K is successively: 200, 400, . . . 2000.

Partial Solution to Review Problem 15

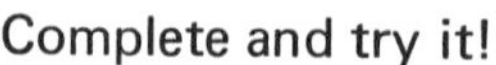

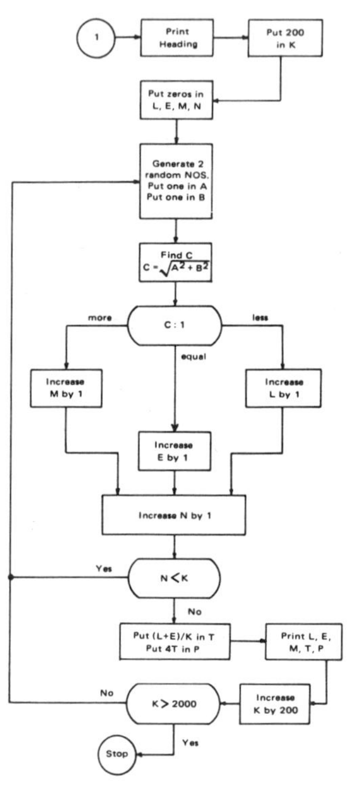


```
 9 PRINT "INSIDE", "ON
   CIRCLE", "OUTSIDE",
   "IN/TOTAL", "PI"
10 LET K = 200
11 PRINT
12 LET L = 0
13 LET E = 0
14 LET M = 0
15 LET N = 0
18 REM RANDOM
20 LET A = RND(X)
24 LET B = RND(X)
30 LET C = SQR(A*A+B*B)
32 IF C = 1 THEN 48
34 IF C <1 THEN 42
38 LET M = M + 1
40 GO TO 50
42 LET L = L + 1
44 GO TO 50
48 LET E = E + 1
50 LET N = N + 1
52 IF N < K THEN 20
```

Review Problem 16
Test Your Random Selection

Assume an array of 20 cells with 4 rows and 5 columns as shown below.

<table>
<tr><td></td><td></td><td></td><td>4</td><td>8</td></tr>
<tr><td></td><td>1</td><td></td><td>7</td><td></td></tr>
<tr><td>3</td><td></td><td>6</td><td>10</td><td>2</td></tr>
<tr><td>5</td><td></td><td></td><td>9</td><td></td></tr>
</table>

The computer generates 10 random numbers in the range 11, 12, 13, . . . 30. The order of appearance is marked in the squares. For example, if random numbers are: 17, 25, 21, 14, 26, 23, 19, 15, 29, 24; 1 is put in square 7, 2 in square 15, etc. (Cell number is 10 less than random number).

A person is then told to input any 10 numbers from 11 through 30. The computer prints the 2 matrices; one showing the person's choices, the other showing the random choices; and also a <u>score.</u> The score is the sum of the absolute differences of the two matrix cells. (Perfect score = 0, poor = 100.) How well can you match the computer? Try it!

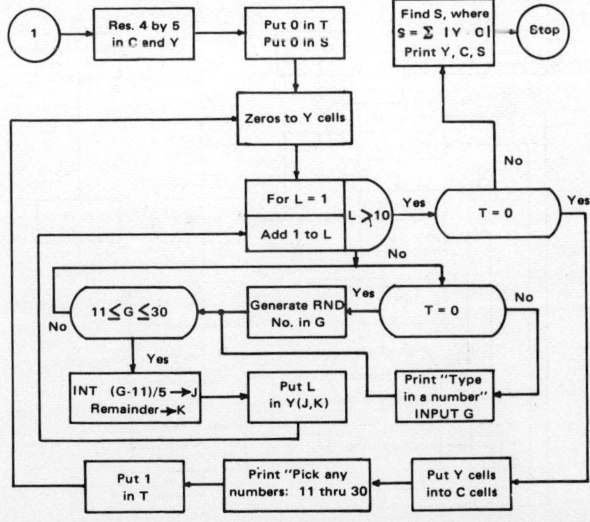

Review Problem 17

Numbers which can represent a triangular pattern of dots are called "triangular numbers". Thus:

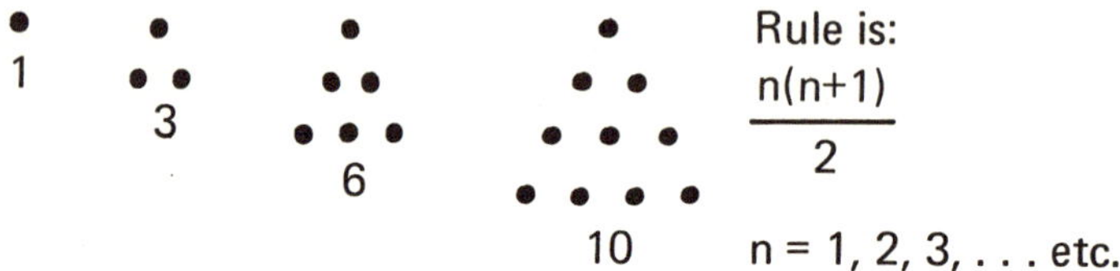

Numbers which can represent a square pattern of dots are called "square numbers". Thus:

1, 4, 9, 16

Rule is:

m^2

m = 1, 2, 3, . . . etc.

Are there numbers that are both triangular and square? Why not find out? Write a BASIC program to print the first 50 triangular numbers in an array 10 by 5. Then print out the first 5 numbers that are both triangular and square.

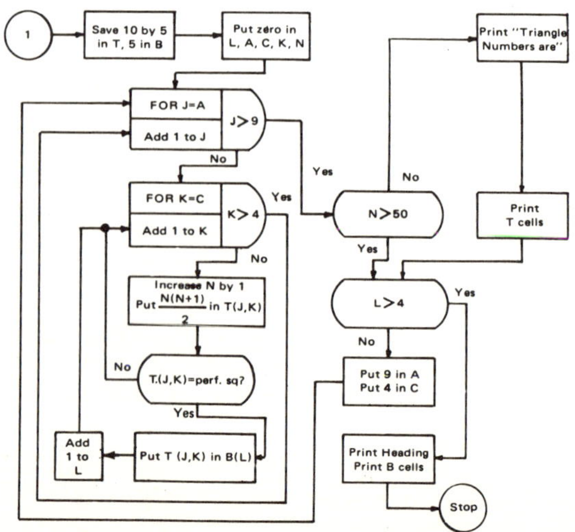

Review Problem 18
The Gilbreath Principle

If you do not know this principle - long a favorite with card "sharps" - perhaps this program will explain it to you. Reserve an array of 60 cells in D (any length can be used - you card players can use 52 if you wish). Now, type in two numbers: F and N. The first, F, indicates the starting number; the second, N, must be an exact divisor of the total number of cells, and this indicates how many items are in each sequence. The computer uses F and N to assign values to each cell. For example, assume one types in 11 for F and 3 for N. The computer then assigns values as follows: 11, 12, 13; 11, 12, 13; 11, 12, 13; 11, 12, 13; . . . etc. If one types in 4 (for F) and 5 (for N) the assignments are: 4, 5, 6, 7, 8; 4, 5, 6, 7, 8; 4, 5, 6, 7, 8; . . . . etc.

Since exact divisors less than 60 must be used for N; the largest possible N is 30. (If 52 is being used, 2, 4, 13, 26 can be used for N.)

Now type in a third number, C, to indicate where to cut the deck. For simplicity, let us limit C to any integer between 1 and 21. The computer removes C "cards" from the bottom of "deck" D, and lists these in reverse order. This list is the cut or second deck. The numbers left in D are the first deck.

Now for each listed number in the cut deck, one must indicate (by a type in) where to insert that number in the first deck. (This is the "shuffle"). More than one number can be inserted at the same place but insertions must be by increasing type ins. For example, type ins of 4, 4, 4, 7, 8 will put first three of cut deck in front of card 4, the next in front of card 7, the next in front of card 8, . . . etc.

Finally, the "shuffled" deck is printed. If you are surprised, try it again - it is the Gilbreath Principle!

The Gilbreath Principle

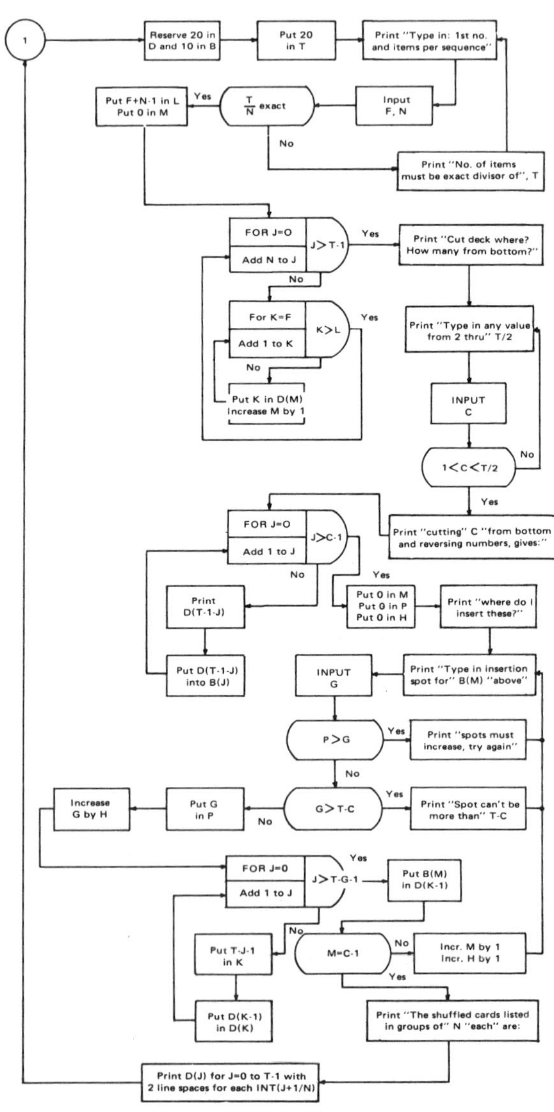

Review Problem 19

The area of a triangle in terms of its three sides (a,b,c) is given by the formula:

$$K = \sqrt{s(s - a)\ (s - b)\ (s - c)}$$

where $s = (a + b + c)/2$

Find and print (under heading below) the triangles whose areas are integral and whose sides are consecutive integers less than 1000.

SIDE A SIDE B SIDE C AREA OF TRIANGLE

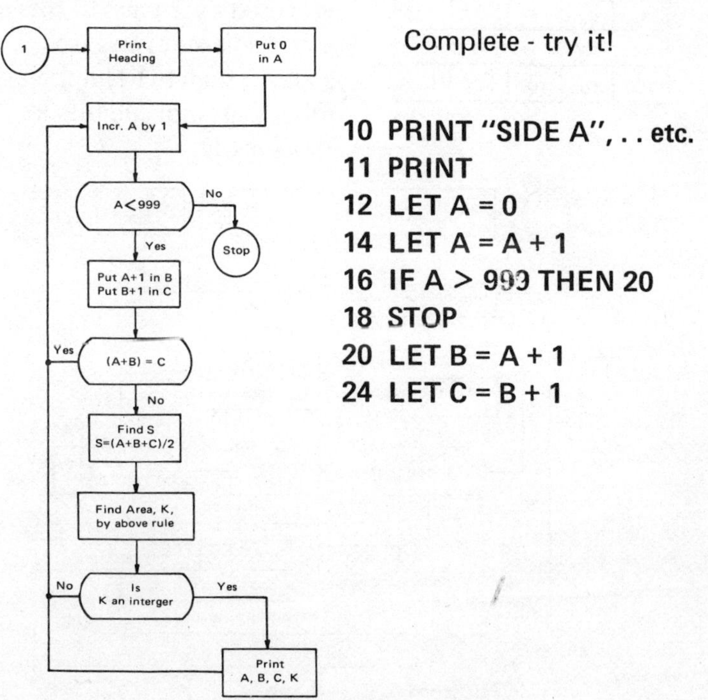

Complete - try it!

```
10 PRINT "SIDE A", . . etc.
11 PRINT
12 LET A = 0
14 LET A = A + 1
16 IF A > 999 THEN 20
18 STOP
20 LET B = A + 1
24 LET C = B + 1
```

Review Problem 20
Computer Target Search

An ammunition dump is made up of 50 underground caves with 10 rows of 5 caves each. Bombs landing in an $\begin{pmatrix} x & x \\ x & x \end{pmatrix}$ pattern in any 2 adjacent rows destroy the whole dump. (See sketch for sample distribution.) Write a BASIC program to indicate how many firings a battery of 4 guns will require to make such a pattern. Also print out the whole matrix showing number of hits in all caves. Assume each gun in the battery is aimed at random caves.

110	107	107	101	106
X	117	X	124	120
X	212	X	110	116
⋮				⋮
105	109	100	111	112

Number the caves in order as: 11, 12, 13, . . . 60. An impact is caused by 2 pairs of hits in any 2 adjacent rows (see x spots in sketch.) Numbers in other cells indicate hits in those spots.

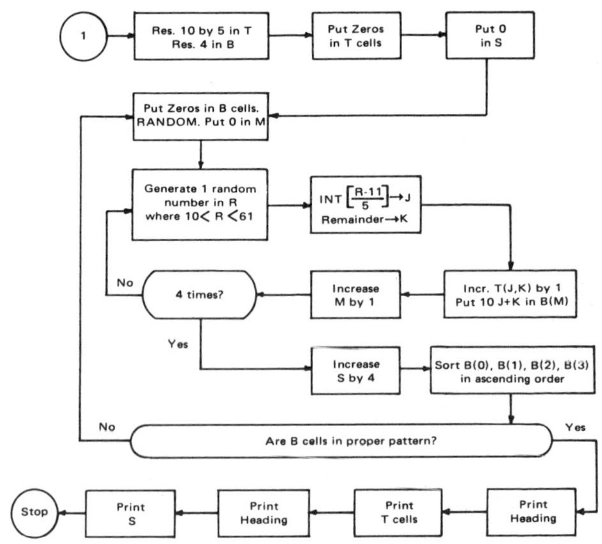

Review Problem 21

A famous Egyptian Pharaoh, after a great victory, granted his slaves the following reward: "In this pile", he said, "are 99 rods, each an integral length, ranging from 1 through 99 units. Each of you can select any length from 1 thru 99. My number experts will then calculate all possible triangles of integral areas that can be formed by the rod equal to your chosen length and any two larger rods of this pile".

"Each of you", he continued, "will receive a parcel of land equal to the sum of the areas of all triangles whose one side is your chosen length".

Some received a lot of land, some received a little – and perhaps, some received none? Why not let the computer give you the details?

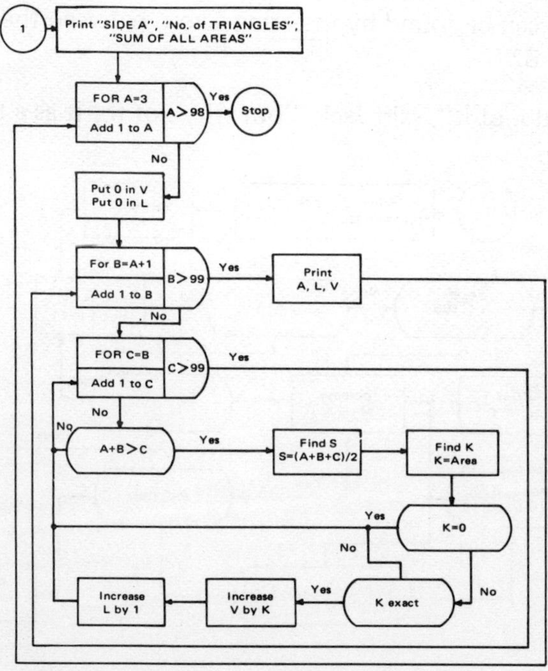

Review Problem 22

"An interesting thought came to me", said Tom. "Have you noticed that 10 times 40 = 400 can be considered in the following way:

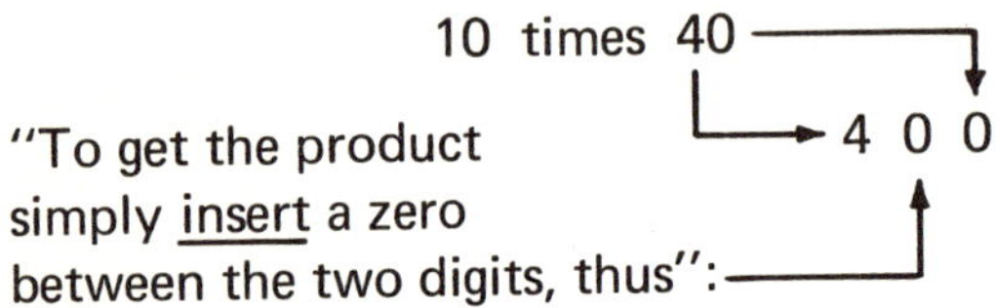

"So what", quipped Jack, "10 times 20 is 200, 10 times 90 is 900, etc.".

"Yes", answered Tom, "however, there may be other numbers where the product can be found the same way. In other words, are there integers A, B, where the product of A and B can be found by inserting a zero between the two digits of B?"

"I doubt it", said Jack, "but why not try it as a BASIC program?"

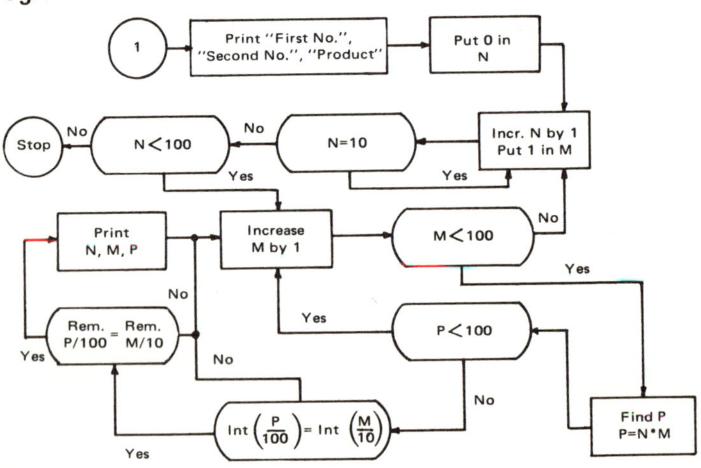

Review Problem 23

A union signed the following work contract:

(a) Ten separate jobs are to be done requiring respectively: 10, 20, 30, 40, ... 100 hours of work.

(b) Three workers are to be assigned to each job.

(c) Each worker must work an exact number of hours and no two workers on a job can work the same number of hours.

(d) The union shall receive, for each job, an amount equal to the product of the hours worked by the three workers. For example, if workers on the 10 hour job worked 2, 3, and 5 hours (note sum is 10) the total pay is $30 (product of 2, 3, and 5).

Write a BASIC program to show "best plan" for the union to follow. Use heading such as:

JOB LENGTH MAN-1 MAN-2 MAN-3 AMOUNT

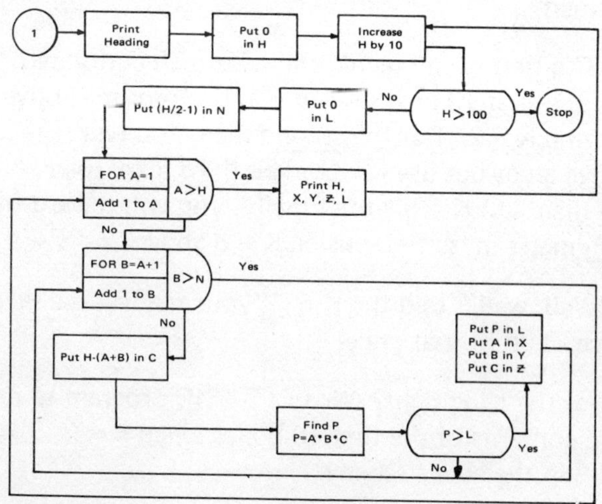

Review Problem 24

"Ask what you wish", said the King, "and I will grant you and your men what you ask".

"Agreed", replied the wise man, "there are 7 of us to be rewarded. I ask the following of your kingdom".

"Set aside 100 safety boxes. First, place in each an amount of dollar bills equal to the box number. Thus boxes will initially contain: $1, $2, $3, . . . $100. Second, empty every Kth box where K is initially 2. Third, shift money in boxes from right to left so that only boxes on the extreme right will be empty. For example, if boxes contain 1, 0, 3, 0, 5, 0, . . . etc., after shifting, they will contain 1, 3, 5, . . . 000. Fourth, find the partial sums and put these sums in the 100 boxes. Partial sums are found by adding the contents of all boxes preceding and including the box itself. Thus, partial sum of first box is 1; partial sum of second box is sum of boxes 1 and 2; partial sum of third box is sum of boxes 1, 2, and 3; etc. Fifth, give the contents of the first 10 boxes to one of my men".

"The first of my men", the wise man continued, "will receive the first 10 boxes when you perform the above five steps using K = 2. For the second man, you will repeat the same five steps but use K = 3. The third man, use K = 4; the fourth man, use K = 5, etc. Finally, you will reward the seventh man - myself - by using K = 8 above".

"Well, well", said the King, "your request is a mere pittance. I grant it at once!"

Was the King right? Write a BASIC program to print out the contents of the first 10 boxes when K = 2, 3, 4, 5, 6, 7, and 8 in the above scheme.

The King Grants a "Pittance" Request

Write, try it, think!

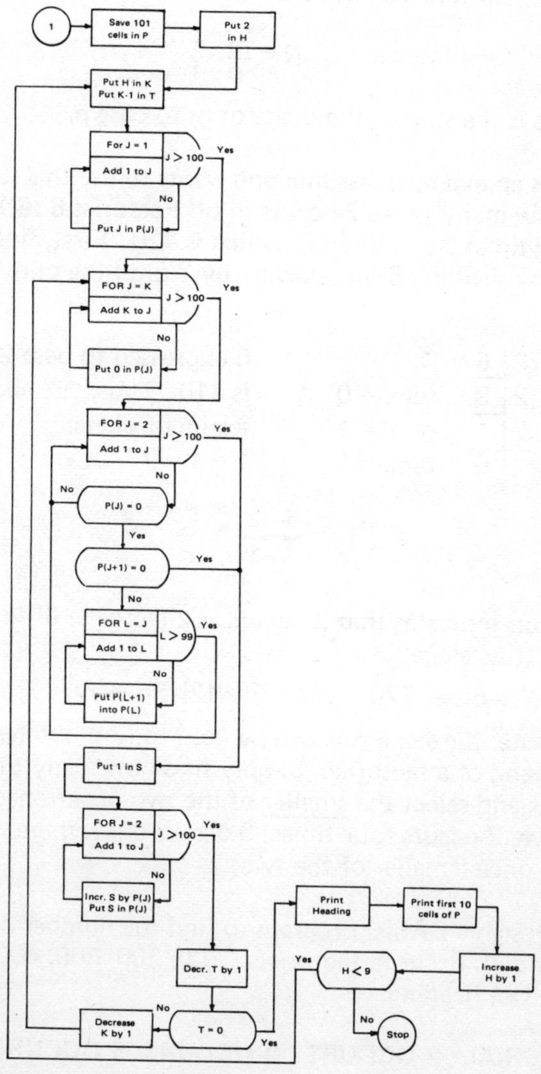

Review Problem 25

To find how many times a prime, p, occurs in any factorial, m!, one can use the rule:

$$N = \frac{m - s}{p - 1}$$

where s is the sum of the digits of m to base p.

As an example, assume one wants to use this rule to find how many times 2 occurs in 6! Factorial 6 (6!) is 1 times 2 times 3 . . . times 6, which is 720. First, find "s" above by dividing 6 successively by 2 until the quotient is zero.

2 | 6		6 expressed to base 2
2 | 3	rem. = 0	is 110. Thus, "s" above
2 | 1	rem. = 1	= sum of digits:
0	rem. = 1	1 + 1 = 2

$$N = \frac{6 - 2}{2 - 1} = \frac{4}{1} = 4$$

This indicates that 2 occurs as a factor in 6! four times. This is true, since:

6! = 720 = (2)(2)(2)(2)(3)(3)(5)

Note, the same rule can be used to find number of zeros on the end of a factorial. Simply find how many times 2 and 5 occur and select the smaller of the two occurrences. Thus, in above, 2 occurs four times; 5 occurs once; therefore 10 occurs once (smaller of the two).

Design a BASIC program to find the number of times 2, 3, 5, and 10 occur in factorials: 100, 200, 300, 400, ... , 2000. Use heading:

FACTORIAL 2 OCCURS 3 OCCURS 5 OCCURS 10 OCCURS

Review Problem 26
Computer "Guesses" Your Number

If one knows the sums of certain digits in a number, he can work out what the number is. The following example uses this in order to enable the computer to "discover" what number you were thinking about. Try it and discover how it works.

```
08  DIM T(15)
09  PRINT
10  PRINT "WRITE ANY NUMBER, 3 TO 9 DIGITS, ON A PIECE OF PAPER"
11  PRINT "WHEN READY, TYPE IN THE NUMBER- -THEN A CAR. RETURN"
12  INPUT W
13  LET S=0
14  LET E=0
15  LET H=-1
16  MAT T=ZER
17  PRINT "HOW MANY DIGITS ARE THERE IN YOUR NUMBER?
18  PRINT
19  INPUT N
20  LET G=N/2
21  IF G <> INT(N/2) THEN 23
22  LET E=1
23  FOR J=0 TO N-2
24  LET K=J+1
25  PRINT
26  PRINT "WHAT IS SUM OF DIGIT "K" AND DIGIT "K + 1. "
27  PRINT
28  INPUT T(J)
29  NEXT J
30  PRINT "WHAT IS SUM OF DIGIT "E + 1 AND LAST DIGIT?"
31  PRINT
32  INPUT T(K)
36  FOR J=E TO N-1
38  LET H=-1 * H
40  LET S=S+T(J) * H
41  NEXT J
42  LET S=S/2
43  LET T(K+1)=S
44  LET G=1
45  LET S=0
46  FOR J=0 TO N-1
50  LET L=N-J-1
52  LET T(L) = T(L) - T(L+1)
53  LET S=S+T(L) * G
54  LET G= 10 * G
56  NEXT J
58  PRINT
60  PRINT "YOUR NUMBER IS- -S"
62  GO TO 9
65  END
```

Review Problem 27
Simulating a Dice Game; A versus B

Rules: On first throw, the thrower (A or B) wins if he gets 7 or 11. He loses if it is: 2, 3, or 12. Any other sum becomes his "point". If he rolls this "point" on successive throws, he wins. However, a 7 while trying to get a "point" is a loss. Dice change hands on each loss.

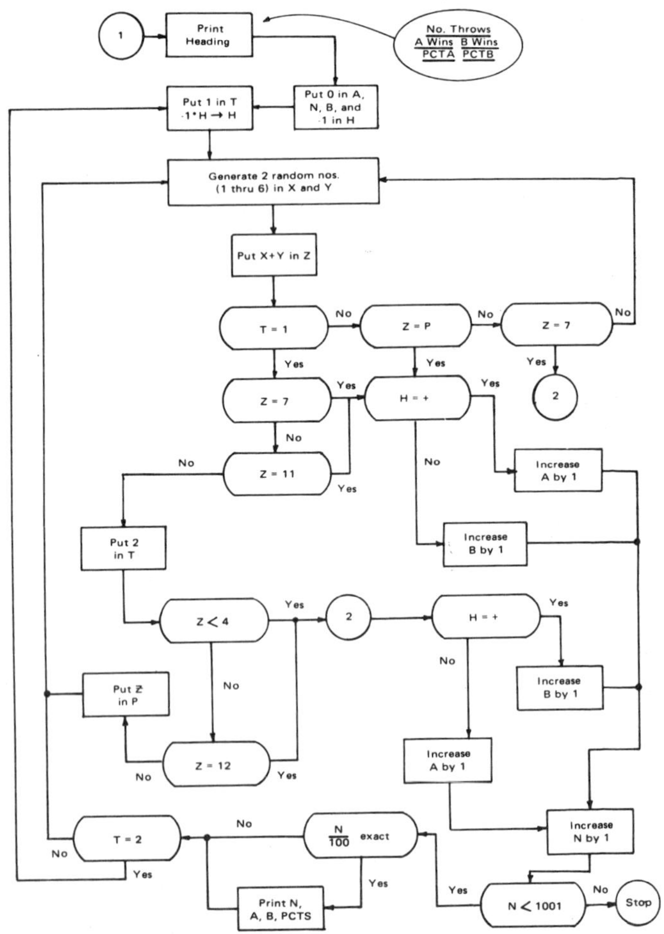

Review Problem 28
Radix Sorting

"Radix sorting" is often useful. In this scheme, one first sorts all numbers by order of each <u>unit</u> digit; then each tens digit; hundreds digit, etc.; until the leftmost digits have been thus sorted. As an example, the following are radix sorted.

Original numbers: 3126, 3025, 3120, 7177, 7241, 5146, 5357, 5124, 1700, 1214, 1705, 132, 150, 799, 610

<u>First</u>, they are sorted by the units digits:

3120, 1700, 150, 610, 7241, 132, 5124, 1214, 3025, 1705, 3126, 5146, 7177, 5357, 799. Note zero units digits appear first, then 1, 2, 3, . . . etc. This is called a "pass".

<u>Second</u> pass; sort the above by order of tens digits:

1700, 1705, 610, 1214, 3120, 5124, 3025, 3126, 132, 7241, 5146, 150, 5357, 7177, 799

<u>Third</u> pass; sort the above by order of hundreds digits (the 3rd digit from right):

3025, 5124, 3120, 3126, 132, 5146, 150, 7177, 1214, 7241, 5357, 610, 1700, 1705, 799

Finally, the last pass is to sort on the <u>fourth</u> digit from the right. (This is zero if number is less than 4 digits.)

0132, 0150, 0610, 0799, 1214, 1700, 1705, 3025, 3120, 3126, 5124, 5146, 5353, 7177, 7241

The following flow chart uses this method to sort 40 random numbers of up to 4 digits each, printing out each "pass". Try it!

Radix Sort

1
Save 40 cells in each R, T
Put zero in V
FOR J = 0
Add 1 to J
J > 39
Yes
No
Put 4 digit random no. in R(J)
Put 0 in K
Put 0 in L
FOR J = 0
Add 1 to J
J > 39
Yes
No
Yes
R(J) = 1
No
Put R(J) in H
FOR M = 0
Add 1 to M
M > V
Yes
No
Put INT (H/10) in Z
Put H-10Z in G
Put Z in H
No
G = L
Yes
Put R(J) in T(K)
Put 1 in R(J)
Incr. K by 1
Increase L by 1
Yes
L < 10
No
No
V < 4
Change dim. of T to 40.
Put T in R
Change dimension of T to 8 by 5
Print T cells
Yes
Stop
Increase V by 1

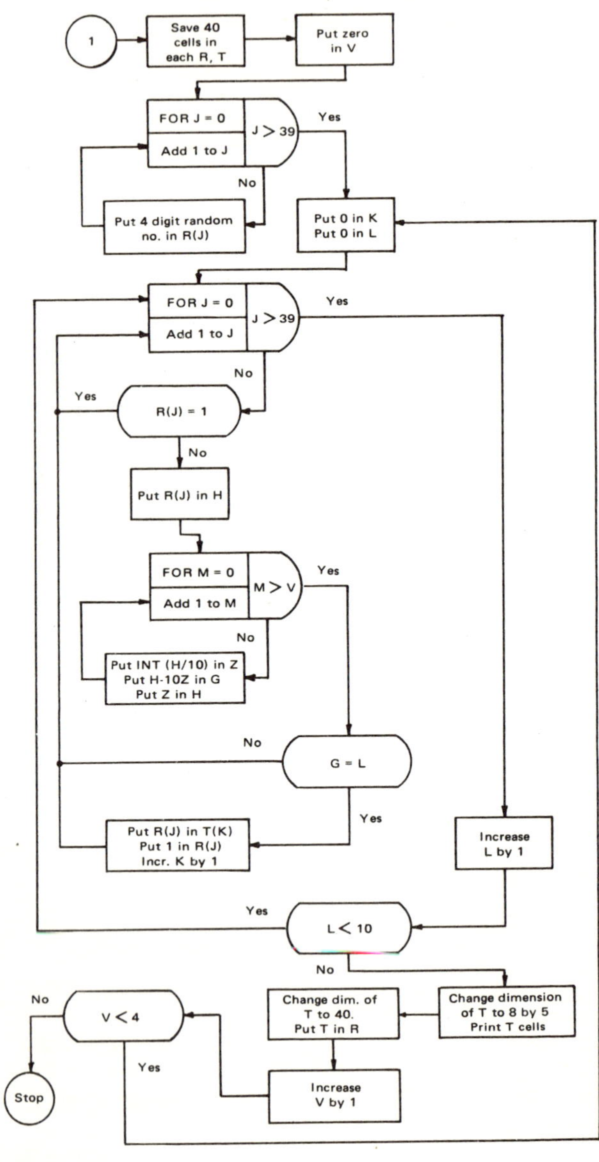

Review Problem 29
The Largest Monotone Increasing Subsequence

Any series of numbers is a sequence. Thus:

3 7 6 5 11 8 13

If one crosses out terms, a "subsequence" is left.

3 ~~7~~ 6 ~~5~~ 11 ~~8~~ 13

3, 6, 11, 13 is a "monotone" increasing subsequence. It is called "monotone" if it is either increasing or decreasing. Can we design a BASIC program to find the largest monotone increasing subsequence from a series? That is our problem.

First, each term itself forms a subsequence of 1. Thus, we can assign 1 to each term to start.

Second, if any term X is larger than a preceding term; its subsequence is one more than the maximum subsequence of its lesser terms. For example, 3, 4, 5 forms the following subsequences:

Subseq. of 1st Term	**Subseq. of 2nd Term**	**Subseq. of 3rd Term**
~~1~~	~~1~~	~~1~~
1	2	3

First we assign 1 to each as its subsequence. Now since, the second term is more than the first, we assign one more than the subsequence of the first term to the second. But the third term is more than the first and the second. Therefore, we assign 1 more than the maximum of these – in other words, we assign 1 more than 2 (of second) to the third. The subsequence ratings are: 1, 2, 3; and the longest is the one ending with the third term. Thus, the longest subsequence is 3, 4, 5.

Design a BASIC program to generate and print 100 random integers of 3 digits. Then find and print the longest monotone increasing subsequence of the 100 terms.

Largest Subsequence Flow Chart

Write it and try it!

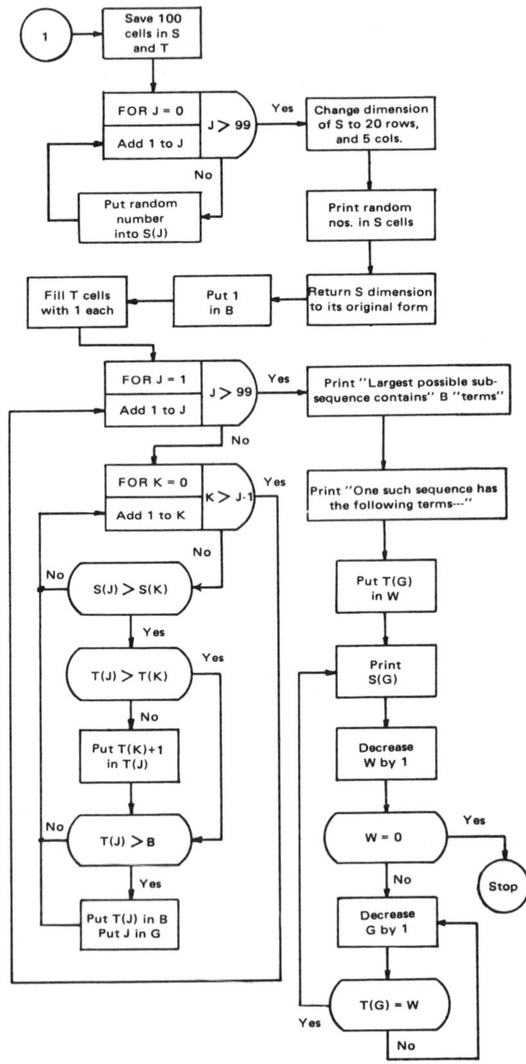

Review Problem 30
Angle, Arc Measurement in Mils

The Mil unit is often neglected, yet is very useful for some special aspects of angle and arc measurement. The Mil unit is:

1 degree = 17.777778 mils
90 degrees = 1600 mils
1 mil = .05625 degrees
1 mil = .00098175 radians

Length of arc on circumference of a circle of radius γ is approx. $\frac{\gamma\alpha}{1000}$ where α is the subtended angle in mils.

Design a BASIC program to print a table (see heading) for angles 0, 5, 10, . . . 90 degrees and showing mils, radians, and arc length.

ANGLE NO. OF MILS NO. RADIANS ARC LENGTH

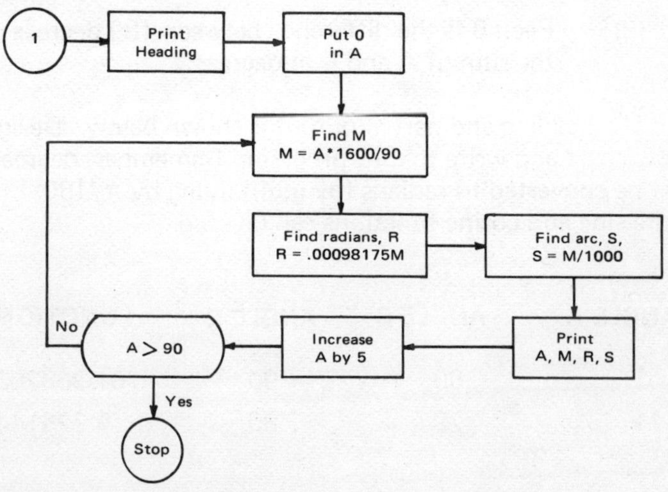

Review Problem 31

A Special Function of an Acute Triangle

Let A, B, C be the angles of an acute triangle (A, B, C each less than or equal to 90 degrees). Examine the following function and decide what value, if any, the function appears to have as a lower limit.

$$G = \frac{\sqrt{1 + 8\cos^2 A}}{\sin C} + \frac{\sqrt{1 + 8\cos^2 B}}{\sin A} + \frac{\sqrt{1 + 8\cos^2 C}}{\sin B}$$

Design a BASIC program to print the values of A, B, C, and G using the heading shown below and the following relationships:

(1) Let C start with 90 degrees and decrease by 10 degrees until C = 0.

(2) For each value of C, let A start with 1 degree and increase by 10 degrees until A = 46 degrees.

(3) Each B is the difference between 180 degrees and the sum of A and C in degrees.

The heading and partial output is shown below. Design a flow chart and write BASIC program. Remember, degrees must be converted to radians (by multiplying by $\pi/180$) before sine and cosine functions can be used.

ANGLE A	ANGLE B	ANGLE C	FUNCTION
1	89	90	61.3682039
11	79	90	9.9251448

Review Problem 32
Finding Value of a Polynomial Function

A polynomial function, Y, can be represented as:

$$(1)\ Y = C(0) + C(1)X + C(2)X^2 + C(3)X^3 + C(4)X^4 + C(5)X^5$$

where C(0), C(1) . . . (C5) are constants.

To find the value of Y for a particular X, one substitutes the X value in the above and finds a unique Y value. For example:

$$Y = 3 + 3X - 2X^3 + X^4;\ \text{when } X = 2$$
$$Y = 3 + 3(2) - 2(2)^3 + (2)^4$$
$$Y = 9$$

Design a BASIC program to solve the above polynomial (Equation 1), permitting one to type in a value, X.

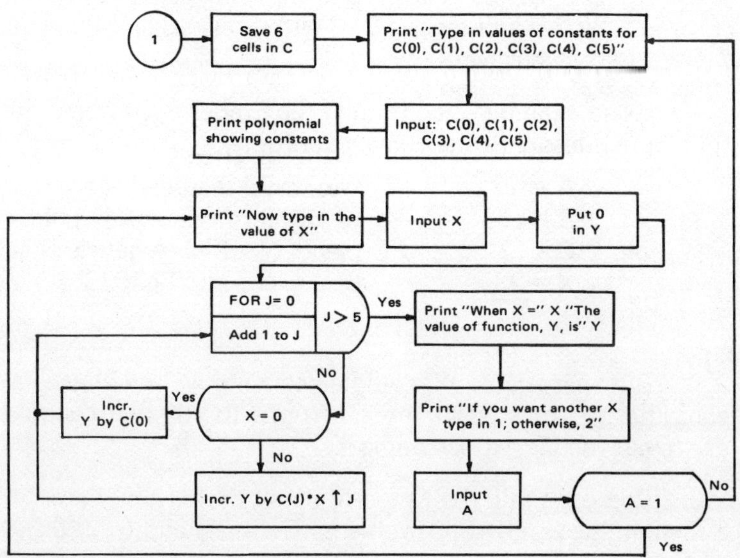

Review Problem 33
Three Kings and the Emperor

"We will divide up the produce of our slaves in the following way", said the Emperor to the three Kings (A, B, C) who ruled his provinces.

"First, King A may choose any of the integers 1 thru 99.

Second, Once A makes a choice, King B must choose an integer 1 more than A; and King C must choose an integer 1 more than B.

Third, As Emperor, my integer, X, which must be less than 100 will be found by the following: $(A^2 - X)(B^2 - X) = (C^2 - X)$.

Fourth, Once choices are made, we will divide up all the wealth into gold equal to the sum of A, B, C, and X and from this sum; A will receive A, B will receive B, C will receive C and I will receive X".

"As an example", continued the Emperor, "assume the following integers fit the above conditions:

	A = 5	We would then divide all wealth into units of 41 gold pieces of which A gets 5, B gets 6, C gets 7 and I get 23".
	B = 6	
	C = 7	
	X = 23	
Total	41	

"But that is unfair", complained King A, "I will need a computer to know which integer from 1 to 100 that I should use to get the largest percentage".

"Correct", said the Emperor, "and that is why I am assigning this as a BASIC problem. Get busy and try it using a heading such as:

KING A KING B KING C EMPEROR PCT FOR A

Review Problem 34
How About a "Fair" Card Game?

Let us simulate the following card game. We will choose 2 cards from the deck of 52 cards. If at least one card is a spade, you win $1. If neither card is a spade, I win $1. Let us consider each drawing of 2 cards a "game" and let us play 100, 200, 300, 400, . . . 1000 games, determining your wins and losses for each 100 games. Let us further agree to form our card "deck" by random numbers; where spades, hearts, clubs, and diamonds are as follows:

Spades = 1 thru 13 Clubs = 27 thru 39
Hearts = 14 thru 26 Diamonds = 40 thru 52

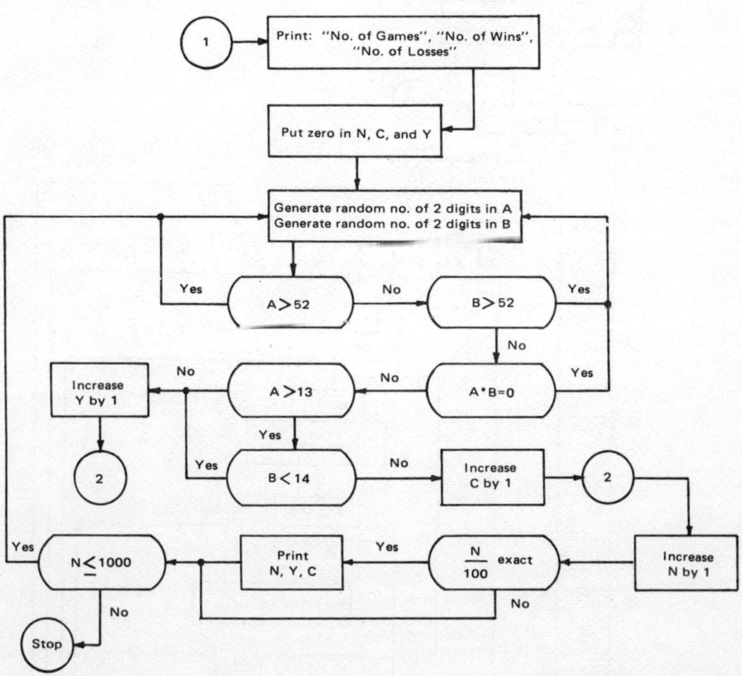

Review Problem 35
Searching for Special Numbers

Are there integers less than 10000 that are equal to the sum of their digits raised to the 3rd or 4th powers. For example, are there numbers:

$$100\,h + 10th + u = h^3 + t^3 + u^3$$

$$1000X + 100h + 10t + u = X^4 + h^4 + t^4 + u$$

An example is the number, 153

$$153 = 1^3 + 5^3 + 3^3$$

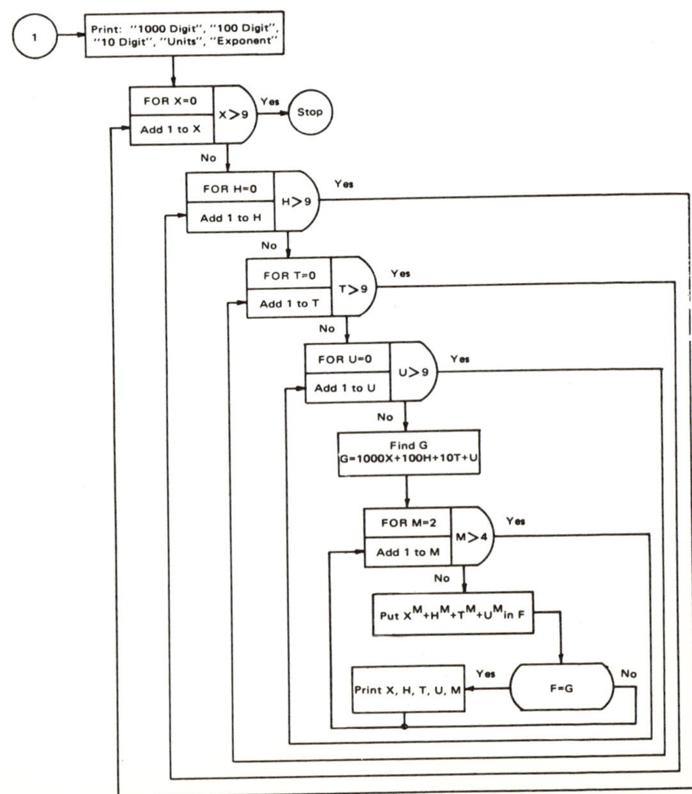

Review Problem 36
A Rank Correlation

Assume two tests are given to each of several students. Is there any relationship (correlation) between results? One such measure is the rank correlation, R, by the formula:

$$R = 1 - \frac{6\sum d^2}{N(N^2-1)}$$

where $\sum d^2$ is the sum of the squared differences between corresponding ranks of scores and N is the number of paired scores. As an example, assume scores on two tests by 5 students are:

Score X	Score Y	Rank X	Rank Y	d^2
32	45	5	4	1
62	34	2	5	9
42	70	4	1	9
80	50	1	2.5	2.25
55	50	3	2.5	.25
			$\sum d^2 =$	21.50

$$R = 1 - \frac{6(21.50)}{5(25-1)} = -.07 \text{ approx.}$$

Perfect positive correlation (high on one = high on other, low on one = low on other) is R = +1. Perfect negative correlation (high on one = low on other) is R = -1. The example indicates almost zero correlation.

Note how ranks are determined. Highest is rank 1, next is rank 2, etc. Note how ties are ranked. It is the average of the positions (see two 50 scores in Y, average of position 2 and 3 is 2.5).

We will now program this application!

Rank Correlation (Continued)

Assume two tests are given to three classes containing 10, 20, 30 students. Find and print a table similar to previous example for each class. Use random number generation to determine test scores. (If random numbers determine test scores, correlation, R, should be approximately zero.)

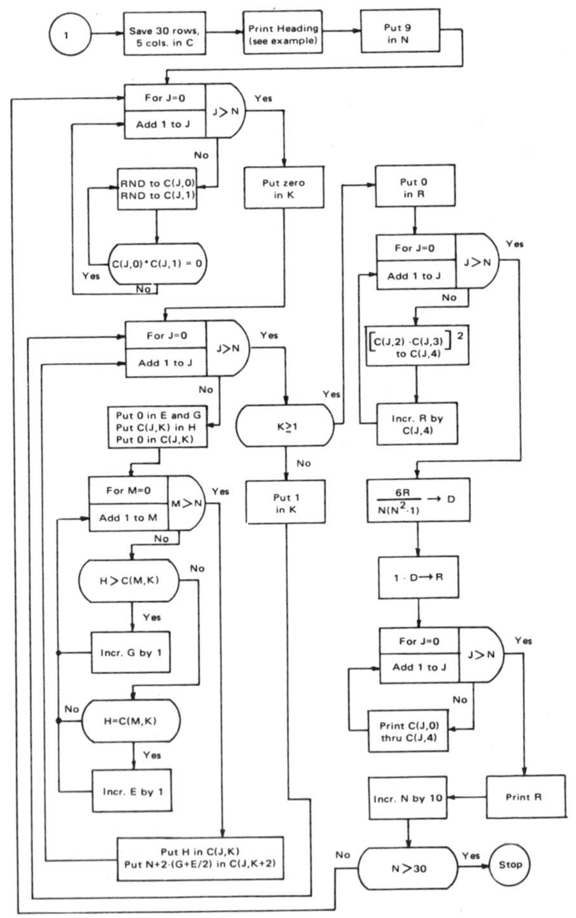

Review Problem 37
The Theory of Runs

A "run" is defined as a succession of similar responses or results. For example:

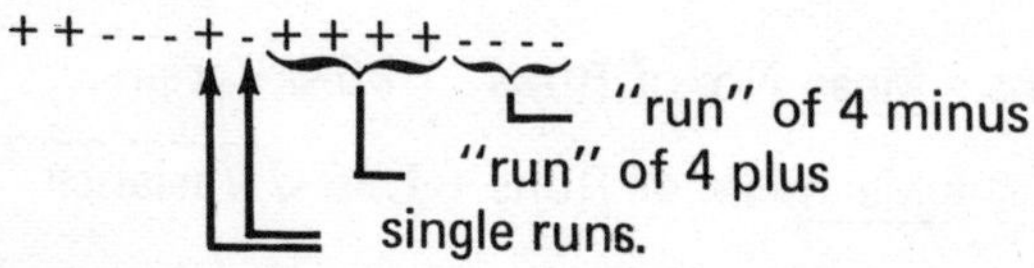

The above example contains 6 "runs" altogether. It is possible to define limits of runs statistically. As a result, various agricultural experiments and other research conducive to "run theory" can use runs to determine if crop treatment, etc. has been effective. In a "normal statistical distribution" of runs the Mean, M, and Variance, V, is:

$$M = \frac{2(N1)(N2)}{N1 + N2} + 1$$

$$V = \frac{2(N1)(N2)\left[2(N1)(N2) - N1 - N2\right]}{(N1 + N2)^2 (N1 + N2 - 1)}$$

where N1, N2 are the number of cases in each of two distributions being compared.

Let us use the run theory to test how well we are able to select "chance numbers". Here is the plan. Permit a person to select any 30 numbers of 2 digits each. At the same time, have the computer select 30 random numbers. To distinguish the two sets, multiply each by 10 and add 1 to the set selected by the computer. Thus, if the person selects 27, 62, 43 . . . . and the computer selects 13, 97, 14 . . .; after multiplying and adding 1 to computer choices, these become 270, 620, 430 . . . and 131, 971, 141 . . . . Now put all 60 in order from high to low and use run theory to determine if both sets came from about the same distribution.

Theory of Runs (Continued)

Runs are determined by succession of same units digits (0 or 1). Number of single, double, triple, and more than 3, runs are also found. The least and highest number of runs is found by the rules:

$$\text{Least Runs} = \underline{\text{Mean}}\ \text{No. of Runs} - 1.96\sqrt{\text{Variance}}$$

$$\text{Most Runs} = \underline{\text{Mean}}\ \text{No. of Runs} + 1.96\sqrt{\text{Variance}}$$

If total runs do not fall within these limits the chances are about 3/100 the two distributions are not similar - in this case, your choice of 30 numbers is not random. Give it a try!

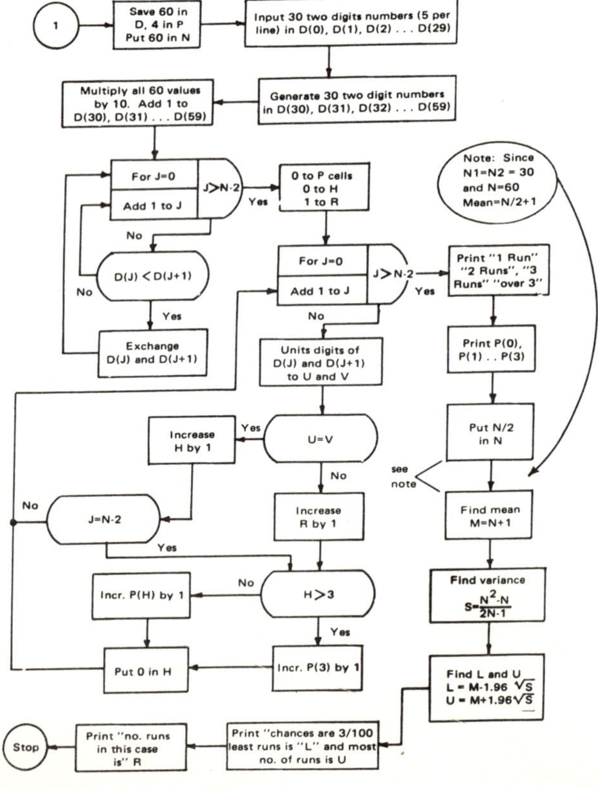

Review Problem 38
Ordinary Annuities

A sequence of equal payments at equal time intervals is an "annuity". Thus, payments of rent, car payments, some insurance, etc. are annuities. When payments are made at the end of each interval, it is an "ordinary" annuity. If the rate of interest is an annual rate it is called "effective."

We will make use of two formulae for an ordinary annuity using effective rates of interest:

$$(1) \qquad V = P\,\frac{(1+R)^N - 1}{R(1+R)^N}$$

$$(2) \qquad S = P\,\frac{(1+R)^N - 1}{R}$$

where: P, R, N, V, and S are respectively:

Payments, Rate, No. of years, Present Value, Sum.

Thus, there are five parameters in the two formulae: P, R, N are in both; V is in the first, and S in the second.

Present Value, V, is the worth of the annuity at the start of its term. Sum, S, is the total sum of the values of all the periodic payments at the end of the term.

Write a BASIC program to find and print the five parameters above if any two, with the exception of Rate, R, are unknown. In other words, the following combinations of parameters can be unknown: V and S; Vand P; V and N; S and P; S and N; and P and N.

Annuity (Continued)

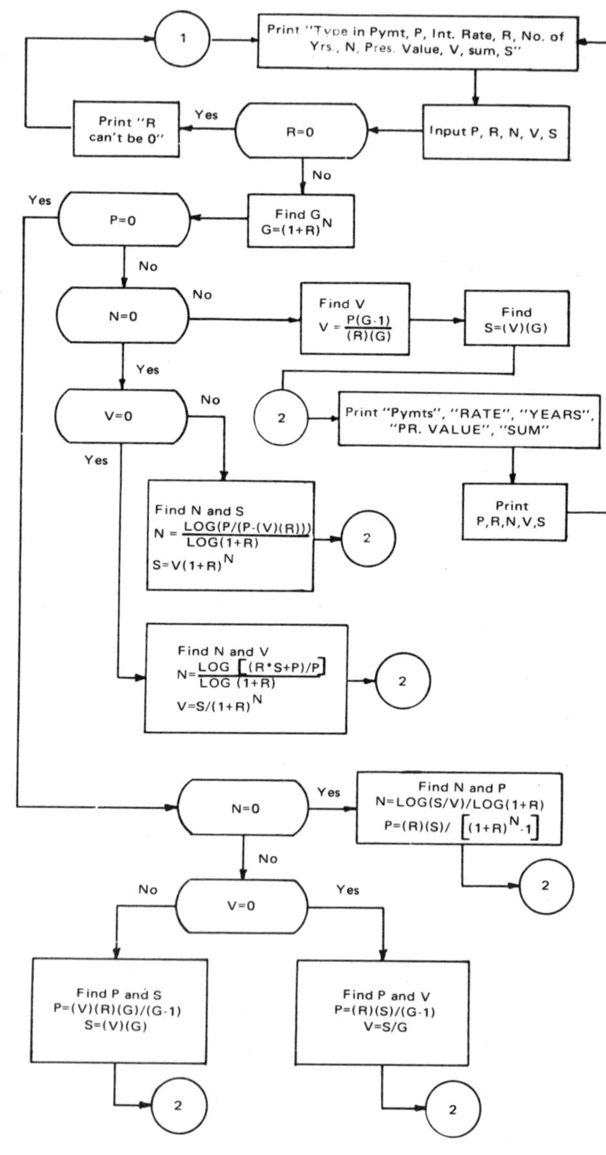

Review Problem 39

Finding the Rate of Interest of an Annuity

A previous application involved finding P, N, V, and S of an annuity. At that time, finding rate of interest, R, was excluded. Let us now add this. We start with two rules and derive two others:

(1) $V = P\,\dfrac{G - 1}{RG}$ (3) $V = S/G$

(2) $S = P\,\dfrac{G - 1}{R}$ (4) $R = P\left(\dfrac{1}{V} - \dfrac{1}{S}\right)$

where $G = (1 + R)^N$

Finding R is difficult unless rule 4 can be used. However, Rule 4 is only applicable if P, V, S are all known. Rule 4 is found by substituting the value of G of (3) into equation (2).

To find R, equations (1) and (2) must be used. These two rules can be written as follows:

(1) $\dfrac{V}{P} = \dfrac{1}{R}\left[1 - \dfrac{1}{1 + R(N + F)}\right]$

(2) $\dfrac{S}{P} - N = F$; where F, in each rule, is:

$$F = \frac{N(N - 1)}{2!}R + \frac{N(N - 1)(N - 2)}{3!}R^2 + \ldots.\, R^{N - 1}$$

In each of these, one starts with a "guessed" R. In (1), the guess can be R = P/V. In (2), it can be R = 2 (S/P - N)/ N(N - 1). The right hand side of each rule is then calculated and compared to the left side. If larger, and rule (1) is being used, R is decreased; if rule (2) is being used, R is increased. If smaller, the opposite adjustment is made.

The following BASIC program finds: P, R, N, V, S where R is unknown and any one of P, N, V, or S can also be unknown. Try it - it is not an easy program!

Find Rate R (Continued)

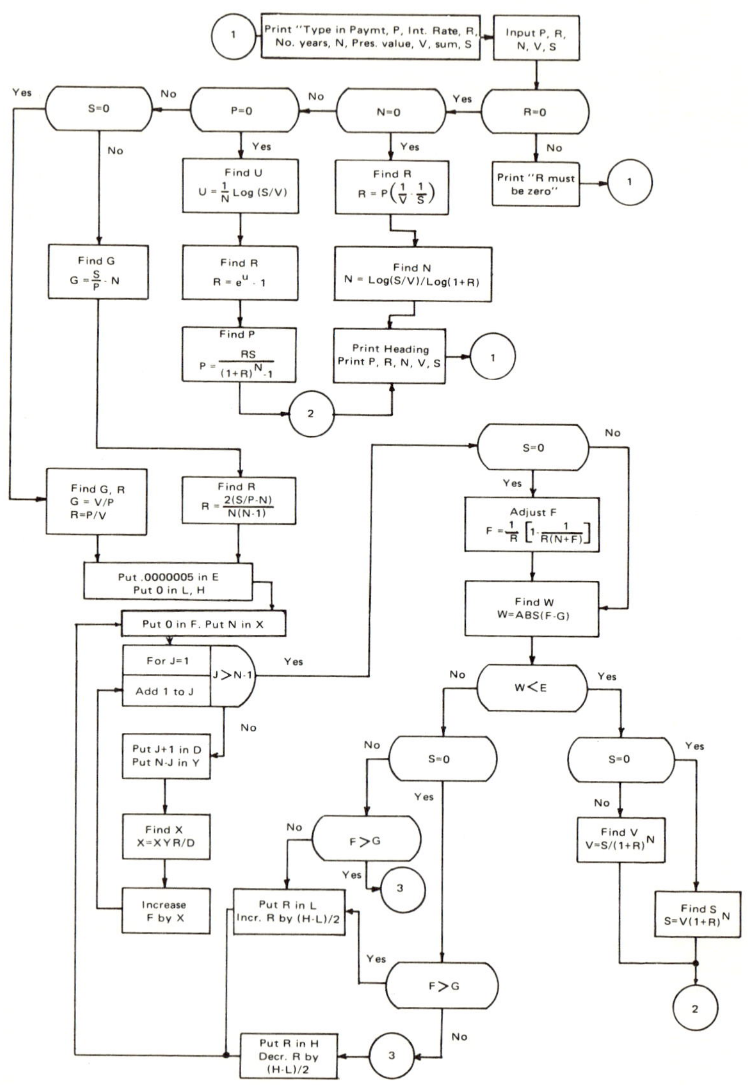

Review Problem 40
Extended Annuity Calculations

Review Problem 38 enabled one to find: P, R, N, V, and S for an ordinary annuity but required the interest rate, R, to be given. Review Problem 39 calculated R when the other parameters were present.

In this application, try combining the two (38 and 39) so that one can find <u>any</u> two missing parameters. The following broad flow chart indicates the problem.

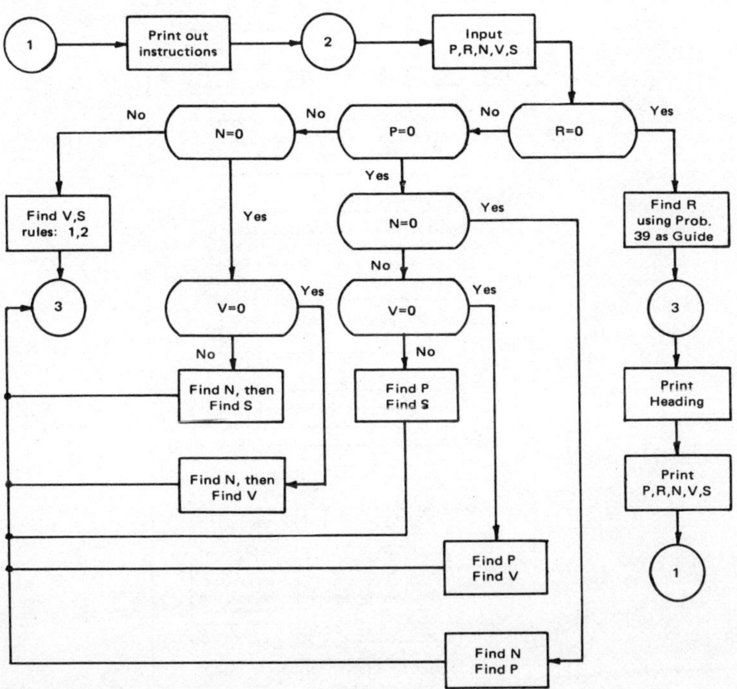

Review Problem 41
The Beggar and the King

"I have less than 100 boxes in this room", said the King. "I have placed a priceless gem in each of the first "X" boxes. Tell me how many boxes contain coins and the fortune is yours".

"I will tell you", said the beggar, "but you must be willing to follow certain procedures and it requires making use of this Bag, my Hat, and your court Jester. I can best present the plan by the following flow chart."

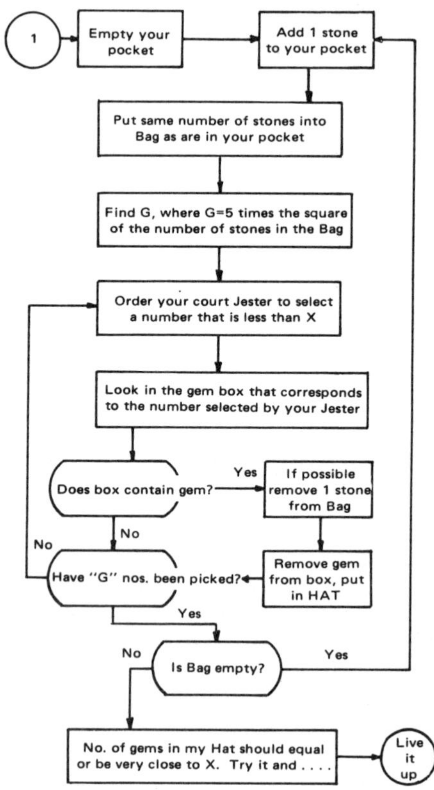

Review Problem 42
Amortization Schedules

A debt is "amortized" if it and the interest on it are paid off by a sequence of equal payments at equal intervals. Each payment is used to pay periodic interest and to decrease outstanding principal. This is the case of most home or property "ownership" – a mortgage payment plan.

Very few home "owners" realize the enormity of interest payments over the life of the mortgage. These interest payments are large since interest is compounded monthly and over a total time of 20 to 30 or more years. This is considerable.

Although most lending banks and loan associations release "amortization schedules" which show payments to interest, principal, etc. each month; few issue summary schedules that indicate total interest payments. Likewise, the public seldom sees a summary of possible savings by making extra payments each month in an open contract.

The following BASIC program prints such summary tables. First, it shows payments: 1, 12, 24, 36, . . . etc. for life of the contract; second, it shows total payments in a summary table; third, it shows summary of possible savings if one pays \$10, \$20, \$30, ... up to \$100 extra per month.

The formula used to calculate the monthly payment on the mortgage is:

$$P = \frac{(R)\,(V)\cdot(G)}{12\,(G - 1)} \qquad \text{where } G = \left(1 + \frac{R}{12}\right)^{12N}$$

R = interest rate per year
V = mortgage value
N = number of years for mortgage

Amortization (Continued)

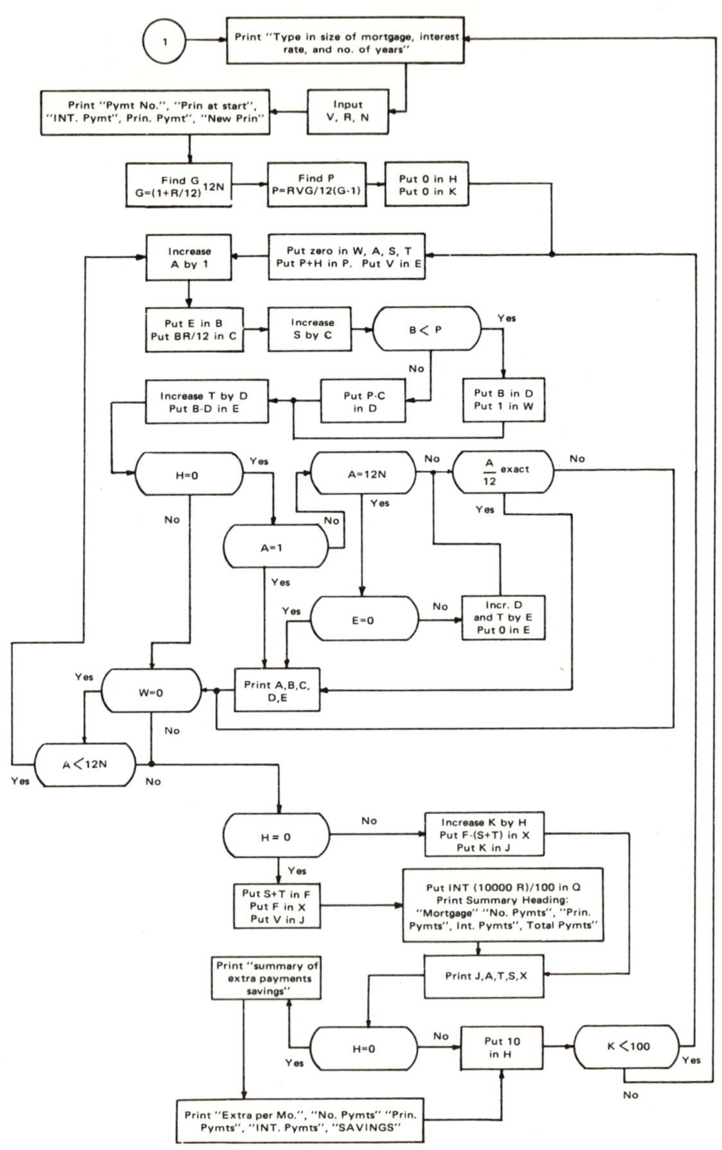

Review Problem 43

The chances of exactly "S" wins and "N-S" losses; when the chance of each win is "P" and the chance of each loss is "Q", can be found by:

$$\text{Chances} = \frac{N!}{S!\,(N-S)!}\quad P^S\,Q^{N-S}$$

where N! = (1)(2)(3)(4) . . . . . . N

An example: Assume 6 dice are thrown. The chance of each dice being 6 is 1/6. The chance of each not being 6 is 5/6.. Find the chances that exactly 2 die will be 6.

$$P(2) = \frac{6!}{2!\,4!}\left(\frac{1}{6}\right)^2\left(\frac{5}{6}\right)^4 = \text{approx.} \frac{20}{100}$$

Another example: Assume 6 dice are thrown, find the chances of exactly 4 dice being six.

$$P(4) = \frac{6!}{4!\,2!}\left(\frac{1}{6}\right)^4\left(\frac{5}{6}\right)^2 = \text{approx.}\ \frac{1}{100}$$

Design a BASIC program to simulate the tosses of 6 dice for 100 times, using random numbers. Compare the number of times 1, 2, 3, 4, 5, and 6 dice are exactly equal to six with the above rule results. Results should be printed in a table as follows:

No. of 6's	in 100 times	by rule	abs. diff.
1	.	40	.
2	.	.	.
3	.	.	.
.	.	.	.
.	.	.	.
6	.	.	.

Chances of Six Dice Being Six

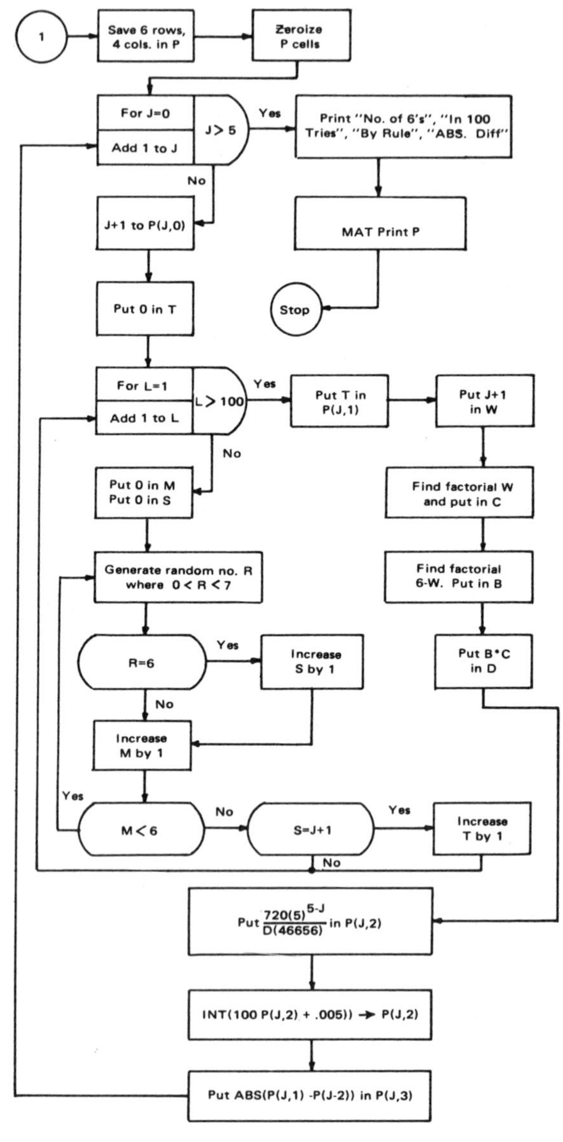

Review Problem 44
Retirement of Bonded Debt

Public schools and other buildings are often paid for by selling bonds. These bonds are really promises to pay back borrowed monies at interest over a term of years. Many are tax free to make the lower interest rates more attractive to investors.

The payments by school officials to retire these bonds - along with number of bonds paid off (retired) make up a "Bond Retirement Schedule". Many businesses use the annuity formula to find the annual payment P, which in turn, is used to pay off as many bonds as possible for that amount.

As an example, assume a village library is paid for by issuing 100 bonds at $1000 each, with interest at 4 per cent. If the debt is to be paid in 10 years, a schedule such as the following is possible:

First use Present Value of 100000 to find annual payment, P.

$$100000 = P \frac{1 - (1 + R)^{-N}}{R} \qquad P = \text{approx. } \$12,330$$

Year	Value	Interest	Payment	Amt. Retired
1	100000	4000	12000	8000
2	92000	3680	12680	9000
3	83000	3320	12320	9000
;	;	;	;	;
10	12000	480	12480	12000

Note: Interest (col. 3) = Value (col. 2) times rate (.04). Payment (col. 4) = Interest (col. 3) + Amt. Retired (col. 5). Amt. Retired (col. 5) = Value of nearest no. of bonds contained in Payment P minus Interest.

The following program prints such a schedule. Try it!

Bond Retirement (Continued)

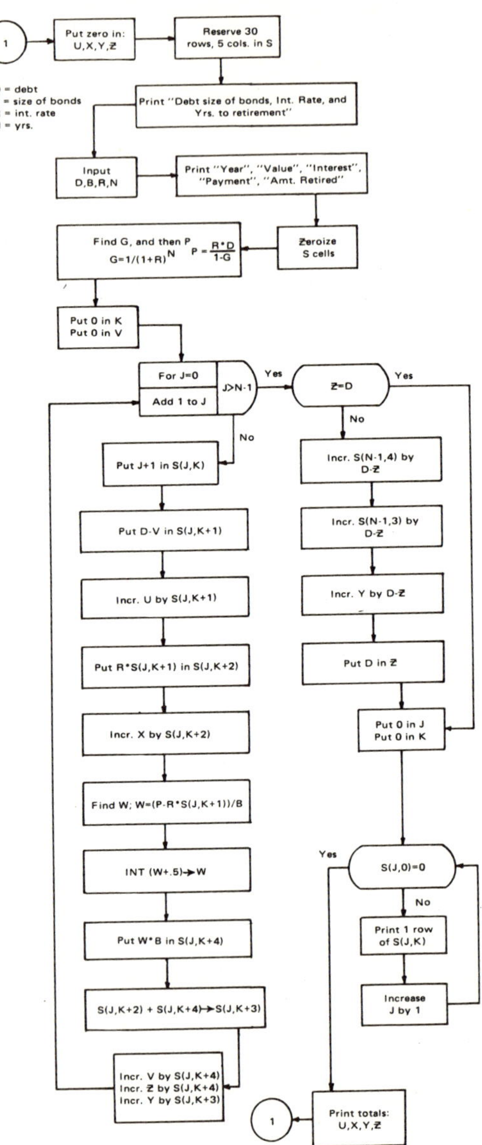

Review Problem 45

Are there numbers that equal the sum of the factorials of their digits? For example, is there a three digit number such that:

$$100\,H + 10t + u = h! + t! + u!$$

Let's look at the problem in another way. Does the number 1626 satisfy the conditions?

1 6 5 6

6!	=	720
5!	=	120
6!	=	720
1	=	1
		1561

It is obvious, that 1656 does not satisfy the problem conditions since the sum of the factorials of its digits does <u>not</u> equal 1656.

Thc following problem examines numbers less than 50000 for these conditions. You may wish to extend or change the solution strategy.

In the solution presented here, 5 cells D(0), D(1), D(2), D(3), D(4) hold the 5 digits of each number. Thus, number 145 is held in:

0	0	1	4	5
D(0)	D(1)	D(2)	D(3)	D(4)

Each of these cells never exceed the digit 9. By the way, is 145 a solution?

Sum of Factorials (Continued)

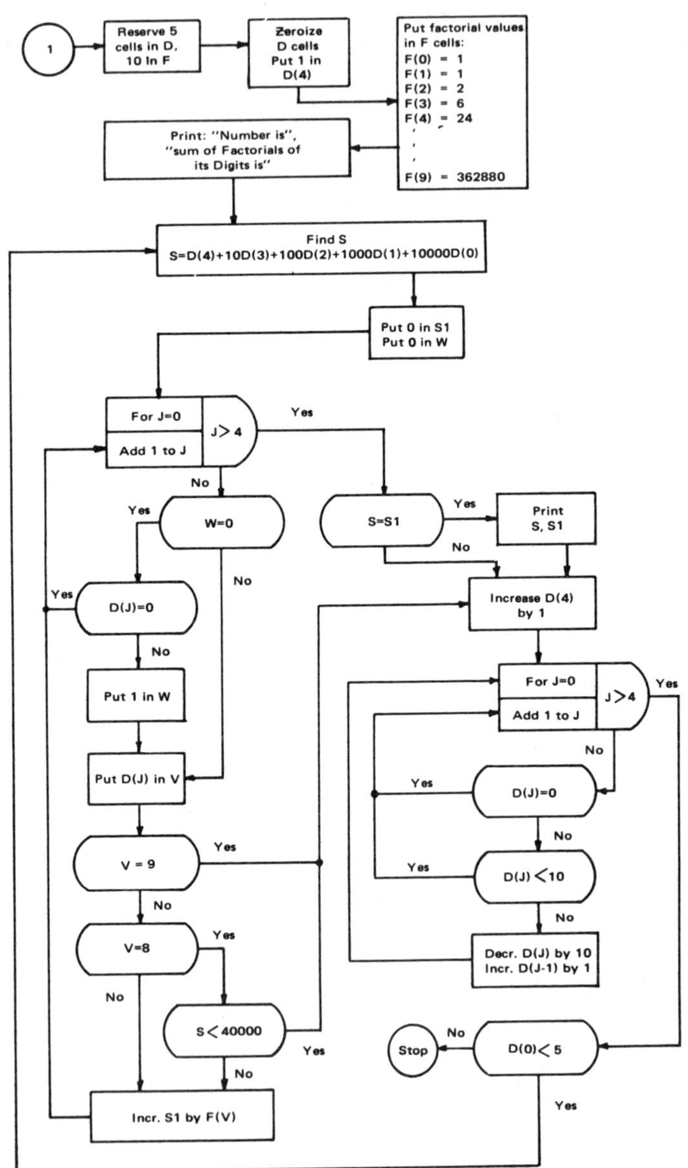

Review Problem 46
Chances of Living or Dying

The Commissioners Standard Ordinary (C.S.O.) Mortality Table was established in 1941 by a Committee of the National Association of Insurance Commissioners. Mortality data was collected from many sources. It essentially is a study of 1,023,102 persons that indicates how many of these persons were living at ages 0, 1, 2, 3, ... thru 99. For example, at age 0, all of these persons were living; whereas, at age 99, only 125 were still alive. Certain symbols are used in actuarial mathematics. For example,

l_x = no. of persons living at age x

d_x = no. of persons dying at age x

(x) = a person whose age is x

P_x = probability that (x) will live one year

$$\text{where } P_x = \frac{l_{x+1}}{l_x}$$

The heart of the C.S.O. Table is the column l_x which shows the number living at each age. We can put these into the computer and easily find the other columns of the C.S.O. if we desire.

Let us design a BASIC program that will place the living data (l_x) into the computer and then find and print a table showing the following:

			Chances of Living Until	
Age	No. Living	No. Dying	2000	2025
1	1000000	5770	0.91	0.71
5	'	'	'	'
10	'	'	'	'
'	'	'	'	'
99	125	125	0.0	0.0

Problem 46 (Continued)

The second column of the previous table is first read into the computer. The third column is easily found by subtracting each l_x (col. 2) from the next l_{x+1}. The last 2 cols. are found by the P_x rule? For example: a person age 20 (in 1968) must live 32 more years to reach year 2000. Therefore his chances are:

$$\frac{l_{20+32}}{l_{20}} = \frac{l_{52}}{l_{20}} = \frac{790282}{951483} = \text{approx. } \frac{83}{100}$$

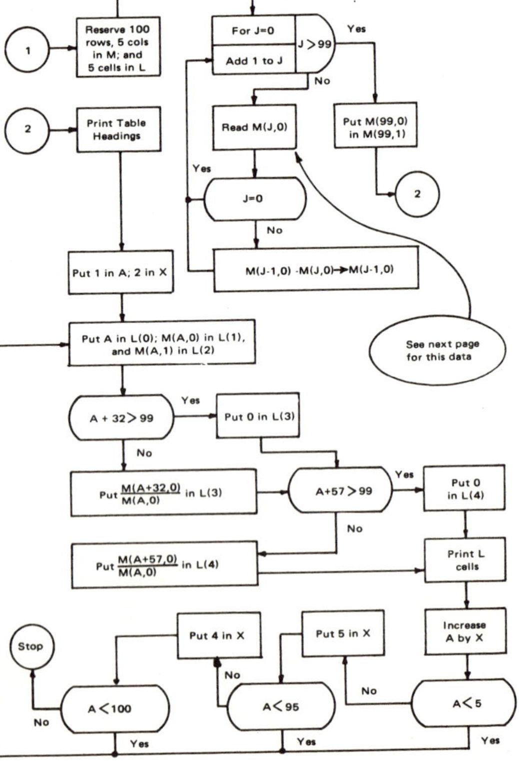

Data for Mortality Table

In order to do problems based on the C.S.O. Mortality Table, it is necessary to read data into the computer. This data consists of the number of persons living at ages: 0, 1, 2, 3, ... 99; and is given below. Starting with the first DATA row, ages are 0, 1, 2, 3, and 4. Second DATA row is number living at ages: 5, 6, 7, 8, 9; third DATA row is number living at ages: 10, 11, 12, 13, 14, etc.

```
DATA  1023102  1000000  994230  990114  986767
DATA   983817   981102  978541  976124  973869
DATA   971804   969890  968038  966179  964266
DATA   962270   960201  958098  955942  953743
DATA   951483   949171  946789  944337  941806
DATA   939197   936492  933692  930788  927763
DATA   924609   921317  917880  914282  910515
DATA   906554   902393  898007  893382  888504
DATA   883342   877883  872098  865967  859464
DATA   852554   845214  837413  829114  820292
DATA   810900   800910  790282  778981  766961
DATA   754191   740631  726241  710990  694843
DATA   677771   659749  640761  620782  599824
DATA   577882   554975  531133  506403  480850
DATA   454548   427593  400112  372240  344136
DATA   315982   287973  260322  233251  206989
DATA   181765   157799  135297  114440   93378
DATA    78221    63036   49838   38593   29215
DATA    21577    15514   10833    7327    4787
DATA     3011     1818    1005     454     125
```

Review Problem 47
Your Chances of Living and Dying

Using the previous DATA of persons living at ages: 0, 1, 2, ... 99; and the rules of problem 46, design a BASIC program to find chances of living and dying during years 1970, 1980, 1990, ... 2040. Print results in a table similar to:

Your Chances of Living		Your Chances of Dying	
Before	**Are**	**Before**	**Are**
1970	0.99	1970	0.01
1980	0.95	1980	0.05
;	;	;	;

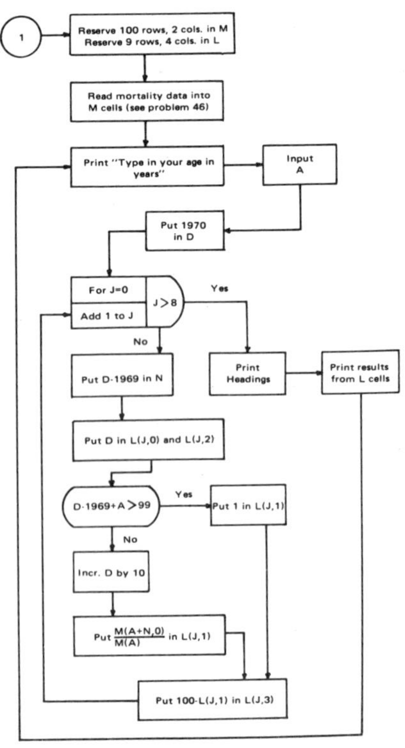

Review Problem 48
Finding the Mean and Median

Two measures that are often used to describe a group of socres are: mean and median. The mean is the average, found by the rule:

$$\text{Mean} = \frac{\sum X}{N} \quad \text{where X is ``sum of X scores''}$$

N = no. of scores

The median is the middle score. If there are an odd number of scores, the middle score is the median. However, if there are an even number of scores, the median is the average of two "middle scores." For example:

Of the 6 scores shown, the "middle scores" are 20 and 32.

	Scores
	10
	15
"Middle" scores →	20
	32
	60
	64

The median is the average of these two middle scores

$$\frac{20 + 32}{2} = 26$$

The following BASIC program permits one to enter up to 100 scores. The program puts these scores in descending order (high to low), and prints: the scores, number of scores, mean, and median.

Give it a try!

Mean and Median

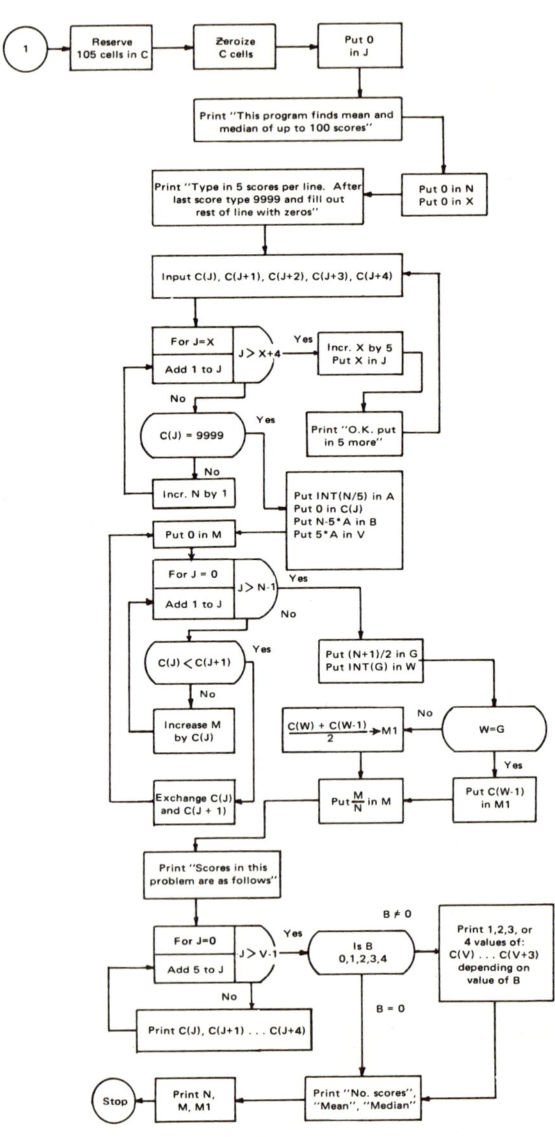

Review Problem 49
Ƶ Scores and Percentile Ranks

A raw score, along with mean or median, is not as meaningful as some measure of spread from the mean. The Standard Deviation, often called "Sigma" is such a measure. It is:

$$\text{Sigma} = \sqrt{\frac{\Sigma (M - X)^2}{N}}$$

where M = mean
N = no. of scores
X = raw score

Using the Normal Curve philosophy, one can interpret scores relative to sigma. Such scores are called "Ƶ scores". One simply changes the raw score to sigma units by the rule:

$$Z \text{ score} = \frac{X - M}{\text{Sigma}}$$

This will be negative if the raw score (X) is <u>below</u> the mean (M), and positive if <u>above</u> M.

Another measure is a percentile rank. This indicates the area of the "normal distribution" below a score. One who is at the 60 percentile is above 60% of the scores; 80 percentile is above 80%; etc. To find a percentile rank, one finds Ƶ score and the <u>area</u> of normal curve <u>below</u> that Ƶ score. To find area of normal curve below a Ƶ score, we will use the rule:

$$G = \frac{1}{\sqrt{2\pi}} \left[Z - \frac{Z^3}{6} + \frac{Z^5}{40} - \frac{Z^7}{336} + \frac{Z^9}{3456} - \frac{Z^{11}}{42240} \right] + 50$$

The following BASIC program calculates sigma, Ƶ score, and Percentile Rank for up to 100 raw scores. Each score is entered with a student number, rather than a student's name.

Try it!

Ƶ Scores and Percentiles (Continued)

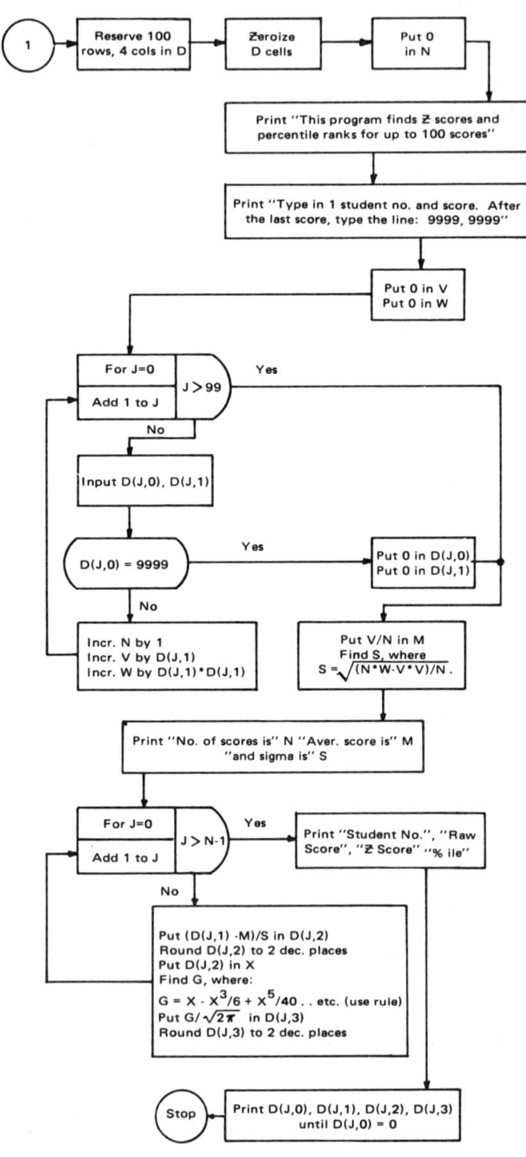

Review Problem 50

Linear Correlation Between Sets of Scores

One is often interested in the relationship between two sets of scores. Previously, (see problem 36) we wrote a BASIC program for "rank correlation"). Another technique is the Pearson Correlation, R, which ranges between -1 and +1. Perfect positive correlation is +1, perfect negative is -1, and no relationship is 0.

There are several rules for finding the value, R. We will use that rule which calculates R from the raw scores (X and Y) directly.

$$R = \frac{N\sum XY - \sum X \sum Y}{N^2 (\text{sigma } X)(\text{sigma } Y)}$$

where $\sum$ means: "the sum of".

As an example assume the following:

X Scores	Y Scores	XY
1	10	10
2	9	18
3	8	24
4	7	28
$\sum X = 10$	$\sum Y = 34$	$\sum XY = 80$

Sigma X = 1.12

Sigma Y = 1.12

$$R = \frac{4(80) - 10(34)}{16(1.12)(1.12)} = \frac{-20}{20.1} = -1$$

Since low score in X seems to indicate a high score in Y, the R should be close to negative 1.

Write a BASIC program to enable one to type in up to 100 sets of student numbers followed by two scores. Show this data and find mean of X, mean of Y, sigma X, sigma Y, and correlation, R.

Pearson Correlation (Continued)

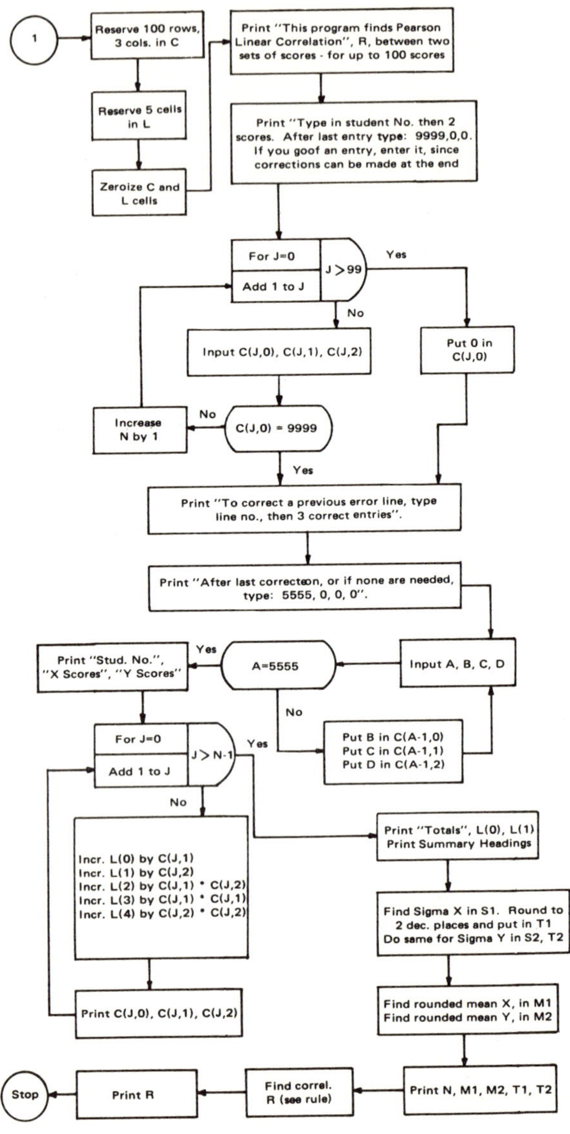

Program Solutions to Problems in Text

PAGE 3

```
WHAT SYSTEM? BASIC

NEW OR OLD--NEW
NEW FILE NAME--AA
READY

10 LET K=2
20 LET G=3
30 LET R=K*G
40 PRINT K,G,R
50 END

RUN

 2              3       6

TIME: 0 SEC.

30 LET R=K+G

RUN

 2              3       5

TIME: 0 SEC.

30 LET R=K-G

RUN

 2              3      -1

TIME: 0 SEC.

30 LET R=K/G

RUN

 2              3       0.666667

TIME: 0 SEC.
```

PAGE 4,5

```
10 LET K=2
20 LET G=3
30 LET R=K*G
40 PRINT K,G,R
50 END

RUN

 2              3       6

TIME: 0 SEC.

NEW
NEW FILE NAME--AA
READY

10 LET X=5+10/5*2-6
20 PRINT X
30 END

RUN

 3

TIME: 0 SEC.

NEW
NEW FILE NAME--A
READY

10 LET X=5+10/5*2↑3-6
20 PRINT X
30 END

RUN

 15

TIME: 0 SEC.
```

PAGE 6

```
10 LI-ET X=5+10/5*(2↑3-6)
20 LET Y=5+10/5*2↑3-6
30 LET Z=5+10/(5*2↑3)-6
40 LET W=(5+10)/5*(2↑3-6)
50 LET W1=5+(-10↑2/5)*(2↑3-6)
60 PRINT X,Y,Z,W,W1
70 END

RUN

 9              15      -0.75     6      45

20 LET Y=(5+10)/5*2↑3-6

RUN

 9              18      -0.75     6      45
```

PAGE 11

```
10 LET X=976525
20 LET Y=SQR(X)
30 PRINT Y
40 END

RUN

 988.192795
```

```
20 LET Y=SQR(976525)
30 PRINT Y
40 END

RUN

 988.192795
```

PAGE 8

```
TIME: 0 SEC.
NEW
NEW FILE NAME--A
READY

10 LET R=3
20 LET W=LOG(R)
30 PRINT W
40 END

RUN

 1.09861229

TIME: 0 SEC.

LIST

10 LET R=3
20 LET W=LOG(R)
30 PRINT W
40 END
```

```
NEW OR OLD--NEW
NEW FILE NAME--A
READY

10 LET Z=100
20 LET Y=.434294482*LOG(Z)
30 PRINT Y
40 END

RUN

 2

TIME: 0 SEC.

NEW
NEW FILE NAME--A
READY

10 LET X=30*3.14159/180
20 LET Y=SIN(X)
30 PRINT Y
40 END

RUN

 0.5
```

PAGE 9

```
NEW
NEW FILE NAME--A
READY

10 LET N=1
20 PRINT N
30 LET N=N+1
40 IF N<26 THEN 20
50 END

RUN

 1
 2
 3
 4
 5
 6
 7
 8
 9
 10
 11
 12
 13
```

```
 14
 15
 16
 17
 18
 19
 20
 21
 22
 23
 24
 25
10 LET N=10
20 PRINT N
30 LET N=N+10
40 IF N<110 THEN 20
50 END
RUN

 10
 20
 30
 40
 50
 60
 70
 80
 90
 100
```

PAGE 10

```
LIST
10 LET X=110
20 LET Y=SQR(X)
40 LET X=X-10
50 IF X>0 THEN20
60 END

10 LET X=100

30 PRINT Y
RUN

 10
 9.48683298
 8.94427191
 8.36660027
 7.74596669
 7.07106781
 6.32455532
 5.47722558
 4.47213596
 3.16227766
```

```
10 LET X=110
20 LET X=X-10
30 IF X=0 THEN 70
40 LET Y=SQR(X)
50 PRINT Y
60 GO TO 20
70 END
RUN

 10
 9.48683298
 8.94427191
 8.36660027
 7.74596669
 7.07106781
 6.32455532
 5.47722558
 4.47213596
 3.16227766
```

```
10 LET X=1
20 LET Y=X+1
30 LET Z=X/Y
40 PRINT Z
50 LET X=X+1
60 IF X<10 THEN 20
70 END
RUN

 0.5
 0.666667
 0.75
 0.8
 0.833333
 0.857143
 0.875
 0.888889
 0.9
```

```
10 LET J=10
20 PRINT J
30 LET J=J-.5
40 IF J>0 THEN 20
50 END
RUN
 10
 9.5
 9
 8.5
 8
 7.5
 7
 6.5
 6
 5.5
 5
 4.5
 4
 3.5
 3
 2.5
 2
 1.5
 1
 0.5
```

```
10 LET X=1
20 LET Y=X↑3
30 PRINT Y
40 LET X=X+2
50 IF X<13 THEN 20
60 END
U←RUN

 1
 27
 125
 343
 729
 1331
```

PAGE 12

```
NEW
NEW FILE NAME--A
READY
10 LET X=1
20 LET Y=SQR(X)
30 LET X=X+1
25 PRINT X,Y
40 IF X< 51 THEN 20
50 STOP
60 END
RUN

 1               1
 2               1.41421356
 3               1.73205081
 4               2
 5               2.23606798
 6               2.44948974
 7               2.64575131
 8               2.82842712
 9               3
 10              3.16227766
 11              3.31662479
 12              3.46410162
 13              3.60555128
 14              3.74165739
 15              3.87298335
 16              4
 17              4.12310563
 18              4.24264069
 19              4.35889894
 20              4.47213596
 21              4.58257569
 22              4.6904576
 23              4.79583152
 24              4.89897949
 25              5
```

PAGE 13

```
NEW
NEW FILE NAME--A
READY
10 LET A=2
20 LET B=3
30 LET C=4
40 PRINT "DAYS","DAILY AMOUNT","TOTAL SAVED"
50 PRINT
60 PRINT A,B,C
70 END
RUN

DAYS            DAILY AMOUNT    TOTAL SAVED

 2               3               4

TIME: 0 SEC.

10 LET A=.023456
RUN

DAYS            DAILY AMOUNT    TOTAL SAVED

 2.3456E-02      3               4

TIME: 0 SEC.

40 PRINT "   DAYS","DAILY AMOUNT","TOTAL SAVED"
RUN
   DAYS         DAILY AMOUNT    TOTAL SAVED

 2.3456E-02      3               4
```

PAGE 15

```
10 PRINT "   DAYS","DAILY AMOUNT","TOTAL SAVED"
20 PRINT
22 PRINT
25 LET N=1
30 LET D=.01
40 LET A=0
50 LET A=A+D
60 PRINT N,D,A
70 LET D=2*D
80 LET N=N+1
90 IF N<30 THEN 50
95 STOP
99 END


RUN


   DAYS         DAILY AMOUNT    TOTAL SAVED


 1               0.01            0.01
 2               0.02            0.03
 3               0.04            0.07
 4               0.08            0.15
 5               0.16            0.31
 6               0.32            0.63
 7               0.64            1.27
 8               1.28            2.55
 9               2.56            5.11
 10              5.12            10.23
 11              10.24           20.47
 12              20.48           40.95
 13              40.96           81.91
 14              81.92           163.83
 15              163.84          327.67
 16              327.68          655.35
 17              655.36          1310.71
 18              1310.72         2621.43
 19              2621.44         5242.87
 20              5242.88         10485.75
 21              10485.76        20971.51
 22              20971.52        41943.03
 23              41943.04        83886.07
 24              83886.08        167772.15
 25              167772.16       335544.31
 26              335544.32       671088.63
 27              671088.64       1342177.27
 28              1342177.28      2684354.55
 29              2684354.56      5368709.11
STOP

TIME: 0.432 SEC.
```

PAGE 16

```
10 LET N=5
20 LET J=INT(100*RND(X))
30 LET K=INT(100*RND(X))
40 LET L=INT(100*RND(X))
45 LET A1=J+L
50 LET B1=L-(J+K)
55 LET C1=K+L
60 LET A2=K+L-J
65 LET B2=L
70 LET C2=J+L-K
75 LET A3=L-K
80 LET B3=J+K+L
85 LET C3=L-J
90 PRINT A1,B1,C1
91 PRINT
92 PRINT A2,B2,C2
93 PRINT
94 PRINT A3,B3,C3
95 PRINT
96 PRINT
97 PRINT
98 LET N=N-1
99 IF N>0 THEN 20
100 STOP
101 END

RUN
 93     6     72

 36    57     78

 42   108     21


 74  -110     51

-18     5     28

-41   120    -64


118   -41    121

 69    66     63

 11   173     14


141     0    120

 66    87    108

 54   174     33


 31   -62     55

 32     8    -16

-39    78    -15


STOP
```

PAGE 17

```
10 LET S=0
15 LET R=1
20 LET V=-1
25 LET L=10000
30 LET N=0
35 LET T=2*R-1
40 LET V=-1*V
45 LET S=S+V/T
50 IF N=L THEN 70
55 LET R=R+1
60 LET N=N+1
65 GO TO 35
70 LET G=4*S
75 PRINT N,G
80 LET L=L+10000
90 IF L<110000 THEN 35
95 STOP
99 END
RUN

 10000     3.14169264
 20000     3.14154265
 30000     3.14162598
 40000     3.14156765
 50000     3.14161264
 60000     3.14157597
 70000     3.14160693
 80000     3.14158014
 90000     3.14160375
 100000    3.14158264
```

```
90 IF L<150000 THEN 35
RUN

 10000     3.14169264
 20000     3.14154265
 30000     3.14162598
 40000     3.14156765
 50000     3.14161264
 60000     3.14157597
 70000     3.14160693
 80000     3.14158014
 90000     3.14160375
 100000    3.14158264
 110000    3.14160173
 120000    3.14158431
 130000    3.14160033
 140000    3.1415855
```

PAGE 19

```
TIME: 0.512 SEC.
NEW
NEW FILE NAME--A
READY
20 LET W=Y/7
10 LET Y=INT(1000*RND(X))
30 LET P=INT(W)
40 IF P=W THEN 70
50 PRINT "NOT EXACT",Y
60 STOP
70 PRINT "MULTIPLE OF 7 =" Y
80 STOP
90 END
RUN

NOT EXACT        361
STOP
```

PAGE 18

```
NEW
NEW FILE NAME--A
READY
10 LET N=0
15 LET E=0
20 LET T=INT(R+100*RND(X))
25 LET R=T/2
30 LET G=INT(R)
35 IF R<>G THEN 45
40 LET E=E+1
45 LET N=N+1
50 IF N<=1000 THEN 20
60 PRINT "NO. OF EVENS="E,"NO, OF ODD="N-E
70 STOP
80 END
RUN

NO. OF EVENS= 503               NO, OF ODD= 498
STOP
```

PAGE 20

```
NEW
NEW FILE NAME--A
READY

LET N=1234

10 LET N=1234
20 PRINT "YOU CN+AN'T EVEN COUNT"N
RUN

YOU CAN'T EVEN COUNT 1234

TIME: 0 SEC.
20 PRINT N"  DON'T ASK ME FOR MORE"
RUN

 1234  DON'T ASK ME FOR MORE
```

PAGE 22

```
NEW
NEW FILE NAME--A
READY

10 LET N=6
15 LET L=0
20 LET J=N
25 LET J=J-1
30 LET M=J/5
35 LET K=INT(M)
40 IF M<>K THEN 70
45 LET L=L+1
50 IF L<6 THEN 60
55 PRINT"NUMBER OF COCONUTS = "N
60 LET J=4*J/5
65 GO TO 25
70 LET N=N+5
75 IF N<100000 THEN 15
80 STOP
85 END
RUN


NUMBER OF COCONUTS =  15621
NUMBER OF COCONUTS =  31246
NUMBER OF COCONUTS =  46871
NUMBER OF COCONUTS =  62496
NUMBER OF COCONUTS =  78121
NUMBER OF COCONUTS =  78121
NUMBER OF COCONUTS =  93746
STOP
```

PAGE 25

```
10 LET S=0
12 LET R=1
15 LET C=1
20 READ A
25 LET T=R+C
30 IF T<6 THEN 40
35 LET T=T-5
40 IF A=T THEN 60
45 LET G=C*R
50 PRINT"YOU MISSED QUESTION NO.  "G
51 PRINT
55 GO TO 65
60 LET S=S+1
65 LET C=C+1
70 IF C<6 THEN 20
75 LET R=R+1
80 IF R<5 THEN 15
85 PRINT
90 PRINT"YOU HAD  "S"  CORRECT ANSWERS"
92 PRINT"IF MORE THAN 15, CONGRATULATIONS ! "
95 DATA 2,3,4,5,5
96 DATA 3,4,5,2,2
97 DATA 4,5,1,2,3
98 DATA 5,1,2,3,5
99 END


RUN


YOU MISSED QUESTION NO.   5

YOU MISSED QUESTION NO.   8

YOU MISSED QUESTION NO.   20


YOU HAD   17  CORRECT ANSWERS
IF MORE THAN 15, CONGRATULATIONS !
```

PAGE 27

```
NEW
NEW FILE NAME--A
READY

10 READ X
20 IF END DATA THEN 60
30 LET Y=3*X↑3-X*X+SQR(X)
40 PRINT X,Y
50 GO TO 10
60 STOP
70 DATA 3.8,1,6.78
75 DATA 68.2
80 END

 3.8            152.125359
 1              3
 6.78           891.632699
 68.2           947000.722
STOP
```

PAGE 28

```
10 REM BUILDING A TABLE
15 PRINT"NUMBERS","SQUARES","CUBES","RECIPROCALS","SQ.RT."
16 PRINT
20 READ X
25 IF END DATA THEN 80
30 LET A=X*X
35 LET B=X↑3
40 LET C=1/X
50 LET D=SQR(X)
60 PRINT X,A,B,C,D
65 GO TO 20
80 STOP
90 DATA 17,32,16,25,88
95 DATA 9,15,7,29,33
96 DATA 14,26
99 END
```

NUMBERS	SQUARES	CUBES	RECIPROCALS	SQ.RT.
17	289	4913	5.882353E-02	4.12310563
32	1024	32768	0.03125	5.65685425
16	256	4096	0.0[illegible]25	4
25	625	15625	0.0[illegible]	5
88	7744	681472	1.1[illegible]364E-02	9.38083152
9	81	729	0.11 111	3
15	225	3375	6.66[illegible]667E-02	3.87298335
7	49	343	0.142857	2.64575131
29	841	24389	3.448276E-02	5.38516481
33	1089	35937	3.030303E-02	5.74456265
14	196	2744	7.142857E-02	3.74165739
26	676	17576	3.846154E-02	5.09901951

STOP

PAGE 30

```
10 REM H.C.F PROBLEM
11 PRINT
20 READ A,B
25 IF END DATA THEN 99
30 LET X=A
35 LET Y=B
40 IF X>Y THEN 60
45 LET T=X
50 LET X=Y
55 LET Y=T
60 LET W=INT(X/Y)
65 LET R=X-W*Y
70 IF R=0 THEN 88
75 LET X=Y
80 LET Y=R
85 GO TO 60
88 PRINT
89 PRINT
90 PRINT "ONE NUMBER IS "A,"THE OTHER IS"B
91 PRINT "H.C.F.IS "Y
92 GO TO20
93 DATA 2059,4189
94 DATA 53053,689
95 DATA 1824,6432
96 DATA 1935,1763
97 DATA 18103,5473
98 DATA 148037,44011
99 END
RUN

ONE NUMBER IS  2059        THE OTHER IS 4189
H.C.F.IS  71

ONE NUMBER IS  53053       THE OTHER IS 689
H.C.F.IS  689

ONE NUMBER IS  1824        THE OTHER IS 6432
H.C.F.IS  96

ONE NUMBER IS  1935        THE OTHER IS 1763
H.C.F.IS  43

ONE NUMBER IS  18103       THE OTHER IS 5473
H.C.F.IS  421

ONE NUMBER IS  148037      THE OTHER IS 44011
H.C.F.IS  4001
```

PAGE 32

```
10 PRINT "NUMBERS","SUM OF FACTORS","NUMBER OF FACTORS"
11 PRINT
15 LET F=1133
20 LET F=F+1
25 IF F< 1175 THEN 30
28 STOP
30 LET M=0
32 LET N=0
34 LET D=2
35 LET Y=F/D
40 LET W=INT(Y)
45 IF W<>Y THEN 70
50 LET M=M+D
55 LET N=N+1
60 IF D=Y THEN 70
65 LET M=M+Y
68 LET N=N+1
70 LET D=D+1
75 IF D*D<=F THEN 35
80 PRINT F,M,N
90 GO TO 20
95 END
```

NUMBERS	SUM OF FACTORS	NUMBER OF FACTORS
1134	1769	18
1135	232	2
1136	1095	8
1137	382	2
1138	571	2
1139	84	2
1140	2219	22
1141	170	2
1142	573	2
1143	520	4
1144	1375	14
1145	234	2
1146	1157	6
1147	68	2
1148	1203	10
1149	386	2
1150	1081	10
1151	0	0
1152	2162	22
1153	0	0
1154	579	2
1155	1148	14
1156	992	7
1157	102	2
1158	1169	6
1159	80	2
1160	1539	14
1161	598	6
1162	853	6
1163	0	0
1164	1579	10
1165	238	2
1166	777	6
1167	392	2
1168	1125	8
1169	174	2
1170	2105	22
1171	0	0
1172	885	4
1173	554	6
1174	589	2

PAGE 34

```
10 LET L=100
15 LET N=4
20 LET F=9
25 LET M=L
30 LET D=3
35 IF D*D>F THEN 75
40 LET Y=F/D
45 LET W=INT(Y)
50 IF W=Y THEN 65
55 LET D=D+2
60 GO TO 35
65 LET F=F+2
70 GO TO 30
75 LET N=N+1
80 IF N<>M THEN 65
85 PRINT
87 PRINT N"TH PRIME IS  "F
90 LET M=M+L
95 IF M<= 1000 THEN 65
99 END
RUN

 100TH PRIME IS    541

 200TH PRIME IS    1223

 300TH PRIME IS    1987

 400TH PRIME IS    2741

 500TH PRIME IS    3571

 600TH PRIME IS    4409

 700TH PRIME IS    5279

 800TH PRIME IS    6133

 900TH PRIME IS    6997

 1000TH PRIME IS    7919
```

PAGE 35

```
10 PRINT "TYPE A NUMBER"
20 PRINT
30 INPUT A
40 LET B=A/2
50 LET C=INT(B)
60 IF B=C THEN 80
70 PRINT A" IS ODD"
75 GO TO 10
80 PRINT A" IS EVEN"
90 GO TO 10
95 END
RUN
TYPE A NUMBER

345
 345  IS ODD
TYPE A NUMBER

567
 567  IS ODD
TYPE A NUMBER

78
 78  IS EVEN
TYPE A NUMBER

345678945
 345678945  IS ODD
TYPE A NUMBER
```

PAGE 36

```
10 PRINT
15 PRINT "TYPE ANOTHER NUMBER"
20 INPUT F
25 IF F<10000000 THEN 40
30 PRINT "NUMBER TOO LARGE TRY ANOTHER"
35 GO TO 10
40 IF F=2 THEN 96
45 LET W=F/2
50 LET G=INT(W)
55 IF W=G THEN 94
60 LET D=3
65 IF D*D>F THEN 92
70 LET W=F/D
75 LET G=INT(W)
80 IF W=G THEN 90
85 LET D=D+2
88 GO TO 65
90 PRINT "NOT PRIME,IT IS DIVISIBLE BY  "D
91 GO TO 10
92 PRINT "YES,  "F,"  IS PRIME"
93 GO TO 10
94 PRINT "NOT PRIME, IT IS DIVISIBLE BY 2"
95 GO TO 10
96 PRINT "YES,2 IS THE ONLY EVEN PRIME"
97 GO TO 10
98 END
TYPE ANOTHER NUMBER
17
YES,    17          IS PRIME

TYPE ANOTHER NUMBER
4567
YES,    4567        IS PRIME

TYPE ANOTHER NUMBER
2
YES,2 IS THE ONLY EVEN PRIME

TYPE ANOTHER NUMBER
379
YES,    379         IS PRIME

TYPE ANOTHER NUMBER
93
NOT PRIME,IT IS DIVISIBLE BY    3

TYPE ANOTHER NUMBER
1070639
NOT PRIME,IT IS DIVISIBLE BY    541

TYPE ANOTHER NUMBER
345678999
NUMBER TOO LARGE TRY ANOTHER

TYPE ANOTHER NUMBER
3799999
NOT PRIME,IT IS DIVISIBLE BY    7
```

PAGE 38

```
10 LET F1=0
12 LET F2=0
14 LET F3=0
16 LET N=6
18 LET F=0
20 LET D=2
22 IF D*D>N THEN 40
24 LET W=N/D
26 LET Y=INT(W)
28 IF W<>Y THEN 32
30 LET F=F+1
32 LET D=D+1
34 GO TO 22
40 IF F<=F3 THEN 78
45 IF F>F1 THEN 70
50 IF F>F2 THEN 60
52 LET F3=F
54 LET N3=N
56 GO TO 78
60 LET F3=F2
62 LET N3=N2
64 LET F2=F
66 LET N2=N
68 GO TO 78
70 LET F3=F2
71 LET N3=N2
72 LET F2=F1
73 LET N2=N1
74 LET F1=F
75 LET N1=N
78 LET N=N+1
80 IF N<2000 THEN 18
85 PRINT
86 PRINT"NUMBERS","NO. OF FACTORS"
88 PRINT
90 PRINT N1,F1
91 PRINT
92 PRINT N2,F2
93 PRINT
94 PRINT N3,F3
96 STOP
99 END

RUN


NUMBERS        NO. OF FACTORS

 1680           19

 1260           17

 1440           17
STOP

TIME: 27.768 SEC.
```

PAGE 40

```
7 LET H=7
8 LET D=1000000
9 PRINT
10 PRINT"TYPE IN 3 INTEGERS--EACH LESS THAN "H" DIGITS"
12 INPUT J,E,L
13 LET K=E
14 LET C=L
16 LET A=0
18 LET B=0
20 LET F=0
22 LET T=0
24 LET R=C
25 LET Z=1
26 IF K<= 100 THEN 28
27 LET Z=100
28 LET K=K-Z
30 IF K<=0 THEN65
35 LET C=C+R*Z
38 IF F=0 THEN 40
39 LET B=B+V*Z
40 IF C<D THEN 25
45 LET P=INT(C/D)
46 LET B=B+P
48 LET C=C-P*D
50 IF B<D THEN 25
55 LET P=INT(B/D)
56 LET A=A+P
58 LET B=B-P*D
60 GO TO 25
65 LET K=J
66 LET F=1
67 LET V=B
70 IF T=0 THEN 85
72 PRINT
74 PRINT"THE THREE NUMBERS ARE       "J,E,L
76 PRINT
78 PRINT A,B,C, " IS THE PRODUCT"
79 PRINT
80 GO TO 9
85 LET T=1
95 GO TO 24
99 END

TYPE IN 3 INTEGERS--EACH LESS THAN  7 DIGITS
99999,99999,99999
THE THREE NUMBERS ARE        99999        99999        99999
 999          970000         299999       IS THE PRODUCT

TYPE IN 3 INTEGERS--EACH LESS THAN  7 DIGITS
55555,55555,55555
THE THREE NUMBERS ARE        55555        55555        55555
 171          462620         78875        IS THE PRODUCT
```

PAGE 42

```
10 LET N=6
12 LET T=0
14 LET G=N
16 LET S=1
18 LET D=2
20 IF D*D>G THEN 55
24 LET W=G/D
28 LET Y=INT(W)
30 IF Y<>W THEN 45
32 LET S=S+D
36 IF W=D THEN 45
40 LET S=S+W
45 LET D=D+1
50 GO TO 20
55 IF T<>0 THEN 72
60 IF S<=N THEN 76
64 LET G=S
68 LET T=1
70 GO TO 16
72 IF N=S THEN 90
76 LET N=N+2
80 IF N<10000 THEN 12
84 STOP
90 PRINT
92 PRINT" AMICABLE NUMBERS ARE  "N,G
94 GO TO 76
99 END
 AMICABLE NUMBERS ARE    220     284

 AMICABLE NUMBERS ARE    1184    1210

 AMICABLE NUMBERS ARE    2620    2924

 AMICABLE NUMBERS ARE    5020    5564

 AMICABLE NUMBERS ARE    6232    6368
STOP
```

PAGE 45

```
10 PRINT "TYPE IN YOUR ANSWERS,
WITH A CARRIAGE RETURN AFTER EACH "
11 LET N=0
12 LET S=0
14 LET R=1
16 LET N=N+1
17 IF N>20 THEN 60
18 INPUT X
20 LET Y=INT(R*N/5)
24 LET T=R*N-5*Y+1
25 IF X=T THEN 50
30 PRINT"YOU MISSED QUESTION NO.  "N
32 PRINT
34 LET G=N/5
36 LET P=INT(G)
38 IF P<>G THEN 16
40 LET R=R+1
42 GO TO 16
50 LET S=S+1
55 GO TO 34
60 PRINT
65 PRINT "YOU HAD  "S"  CORRECT ANSWERS "
70 PRINT "IF MORE THAN 15, CONGRATS "
75 END
TYPE IN YOUR ANSWERS, WITH A CARRIAGE RETURN AFTER EACH
1
YOU MISSED QUESTION NO.   1

2
YOU MISSED QUESTION NO.   2

4
5
2
YOU MISSED QUESTION NO.   5

3
4
YOU MISSED QUESTION NO.   7

2
4
1
4
5
YOU MISSED QUESTION NO.   12
2
YOU MISSED QUESTION NO.   13

5
YOU MISSED QUESTION NO.   14

3
YOU MISSED QUESTION NO.   15

5
4
3
2
2
YOU MISSED QUESTION NO.   20

YOU HAD   11  CORRECT ANSWERS
IF MORE THAN 15, CONGRATS
```

PAGE 49

```
10 REM SORTING
15 DIM X(100)
20 LET L=20
25 LET K=1
30 LET J=0
35 INPUT X(J)
40 LET J=J+1
45 IF J<L THEN 35
50 LET J=0
55 PRINT X(J),X(J+1),X(J+2),X(J+3),X(J+4)
56 PRINT
60 LET J=J+5
65 IF J<L THEN 55
70 IF K=0 THEN 98
75 LET J=0
78 IF X(J)>X(J+1) THEN 90
80 LET W=X(J)
84 LET X(J)=X(J+1)
86 LET X(J+1)=W
88 GO TO 75
90 LET J=J+1
92 IF J<L-1 THEN 78
94 LET K=0
95 PRINT
96 GO TO 50
98 STOP
99 END
12,56,78,58,98,5,6,8,789,567,435,97,100,67,75,45,34,23,4,88
 12           56           78           58           98

 5            6            8            789          567

 435          97           100          67           75

 45           34           23           4            88


 789          567          435          100          98

 97           88           78           75           67

 58           56           45           34           23

 12           8            6            5            4
```

PAGE 46

```
10 LET J=0
20 INPUT X(J)
30 LET J=J+1
40 IF J<10 THEN 20
50 LET K=10-J
60 PRINT X(K)
70 LET J=J-1
80 IF J>0 THEN 50
90 END
1,2,3,4,5,6,7,8,9,10
 1
 2
 3
 4
 5
 6
 7
 8
 9
 10
```

PAGE 52

```
10 DIM M(50)
15 LET P=1
16 LET J=0
18 LET N=5
20 LET T=4
24 LET B=.05
26 LET J=J+1
28 LET A=N
29 LET R=B/T
30 LET M(J)=A
32 IF J=N THEN 70
34 LET A=P*(1+R)↑(N*T)
36 LET B=B+.01
38 LET J=J+1
40 GO TO 29
70 LET N=N+5
75 IF N<51 THEN 24
76 PRINT
78 PRINT "YEARS","5 PERCENT",
"6 PERCENT","7 PERCENT","8 PERCENT"
79 PRINT
80 LET J=1
85 PRINT M(J),M(J+1),
M(J+2),M(J+3),M(J+4)
86 PRINT
90 LET J=J+5
95 IF J<51 THEN 85
98 STOP
99 END
```

YEARS	5 PERCENT	6 PERCENT	7 PERCENT	8 PERCENT
5	1.28203723	1.34685501	1.4147782	1.4859474
10	1.64361946	1.81401841	2.00159734	2.20803966
15	2.10718135	2.44321978	2.83181628	3.28103079
20	2.70148494	3.29066279	4.00639192	4.87543915
25	3.46340428	4.43204566	5.66815594	7.24464612
30	4.44021324	5.96932289	8.01918342	10.765163
35	5.69251869	8.03981242	11.3453658	15.996466
40	7.29802091	10.8284616	16.0511762	23.7699069
45	9.35633452	14.5843677	22.7088541	35.3208313
50	11.9951692	19.6430287	32.1279917	52.4848974

STOP

PAGE 54

```
10 DIM M(9,4)
12 LET P=1
14 LET N=10
16 LET T=4
18 LET J=0
19 LET B=.05
20 LET K=0
22 LET M(J,K)=N
25 LET R=B/T
30 LET K=K+1
35 LET A=P*(1+R)↑(N*T)
40 LET M(J,K)=A
42 LET B=B+.01
45 IF K<4 THEN 25
50 LET N=N+10
55 LET J=J+1
60 IF J<10 THEN 19
64 PRINT
65 PRINT "YEARS","5 PERCENT",
"6 PERCENT","7 PERCENT","8 PERCENT"
66 PRINT
70 LET J=0
72 LET K=0
75 PRINT M(J,K),M(J,K+1),
M(J,K+2),M(J,K+3),M(J,K+4)
76 PRINT
78 LET J=J+1
80 IF J<10 THEN 72
85 STOP
90 END
```

YEARS	5 PERCENT	6 PERCENT	7 PERCENT	8 PERCENT
10	1.64361946	1.81401841	2.00159734	2.20803966
20	2.70148494	3.29066279	4.00639192	4.87543915
30	4.44021324	5.96932289	8.01918342	10.765163
40	7.29802091	10.8284616	16.0511762	23.7699069
50	11.9951692	19.6430287	32.1279917	52.4848974
60	19.7154937	35.6328157	64.3073028	115.888735
70	32.4047691	64.6385838	128.717326	255.886923
80	53.2611092	117.255581	257.640258	565.008476
90	87.5409956	212.703783	515.692056	1247.56112
100	143.884085	385.848577	1032.20785	2754.66446

STOP

PAGE 50

```
10 DIM P(200)
12 LET J=0
14 LET N=1
15 LET P(J)=N
18 LET N=N+2
19 LET J=J+1
20 IF N<400 THEN 15
25 LET K=3
30 LET L=(K+1)/2
35 LET J=K+L-1
40 LET P(J)=0
45 LET J=J+K
50 IF J<200 THEN 40
55 LET K=K+2
60 IF K<134 THEN 30
65 LET J=0
70 PRINT P(J),P(J+1),
P(J+2),P(J+3),P(J+4)
75 LET J=J+5
80 IF J<200 THEN 70
85 STOP
90 END
```

```
1    3    7    0    5
11   13   17   19   0
0    23   0    29   0
31   0    37   0    0
41   43   47   0    0
0    53   0    59   0
61   0    67   0    0
71   73   0    79   0
0    83   0    89   0
0    0    97   0    0
101  103  107  109  0
0    113  0    0    0
0    0    127  0    0
131  0    137  139  0
0    0    0    149  0
151  0    157  0    0
0    163  167  0    0
0    173  0    179  0
181  0    0    0    0
191  193  197  199  0
0    0    0    0    0
211  0    0    0    0
0    223  227  229  0
0    233  0    239  0
241  0    0    0    0
251  0    257  0    0
0    263  0    269  0
271  0    277  0    0
281  283  0    0    0
0    293  0    0    0
0    0    307  0    0
311  313  317  0    0
0    0    0    0    0
331  0    337  0    0
0    0    347  349  0
0    353  0    359  0
0    0    367  0    0
0    373  0    379  0
0    383  0    389  0
0    0    397  0    0
STOP
```

PAGE 56

```
10 DIM W(20)
12 DIM V(6,2)
14 LET N=3
15 LET K=0
16 READ W(K)
18 LET K=K+1
20 IF K<21 THEN 16
22 LET J=0
23 LET L=0
24 LET K=0
26 LET V(J,K)=W(L)
28 LET K=K+1
30 LET L=L+1
32 IF K<3 THEN 26
34 LET J=J+1
36 IF J<7 THEN 24
37 LET J=0
38 LET K=0
39 PRINT
40 PRINT
42 PRINT V(J,K),V(J,K+1),V(J,K+2)
43 PRINT
46 LET J=J+1
48 IF J<7 THEN 42
50 PRINT
52 PRINT"WHICH COLUMN HOLDS THE NUMBER YOU ARE THINKING OF ?"
53 PRINT
54 INPUT A
55 PRINT
56 PRINT
57 IF A=2 THEN 80
58 IF A=3 THEN 70
60 LET J=0
61 LET K=0
62 LET Z=V(J,K)
63 LET V(J,K)=V(J,K+1)
64 LET V(J,K+1)=Z
65 LET J=J+1
66 IF J< 7 THEN 62
68 GO TO 80
70 LET J=0
72 LET K=1
73 LET Z=V(J,K)
74 LET V(J,K)=V(J,K+1)
75 LET V(J,K+1)=Z
76 LET J=J+1
77 IF J<7 THEN 72
80 LET L=0
81 LET K=0
82 LET J=0
84 LET W(L)=V(J,K)
86 LET J=J+1
88 LET L=L+1
89 IF J<7 THEN 84
90 LET K=K+1
92 IF K<3 THEN 82
94 LET N=N-1
95 IF N<>0 THEN 22
96 PRINT
97 PRINT
98 PRINT"THE NUMBER YOU CHOSE IS------"W(10)
99 PAUSE
100 DATA 45,29,73,50,19,44,11
101 DATA 7,26,35,43,17,20,9
102 DATA 2,5,13,39,49,64,25
103 END
```

```
45      35      49      45      29      73
7       13      44      50      19      44
2       11      5       11      7       26
19      9       73      35      43      17
17      25      50      20      9       2
20      29      43      5       13      39
64      26      39      49      64      25

WHICH COLUMN HOLDS THE NUMBER YOU ARE THINKING OF ?      2

1

45      50      11
35      20      5
49      29      19
7       43      9
13      64      73
44      26      17
2       39      25

WHICH COLUMN HOLDS THE NUMBER YOU ARE THINKING OF ?

3

THE NUMBER YOU CHOSE IS------ 19
PAUSE
```

PAGE 59

```
9 PRINT
10 PRINT "SIDE A","SIDE B","HYPOTENUSE"
12 LET J=3
14 LET L=J+1
20 FOR K=L TO 99 STEP 1
24 LET N=SQR(J*J+K*K)
28 LET W=INT(N)
30 IF N<>W THEN 70
35 LET D=2
40 IF D*D >N THEN 65
45 LET F=N/D
48 LET W=INT(F)
50 IF F=W THEN 70
55 LET D=D+1
60 GO TO 40
65 PRINT J,K,N
70 NEXT K
75 LET J=J+1
80 IF J<100 THEN 14
85 STOP
90 END
```

```
SIDE A   SIDE B   HYPOTENUSE
 3        4        5
 5        12       13
 8        15       17
 9        40       41
 11       60       61
 12       35       37
 20       21       29
 20       99       101
 28       45       53
 39       80       89
 48       55       73
 60       91       109
 65       72       97
STOP
```

PAGE 60

```
10 PRINT
12 PRINT"SETS","NOS. PER SET",
"NO.OF HITS","THEORY"
15 LET S=100
20 LET H=0
25 FOR J=1 TO S
26 LET P=0
28 LET G=0
30 LET N=S/10
35 FOR K=1 TO N
40 LET Y=INT(1000*RND(X))
42 IF Y<G THEN 48
45 LET G=Y
46 LET P=K
48 NEXT K
50 LET W=INT(N/2.72 + 1)
55 IF W<>P THEN 65
60 LET H=H+1
65 NEXT J
70 LET T=INT(S/2.72)
74 PRINT
75 PRINT S,N,H,T
78 LET S=S+100
80 IF S<=500 THEN 20
85 STOP
90 END
```

```
SETS     NO.OF HITS
100      11
200      11
300      8
400      13
500      11
STOP
NOS. PER SET    THEORY
10              36
20              73
30              110
40              147
50              183
```

PAGE 61

```
10 REM HEADS OR TAILS
12 PRINT"TOSSES","HEADS","TAILS"
14 FOR L=100 TO 1000 STEP 100
16 LET H=0
18 LET T=0
20 RANDOM
24 FOR J=1 TO L
28 LET A=INT(10*RND(X))
30 LET X=5*A
35 LET Y=X/2
40 LET W=INT(Y)
45 IF W=Y THEN 60
50 LET T=T+1
55 GO TO 65
60 LET H=H+1
65 NEXT J
70 PRINT
72 PRINT L,H,T
75 PRINT
80 NEXT L
85 STOP
90 END
```

TOSSES	HEADS	TAILS
100	44	56
200	91	109
300	168	132
400	205	195
500	266	234
600	304	296
700	332	368
800	428	372
900	452	448
1000	486	514

PAGE 62

```
10 DIM M(3)
12 PRINT
14 PRINT"CHANCES","4 ALIKE",
"3 ALIKE","PAIRS","PROFIT,LOSS"
16 LET L=1000
18 LET H=2
20 LET Z=0
22 LET P=0
24 LET F=0
26 LET T=0
30 FOR J=1 TO L
32 LET Y=0
34 LET N=0
37 RANDOM
38 LET W=10*RND(X)
40 LET M(0)=INT(W)
42 LET M(1)=INT(10*RND(X))
44 LET M(2)=INT(10*RND(X))
46 LET M(3)=INT(10*RND(X))
50 FOR K=N TO H
55 IF M(N)<>M(K+1) THEN 60
58 LET Y=Y+1
60 NEXT K
65 LET N=N+1
66 IF N<=2 THEN 50
68 IF Y=3 THEN 75
70 IF Y<3 THEN 83
71 LET Z=Z+100
73 LET F=F+1
74 GO TO 90
75 LET Z=Z+10
78 LET T=T+1
79 GO TO 90
83 IF Y=0 THEN 90
85 LET Z=Z+Y
88 LET P=P+Y
90 NEXT J
92 PRINT
93 PRINT L,F,T,P,(L-Z)
94 LET L=L+1000
96 IF L<=10000 THEN 20
98 STOP
99 END
```

```
CHANCES    4 ALIKE    3 ALIKE

1000       0          50
2000       0          72
3000       0          73
4000       0          99
5000       0.         171
6000       26         172
7000       0          269
8000       27         445
9000       0          502
10000      27         550
STOP
PAIRS           PROFIT,LOSS

524             -24
972             308
1589            681
2078            932
2490            800
2863            -1183
3497            813
3764            -2914
4161            -181
4789            -2989
```

PAGE 64

```
10 PRINT"ANGLES","TAN(X)","TAN(X+90)","TAN(X+180)","TAN(X+270)"
11 PRINT
20 DEF FNT(X)=SIN(X)/COS(X)
22 FOR J=0 TO 90 STEP 5
25 LET X=J
28 LET P=3.1415926536
30 LET X=X*P/180
35 LET A=FNT(X)
40 LET B=FNT(X+P/2)
45 LET C=FNT(X+P)
50 LET D=FNT(X+P+P/2)
60 PRINT J,A,B,C,D
65 NEXT J
70 STOP
75 END
```

```
ANGLES         TAN(X)          TAN(X+90)       TAN(X+180)      TAN(X+270)

0              0               1.645668E+10    -1.215312E-10
5.485558E+09
5              8.748866E-02    -11.4300523     8.748866E-02    -11.4300523
10             0.176327        -5.67128182     0.176327        -5.67128183
15             0.267949        -3.73205081     0.267949        -3.73205081
20             0.36397         -2.74747742     0.36397         -2.74747742
25             0.466308        -2.14450692     0.466308        -2.14450692
30             0.57735         -1.73205081     0.57735         -1.73205081
35             0.700208        -1.42814801     0.700208        -1.42814801
40             0.8391          -1.19175359     0.8391          -1.19175359
45             1               -1              1               -1
50             1.19175359      -0.8391         1.19175359      -0.8391
55             1.42814801      -0.700208       1.42814801      -0.700208
60             1.73205081      -0.57735        1.73205081      -0.57735
65             2.14450692      -0.466308       2.14450692      -0.466308
70             2.74747742      -0.36397        2.74747742      -0.36397
75             3.73205081      -0.267949       3.73205081      -0.267949
80             5.67128182      -0.176327       5.67128181      -0.176327
85             11.4300523      -8.748866E-02   11.4300523
-8.748866E-02
90             3.158382E+10    -1.215312E-10   5.485558E+09
-2.430625E-10
```

PAGE 65

```
10 PRINT"THE FORM OF A QUADRATIC EQUATION IS:  AX↑2 + BX + C"
11 PRINT
12 DEF FND(V)=B*B-4*A*C
14 PRINT "TYPE IN VALUES FOR: A , B , AND C"
15 PRINT
16 INPUT A,B,C
20 LET G=-B+SQR(FND(V))
25 LET H=-B-SQR(FND(V))
30 IF FND(V)<0 THEN 45
32 LET X=G/(2*A)
36 LET X1=H/(2*A)
38 PRINT
39 PRINT
40 PRINT"THE TWO ROOTS OF YOUR EQUATION ARE: "X",""AND "X1
41 PRINT
42 PRINT
43 PRINT
44 GO TO 14
45 PRINT"YOUR A,B,C VALUES GIVE A NEGATIVE DISCRIMINANT"
46 PRINT
48 GO TO 14
50 END
THE FORM OF A QUADRATIC EQUATION IS:  AX↑2 + BX + C

TYPE IN VALUES FOR: A , B , AND C

21,-7,-70


THE TWO ROOTS OF YOUR EQUATION ARE:  2,AND -1.66666667



TYPE IN VALUES FOR: A , B , AND C

40,-13,1


THE TWO ROOTS OF YOUR EQUATION ARE:  0.2,AND  0.125
```

PAGE 66

```
7 PRINT"DEGREES","  SINE X","ARC SIN(RADS)","ARC SIN(DEGREES)"
8 PRINT
9 LET Y=5
10 LET P = 3.1415926536
11 DEF FNF(X)=A+B*X+C*X*X+D*X↑3+E*X↑4
12 LET A=1.57078786
13 LET B=-.21412453
14 LET C=.08466649
15 LET D=-.03575663
16 LET E=.00864884
20 LET X=SIN(P*Y/180)
25 LET W=P/2-(SQR(1-X))*FNF(X)
30 LET R=W*180/P
35 PRINT Y,X,W,R
40 LET Y=Y+2.8
50 IF Y<90 THEN 20
55 STOP
60 END
```

DEGREES	SINE X	ARC SIN(RADS)	ARC SIN(DEGREES)
5	8.715574E-02	8.725837E-02	4.99953627
7.8	0.135716	0.13613	7.79969592
10.6	0.183951	0.185004	10.5999749
13.4	0.231748	0.233878	13.4002215
16.2	0.278991	0.28275	16.2003669
19	0.325568	0.331619	19.0003969
21.8	0.371368	0.380488	21.8003303
24.6	0.416281	0.429355	24.600201
27.4	0.4602	0.478221	27.4000468
30.2	0.50302	0.527088	30.1999008
33	0.544639	0.575955	32.9997874
35.8	0.584958	0.624823	35.7997203
38.6	0.62388	0.673692	38.5997031
41.4	0.661312	0.722562	41.399731
44.2	0.697165	0.771432	44.1997932
47	0.731354	0.820303	46.9998757
49.8	0.763796	0.869173	49.7999638
52.6	0.794415	0.918044	52.6000444
55.4	0.823136	0.966914	55.4001078
58.2	0.849893	1.01578421	58.2001479
61	0.87462	1.06465369	61.0001631
63.8	0.897258	1.11352278	63.8001555
66.6	0.917755	1.16239155	66.6001301
69.4	0.93606	1.21126014	69.4000938
72.2	0.952129	1.26012866	72.2000541
75	0.965926	1.30899725	75.0000179
77.8	0.977416	1.35786599	77.7999904
80.6	0.986572	1.40673494	80.5999749
83.4	0.993373	1.4556041	83.3999718
86.2	0.997801	1.50447346	86.1999795
89	0.999848	1.55334293	88.9999941

PAGE 67

```
10 INPUT A
12 LET X=A
14 GOSUB 50
16 INPUT B
18 LET X=B
20 GOSUB 50
25 INPUT C
28 LET X=C
29 GOSUB 50
30 PAUSE
50 IF X<>0 THEN 60
55 PRINT "ZERO DIVISOR"
58 RETURN
60 LET Y=X+1/X
62 PRINT X,Y
65 RETURN
70 END



RUN


5
 5                  5.2
0
ZERO DIVISOR
8
 8                  8.125
PAUSE
GO TO 10
9
 9                  9.11111111
567
 567                567.001764
1000
 1000               1000.001
PAUSE
```

PAGE 68

```
10 DIM Z(3)
11 DIM M(4)
12 PRINT "NUMBERS","BASE 3","BASE 6","OCTAL","BINARY"
13 PRINT
14 LET Z(0)=3
15 LET N=15
16 LET Z(1)=6
18 LET Z(2)=8
20 LET Z(3)=2
22 LET L=0
24 LET J=0
28 LET M(0)=N
30 LET X=N
32 GOSUB 70
35 LET L=L+1
38 IF L<4 THEN 30
42 PRINT M(0),M(1),M(2),M(3),M(4)
46 LET N=N+31
50 IF N<=511 THEN 22
52 STOP
70 LET B=Z(L)
71 LET W=1
72 LET S=0
74 LET J=J+1
76 LET Q=INT(X/B)
77 LET R=X-B*Q
78 LET S=S+W*R
79 LET W=10*W
80 IF Q=0 THEN 85
82 LET X=Q
84 GO TO 76
85 LET M(J)=S
88 RETURN
90 END
```

```
NUMBERS     BASE 3      BASE 6      OCTAL       BINARY

15          120         23          17          1111
46          1201        114         56          101110
77          2212        205         115         1001101
108         11000       300         154         1101100
139         12011       351         213         10001011
170         20022       442         252         10101010
201         21110       533         311         11001001
232         22121       1024        350         11101000
263         100202      1115        407         100000111
294         101220      1210        446         100100110
325         110001      1301        505         101000101
356         111012      1352        544         101100100
387         112100      1443        603         110000011
418         120111      1534        642         110100010
449         121122      2025        701         111000001
480         122210      2120        740         111100000
511         200221      2211        777         111111111
```

PAGE 69

```
10 DIM M(8)
12 PRINT "NUMBERS",,
"SQUARE OF",,"SQUARE OF"
15 FOR J=1 TO 1000
18 LET K=0
20 LET N=J
24 LET A=1
26 LET B=SQR(N-A*A)
28 IF B=0 THEN 62
29 LET W=INT(B)
30 IF W=B THEN 50
32 LET A=A+1
34 IF A*A>N THEN 62
36 GO TO 26
50 LET M(K)=N
51 LET M(K+1)=A
52 LET M(K+2)=B
54 LET K=K+3
55 IF K>8 THEN 58
56 LET N=N+1
57 GO TO 24
58 PRINT M(0),M(1),M(2)
59 PRINT M(3),M(4),M(5)
60 PRINT M(6),M(7),M(8)
61 PRINT
62 NEXT J
64 STOP
65 END
NUMBERS
 72    SQUARE OF
 73     6       SQUARE OF
 74     3        6
        5        8
 232             7
 233    6
 234    8        14
        3        13
 288             15
 289    12
 290    8        12
        1        15
 520             17
 521    6
 522    11       22
        9        20
 584             21
 585    10
 586    3        22
        15       24
 800             19
 801    4
 802    15       28
        19       24
 808             21
 809    18
 810    5        22
        9        28
STOP             27
```

PAGE 70

```
10 REM UNIT FRACTIONS
11 DIM M(29)
12 PRINT"THIS PROGRAM CONVERTS N/D TO SUM OF ITS UNIT FRACTIONS"
14 PRINT
16 PRINT"TYPE N AND THEN D. REMEMBER, D MUST BE LARGER THAN N."
17 PRINT
18 INPUT N,D
19 FOR J=0 TO 29
20 LET M(J)=0
21 NEXT J
22 IF D<=N THEN 14
23 LET K=0
24 LET P=INT(D/N)+1
35 LET M(K)=P
38 LET K=K+1
40 IF K<30 THEN 50
44 PRINT "TOO MANY FACTORS, TRY ANOTHER FRACTION"
45 PRINT
48 GO TO 14
50 LET R=N*P-D
55 IF R=0 THEN 75
56 LET G=D/10
58 LET D=P*D
60 LET N=R
62 LET W=D/N
64 LET Y=INT(W)
66 IF Y<>W THEN 24
70 LET M(K)=W
75 PRINT
76 PRINT"DENOMINATORS OF THE UNIT FRACTIONS ARE:"
77 PRINT
80 LET K=0
84 IF M(K)=0 THEN 95
86 PRINT
88 PRINT M(K)
92 LET K=K+1
94 GO TO 84
95 PRINT"---------------"
96 PRINT
98 GO TO 16
99 END
THIS PROGRAM CONVERTS N/D TO SUM OF ITS UNIT FRACTIONS

TYPE N AND THEN D. REMEMBER, D MUST BE LARGER THAN N.

37,123

DENOMINATORS OF THE UNIT FRACTIONS ARE:
 4

 20

 1230
---------------

TYPE N AND THEN D. REMEMBER, D MUST BE LARGER THAN N.

43,445

DENOMINATORS OF THE UNIT FRACTIONS ARE:


 11

 175

 171325
---------------
```

PAGE 73

```
10 PRINT"TYPE IN 5 ANSWERS PER LINE SEPARATED BY COMMAS AND WITH"
11 PRINT"A CARRIAGE RETURN AT THE END OF EACH LINE"
12 PRINT
13 PRINT
14 LET J=1
15 LET G=1
18 LET S=0
20 INPUT N(1),N(2),N(3),N(4),N(5)
22 GOSUB 50
24 LET J=J+1
26 IF J<5 THEN 20
30 PRINT
31 PRINT
35 PRINT"YOU HAD "S" CORRECT ANSWERS"
40 PRINT"IF MORE THAN 15, CONGRATS"
45 STOP
50 LET T=0
52 LET K=J+1
54 LET M=1
56 FOR L=J TO K
58 IF N(M)<>L THEN 65
60 LET S=S+1
62 GO TO 70
65 PRINT"YOU MISSED QUESTION " G
70 LET M=M+1
72 LET G=G+1
74 IF G>20 THEN 100
75 NEXT L
80 IF T>0 THEN 96
82 LET T=1
84 LET K=J+2
86 IF K>5 THEN 90
88 GO TO 56
90 LET K=K-1
92 LET T=2
94 GO TO 56
96 IF T<>2 THEN 100
97 LET T=1
98 IF N(M)=1 THEN 60
99 GO TO 65
100 RETURN
101 END
```

```
TYPE IN 5 ANSWERS PER LINE SEPARATED BY COMMAS AND WITH
A CARRIAGE RETURN AT THE END OF EACH LINE


1,2,1,2,3
2,3,3,3,4
YOU MISSED QUESTION   8
3,4,3,4,5
4,4,4,5,1
YOU MISSED QUESTION   17


YOU HAD   18  CORRECT ANSWERS
IF MORE THAN 15, CONGRATS
```

PAGE 75

```
10 DIM A(1,2),B(1,2),C(1,2)
20 INPUT A(0,0),A(0,1),A(0,2)
25 INPUT A(1,0),A(1,1),A(1,2)
30 INPUT B(0,0),B(0,1),B(0,2)
35 INPUT B(1,0),B(1,1),B(1,2)
38 MAT C=A+B
40 MAT PRINT C
50 GO TO 20
60 END
2,3,4
5,6,7
8,9,10
11,12,13

 10             12             14
 16             18             20

5,-8,15
12,15,-34
6,8,10
-4,-8,13

 11             0              25
 8              7             -21

10,20,30
5,5,5
100,200,300
15,30,45

 110            220            330
 20             35             50
```

PAGE 74

```
10 PRINT"NO.FACTORS","LEAST NO."
12 LET N=1
14 LET F=1
15 GO TO 60
16 LET G=F-2
20 LET J=N
22 LET D=2
24 IF D*D<=J THEN 30
25 IF G=0 THEN 60
26 LET N=N+1
28 GO TO 16
30 LET W=J/D
34 LET B=INT(W)
36 IF W<>B THEN 52
40 LET G=G-1
44 IF W=D THEN 52
46 LET G=G-1
52 LET D=D+1
55 GO TO 24
60 PRINT
62 PRINT F,N
64 LET F=F+1
66 IF N<=10 THEN 68
67 LET N=11
68 LET N=N+1
70 IF F<17 THEN 16
74 STOP
75 END
```

```
NO.FACTORS     LEAST NO.

 1              1

 2              2

 3              4

 4              6

 5              16

 6              12

 7              64

 8              24

 9              36

 10             48

 11             1024

 12             60

 13             4096

 14             192

 15             144

 16             120
STOP
```

PAGE 76

```
10 DIM U(3,2),V(3,2),W(3,2)
20 LET R=1
24 FOR J=0 TO 3
28 FOR K=0 TO 2
30 LET U(J,K)=R
40 NEXT K
45 NEXT J
50 GO TO (60,70,80,90) R
60 MAT V=U
62 MAT W=U+V
63 PRINT
64 MAT PRINT U,V,W
66 GO TO 95
70 MAT V=ZER
71 PRINT
72 MAT PRINT U,V
74 GO TO 95
80 MAT V=CON
81 PRINT
82 MAT PRINT U,V
86 GO TO 95
90 MAT W=ZER(0,2)
91 MAT V=CON(3)
92 MAT PRINT V,W
95 LET R=R+1
96 IF R<5 THEN 24
98 STOP
99 END
```

```
1 1 1
1 1 1
1 1 1
1 1 1
1 1 1
1 1 1
1 1 1
1 1 1
2 2 2
2 2 2
2 2 2
2 2 2

2 2 2
2 2 2
2 2 2
2 2 2
0 0 0
0 0 0
0 0 0
0 0 0

3 3 3
3 3 3
3 3 3
3 3 3
1 1 1
1 1 1
1 1 1
1 1 1
1
1
1
1
0 0 0
```

PAGE 77

```
10 DIM X(1,2),Y(1,2)
15 LET T=2
20 MAT X=CON
30 LET R=2
40 MAT Y=(R)*X
42 PRINT
43 PRINT
45 MAT PRINT Y
50 LET R=R+1
60 IF R<6 THEN 40
70 LET T=T-1
80 MAT X=DIM(2,1)
83 MAT Y=DIM(2,1)
85 IF T>0 THEN 20
90 STOP
95 END
```

```
2    2    2
2    2    2


3    3    3
3    3    3


4    4    4
4    4    4


5    5    5
5    5    5
2    2
2    2
2    2
3    3
3    3
3    3
4    4
4    4
4    4
5    5
5    5
5    5
STOP
```

PAGE 78

```
10 DIM R(2,4)
12 MAT R=ZER
15 LET L=2
18 LET M=2
24 FOR J=0 TO 2
28 FOR K=L TO M
30 LET R(J,K)=1
34 NEXT K
40 LET L=L-1
45 LET M=M+1
50 IF M>4 THEN 60
55 NEXT J
60 PRINT
61 PRINT
65 MAT PRINT R
70 MAT R=DIM(4,2)
71 PRINT
72 PRINT
75 MAT PRINT R
80 STOP
85 END
```

```
 0   0   1   0  0
 0   1   1   1  0
 1   1   1   1  1


 0   1   1
 0   1   1
 1   1   0
 0   1   0
 1   0   1
STOP
```

PAGE 79

```
10 DIM P(3,4),R(4,3)
11 MAT P=ZER
12 LET J=0
14 LET T=0
16 LET K=0
20 LET P(J,K)=2
24 LET K=K+1
30 IF K<5 THEN 20
35 IF T>0 THEN 65
40 LET T=1
50 LET J=3
60 GO TO 16
65 LET P(1,2)=2
70 LET P(2,2)=2
80 PRINT
82 PRINT
84 MAT PRINT P
90 MAT R=TRN(P)
92 PRINT
93 PRINT
94 MAT PRINT R
96 STOP
99 END
```

```
 2  2  2  2  2
 0  0  2  0  0
 0  0  2  0  0
 2  2  2  2  2


 2  0  0  2
 2  0  0  2
 2  2  2  2
 2  0  0  2
 2  0  0  2
STOP
```

PAGE 80

```
10 DIM A(4,9),B(9,4)
20 FOR J=0 TO 4
30 FOR K=0 TO 9
40 LET N=5*K+J
50 LET A(J,K)=N
60 NEXT K
70 NEXT J
78 PRINT
80 MAT PRINT A
90 MAT B=TRN(A)
92 PRINT
95 PRINT
96 PRINT
97 MAT PRINT B
98 STOP
99 END
```

```
0        5
25       30
1        6
26       31
2        7
27       32
3        8
28       33
4        9
29       34
0        1
5        6
10       11
15       16
20       21
25       26
30       31
35       36
40       41
45       46
STOP
```

```
10       15       20
35       40       45
11       16       21
36       41       46
12       17       22
37       42       47
13       18       23
38       43       48
14       19       24
39       44       49


2        3        4
7        8        9
12       13       14
17       18       19
22       23       24
27       28       29
32       33       34
37       38       39
42       43       44
47       48       49
```

PAGE 81

```
10 DIM A(2,2),B(2,2),C(2,2)
12 LET N=1
16 FOR J=0 TO 2
20 FOR K=0 TO 2
25 LET B(J,K)=N
30 LET N=N+1
35 NEXT K
40 NEXT J
45 IF N>18 THEN 70
50 MAT A=B
60 GO TO 16
70 MAT C=A*B
80 PRINT
90 MAT PRINT A
91 PRINT
92 MAT PRINT B
93 PRINT
94 MAT PRINT C
96 STOP
99 END
```

```
1        2        3
4        5        6
7        8        9

10       11       12
13       14       15
16       17       18

84       90       96
201      216      231
318      342      366
STOP
```

PAGE 82

```
10 DIM A(2,2),B(2,2),C(2,2)
20 MAT READ B
25 LET T=0
30 MAT A=IDN
40 MAT C=A*B
42 PRINT
43 PRINT
45 MAT PRINT C
50 MAT C=B*A
52 PRINT
53 PRINT
55 MAT PRINT C
60 IF T<>0 THEN 80
65 LET T=1
70 MAT READ A
75 GO TO 40
80 STOP
81 DATA 2,4,6,8,10,12
82 DATA 14,16,18,1,3,5,7,9,11,13,15,17
85 END
```

```
2        4        6
8        10       12
14       16       18


2        4        6
8        10       12
14       16       18


96       114      132
240      294      348
384      474      564


108      132      156
234      294      354
360      456      552
STOP
```

PAGE 83

```
10 DIM A(2,2),B(2),C(2),D(15,2)
15 MAT READ A
20 LET B(0)=0
25 LET B(2)=2
26 LET J=0
30 LET B(1)=0
35 MAT C=A*B
36 LET D(J,0)=C(0)
37 LET D(J,1)=C(1)
38 LET D(J,2)=C(2)
40 LET J=J+1
55 LET B(1)=B(1)+1
60 IF B(1)<=3 THEN 35
65 LET B(0)=B(0)+1
70 IF B(0)<=3 THEN 30
72 PRINT
73 PRINT
74 MAT PRINT D
75 STOP
90 DATA 1,2,3,4,5,6
95 DATA 7,8,9
99 END
```

```
6        12       18
8        17       26
10       22       34
12       27       42
7        16       25
9        21       33
11       26       41
13       31       49
8        20       32
10       25       40
12       30       48
14       35       56
9        24       39
11       29       47
13       34       55
15       39       63
STOP
```

PAGE 84

```
10 DIM M(99)
12 PRINT"CELL NO. = NO. OF DIVISORS; CELL CONTENTS = LEAST NUMBER"
13 PRINT"EXAMPLE: CELL 3 INDICATES LEAST NO. WITH 3 DIVISORS IS 4"
14 PRINT
18 FOR N=0 TO 99
20 LET M(N)=9999
25 NEXT N
30 LET M(0)=1
35 LET M(1)=2
40 FOR N=4 TO 2000 STEP 2
42 LET D=2
44 LET G=2
48 IF D*D>N THEN 80
50 LET J=N
55 LET W=J/D
60 LET B=INT(W)
64 IF B<>W THEN 70
66 LET G=G+1
68 IF W=D THEN 70
69 LET G=G+1
70 LET D=D+1
75 GO TO 48
80 IF N>=M(G-1) THEN 90
85 LET M(G-1)=N
90 NEXT N
91 FOR J=0 TO 99
92 IF M(J)<>9999 THEN 94
93 LET M(J)=0
94 NEXT J
95 MAT M=DIM(19,4)
96 PRINT
97 MAT PRINT M
98 STOP
99 END
```

```
CELL NO. = NO. OF DIVISORS; CELL CONTENTS = LEAST NUMBER
EXAMPLE: CELL 3 INDICATES LEAST NO. WITH 3 DIVISORS IS 4


1        576
2        0
4        0
6        360
16       1296
12       0
64       900
24       960
36       0
48       720
1024     0
60       840
0        0
192      0
144      0
120      1260
0        0
180      0
0        0
240      1680
STOP
```

```
40 FOR N=4 TO 10000 STEP 2

1        576      0        0
2        3072     2880     0
4        0        0        0
6        360      0        7560
16       1296     3600     0
12       0        0        0
64       900      0        0
24       960      2520     0
36       0        0        0
48       720      6480     0
1024     0        0        0
60       840      0        0
4096     9216     0        0
192      0        6300     0
144      5184     0        0
120      1260     6720     0
0        0        0        0
180      0        0        0
0        0        0        0
240      1680     5040     0
STOP
```

PAGE 85

```
10 DIM A(2,2),W(2,2)
12 LET G=0
15 LET N=G
20 FOR J=0 TO 2
25 FOR K=0 TO 2
30 LET A(J,K)=N
35 LET N=N+1
40 NEXT K
45 NEXT J
50 MAT W=INV(A)
51 PRINT
52 PRINT
55 MAT PRINT A
56 PRINT
57 PRINT
58 MAT PRINT W
60 LET G=G+4
65 IF G<20 THEN 15
70 STOP
75 END
```

```
0              1              2
3              4              5
6              7              8


0              -0.5           -0.5
-0.166667      -0.666667      0.5
0.5            -0.5           0


4              5              6
7              8              9
10             11             12


-0.333333      -0.833333      -0.5
-0.5           -1             0.5
0.5            -0.5           0


8              9              10
11             12             13
14             15             16
```

```
-0.666667        -1.16666667      -0.5
-0.833333        -1.33333333      0.5
0.5              -0.5             0


12               13               14
15               16               17
18               19               20


2.147484E+09     -4.294967E+09    2.147484E+09
-4.294967E+09    8.589935E+09     -4.294967E+09
2.14748 1E+09    -4.294967E+09    2.147484E+09


16               17               18
19               20               21
22               23               24


-1.33333333      -1.83333333      -0.5
-1.5             -2               0.5
0.5              -0.5             0
STOP
```

PAGE 86

```
10 DIM A(2,2),B(2,0),C(2,0)
20 MAT READ A,B
30 MAT A=INV(A,R)
32 PRINT
35 MAT PRINT A
40 MAT C=A*B
50 PRINT
55 PRINT C(0),C(1),C(2)
56 PRINT
60 PRINT R
65 STOP
70 DATA 3,2,-1,1,1,1,1,-2,2,4,6,3
80 END
```

```
 0.307692          -0.153846          0.230769
-7.692308E-02       0.538462         -0.307692
-0.230769           0.615385          7.692308E-02

 1                  2                 3


 13
STOP
```

PAGE 87

```
10 DIM L(2,2),M(2),N(2)
15 LET J=0
17 PRINT
18 PRINT"A LINEAR EQUATION IS AX+BY+CZ=D"
19 PRINT
20 LET K=0
25 PRINT
28 PRINT "TYPE IN VALUES FOR A,B,C, AND D"
29 INPUT L(J,K),L(J,K+1),L(J,K+2),M(J)
30 LET J=J+1
32 IF J<3 THEN 20
35 MAT L=INV(L,R)
40 IF ABS(R)>=1 THEN 50
45 PRINT
46 PRINT "INVERSE MATRIX IS SMALL, IT IS ",R
50 MAT N=L*M
55 PRINT
60 MAT PRINT N
65 GO TO 15
70 END

      A LINEAR EQUATION IS AX+BY+CZ=D


      TYPE IN VALUES FOR A,B,C, AND D
      1,1,1,12

      TYPE IN VALUES FOR A,B,C, AND D
      2,-3,1,-1

      TYPE IN VALUES FOR A,B,C, AND D
      4,-3,5,25

       3
       4
       5

      A LINEAR EQUATION IS AX+BY+CZ=D


      TYPE IN VALUES FOR A,B,C, AND D
      2.2,-3.5,1,15

      TYPE IN VALUES FOR A,B,C, AND D
      4.2,6.5,-50,-3

      TYPE IN VALUES FOR A,B,C, AND D
      -1.2,-3,1.8,0

       4.23142509
      -1.56540804
       0.211937
```

PAGE 88

```
10 DIM L(3,3),M(3),N(3)
15 PRINT"A 4TH ORDER LINEAR EQUATION IS AW+BX+CY+DZ=E"
20 FOR J=0 TO 3
24 PRINT
28 PRINT"TYPE IN VALUES FOR A,B,C,D, AND E"
30 INPUT L(J,0),L(J,1),L(J,2),L(J,3),M(J)
35 NEXT J
40 PRINT
42 MAT PRINT L
45 MAT L=INV(L,R)
50 IF ABS(R)>1 THEN 60
55 PRINT"INVERSE IS SMALL, IT IS  "R
60 MAT N=L*M
65 MAT PRINT N
68 GO TO 20
70 END

 A 4TH ORDER LINEAR EQUATION IS AW+BX+CY+DZ=E

 TYPE IN VALUES FOR A,B,C,D, AND E
 3,-2,5,-1,68

 TYPE IN VALUES FOR A,B,C,D, AND E
 1,-1,-1,-1,-16

 TYPE IN VALUES FOR A,B,C,D, AND E
 1,1,1,-1,4

 TYPE IN VALUES FOR A,B,C,D, AND E
 5,5,5,-8,-4

  3              -2             5             -1
  1              -1            -1             -1
  1               1             1             -1
  5               5             5             -8
  2
 -2.85714286
  12.8571429
  8

 TYPE IN VALUES FOR A,B,C,D, AND E
 1,2,3,4,5

 TYPE IN VALUES FOR A,B,C,D, AND E
 4,6,-5,-3,2

 TYPE IN VALUES FOR A,B,C,D, AND E
 10,-42,35,7,-15

 TYPE IN VALUES FOR A,B,C,D, AND E
 6,8,3,11,-12

  1               2             3              4
  4               6            -5             -3
  10            -42            35              7
  6               8             3             11
 -1.71747076
  3.95321637
  5.72404971
 -4.59027778

 TYPE IN VALUES FOR A,B,C,D, AND E
```

PAGE 89

```
10 DIM A(1,2),B(2,0),C(1,0)
12 PRINT
14 PRINT"RAMBLERS","SPLITS",
"COLONIALS","MATERIALS","LABOR"
15 PRINT
20 MAT READ A
25 LET M=0
26 LET L=0
30 FOR R=0 TO 9
34 LET B(0,0)=R+1
36 LET B(1,0)=2*R+1
38 LET B(2,0)=2*R+5
40 MAT C=A*B
45 PRINT
50 PRINT B(0,0),B(1,0),
 B(2,0),C(0,0),C(1,0)
      TOTAL COSTS =",M,L
54 LET M=M+C(0,0)
58 LET L=L+C(1,0)
60 NEXT R
62 PRINT
70 PRINT"
80 STOP
86 DATA 17500,16200,12400
88 DATA 6200,5500,4900
90 END
```

RAMBLERS	SPLITS	COLONIALS	MATERIALS	LABOR
1	1	5	95700	36200
2	3	7	170400	63200
3	5	9	245100	90200
4	7	11	319800	117200
5	9	13	394500	144200
6	11	15	469200	171200
7	13	17	543900	198200
8	15	19	618600	225200
9	17	21	693300	252200
10	19	23	768000	279200
		TOTAL COSTS =	4318500	1577000

STOP

PAGE 91

```
10 DIM A(2,2),B(2,0),C(2,0)
20 PRINT"DACRON","COTTON","WOOL","TOTAL YARDS OF CLOTH"
21 PRINT
24 LET X=10
28 MAT READ A
30 LET B(0,0)=X
32 LET B(1,0)=3*X
36 LET B(2,0)=6*X
38 LET T=0
40 MAT C=A*B
45 MAT C=(3/100)*C
50 LET T=T+C(0,0)+C(1,0)+C(2,0)
55 PRINT C(0,0),C(1,0),C(2,0),T
56 PRINT
60 LET X=X+5
70 IF X<=30 THEN 30
80 STOP
85 DATA 40,45,25,10,30,15,50,25,60
90 END
```

```
DACRON          COTTON          WOOL            TOTAL YARDS OF CLOTH
97.5            57              145.5           300
146.25          85.5            218.25          450
195             114             291             600
243.75          142.5           363.75          750
292.5           171             436.5           900
STOP
```

PAGE 92

```
10 PRINT "PART A","PART B","PART C"
11 PRINT
12 DIM M(2,2),G(2,2),R(2,2),B(2),C(2)
14 MAT READ M,B
20 MAT G=IDN
25 MAT G=G-M
30 MAT R=INV(G)
35 MAT C=R*B
40 PRINT
41 PRINT C(0),C(1),C(2)
45 PRINT
46 PRINT
47 PRINT
48 PRINT "MATRIX M WAS"
50 PRINT
51 PRINT
52 MAT PRINT M
55 PRINT
56 PRINT
58 PRINT"THE INVERSE OF IDN MATRIX MINUS MATRIX M WAS:"
59 PRINT
60 MAT PRINT R
65 STOP
70 DATA 0,0,0,1,0,0,1,2,0,8,0,5
75 END
```

```
PART A          PART B          PART C

8               8               29

MATRIX M WAS

0               0               0
1               0               0
1               2               0

THE INVERSE IF IDN MATRIX MINUS MATRIX M WAS:

1               -1.455192E-11   -0
1               1               0
3               2               1
STOP
```

PAGE 95

```
10 DIM M(6,2),L(4)
12 PRINT"TYPE IN YOUR 20 ANSWERS--5 PER LINE"
14 PRINT"SEPARATE EACH BY COMMAS WITH CAR.RET.AFTER THE 5TH ONE"
16 LET K=-1
18 LET J=0
20 LET N=0
25 INPUT L(0),L(1),L(2),L(3),L(4)
30 LET K=K+1
32 IF K<3 THEN 40
34 LET J=J+1
36 IF J>5 THEN 60
38 LET K=0
40 LET M(J,K)=L(N)
45 LET N=N+1
50 IF N<5 THEN 30
55 GO TO 20
60 LET M(6,0)=L(3)
62 LET M(6,1)=L(4)
64 LET T=1
66 LET S=0
68 FOR J=0 TO 6
70 FOR K=0 TO 2
72 LET G=(J+1)*(K+1)
74 IF G<6 THEN 78
75 LET G=G-5
76 GO TO 74
78 LET R=G-INT(G/6)
80 IF M(J,K)<>R THEN 86
82 LET S=S+1
84 GO TO 87
86 PRINT"YOU MISSED QUESTION NO. "T
87 LET T=T+1
88 IF T>20 THEN 94
90 NEXT K
92 NEXT J
94 PRINT
96 PRINT "YOU HAD "S" CORRECT"
97 PRINT"IF YOU HAD MORE THAN 15, CONGRATS "
98 STOP
99 END
```

```
RUN
TYPE IN YOUR 20 ANSWERS--5 PER LINE
SEPARATE EACH BY COMMAS WITH CAR.RET.AFTER THE 5TH ONE

1,2,3,2,3
1,3,1,3,4
3,2,5,4,5
1,2,3,2,4
YOU MISSED QUESTION NO.  5
YOU MISSED QUESTION NO.  9
YOU MISSED QUESTION NO.  14

YOU HAD  17 CORRECT
IF YOU HAD MORE THAN 15, CONGRATS
STOP
```

PAGE 96

```
 9 DIM L(3)
10 PRINT"NO.OF PEOPLE","  SQ.MI.(IN 1000'S), IF SPACE PER PERSON IS"
12 PRINT"(IN BILLIONS)"," 4 SQ.FT.","1 SQ.YD.","16 SQ.FT.","1 ACRE"
14 PRINT
16 LET P=3.5
18 LET N=0
20 LET F=2
24 LET Y=F/3
30 LET M=P*Y*Y*1600/(88*55)
34 LET L(N)=M
40 LET F=F+1
45 LET N=N+1
50 IF N<3 THEN 24
55 IF N<>3 THEN 65
58 LET F=209
62 GO TO 24
65 PRINT
66 PRINT P,L(0),L(1),L(2),L(3)
70 LET P=P+.5
75 IF P<=10 THEN 18
80 STOP
90 END
```

RUN

NO.OF PEOPLE (IN BILLIONS)	SQ.MI.(IN 1000'S), IF SPACE PER PERSON IS 4 SQ.FT.	1 SQ.YD.	16 SQ.FT.	1 ACRE
3.5	0.514233	1.15702479	2.05693297	5615.55556
4	0.587695	1.32231405	2.35078053	6417.77778
4.5	0.661157	1.48760331	2.6446281	7220
5	0.734619	1.65289256	2.93847567	8022.22222
5.5	0.808081	1.81818182	3.23232323	8824.44444
6	0.881543	1.98347107	3.5261708	9626.66667
6.5	0.955005	2.14876033	3.82001837	10428.8889
7	1.02846648	2.31404959	4.11386593	11231.1111
7.5	1.10192837	2.47933884	4.4077135	12033.3333
8	1.17539027	2.6446281	4.70156107	12835.5556
8.5	1.24885216	2.80991736	4.99540863	13637.7778
9	1.32231405	2.97520661	5.2892562	14440
9.5	1.39577594	3.14049587	5.58310377	15242.2222
10	1.46923783	3.30578512	5.87695133	16044.4444

STOP

PAGE 97

```
10 PRINT"NUMBER","SQ. OF NUMBER","TENS' DIGIT","UNITS DIGIT"
15 LET N=3
20 LET N=N+1
22 IF N>100 THEN 75
23 LET L=N*N
30 LET M=INT(L/10)
35 LET U=L-10*M
40 LET T=M-10*INT(M/10)
45 LET R=T/2
50 LET W=INT(R)
55 IF R=W THEN 20
65 PRINT N,L,T,U
70 GO TO 20
75 STOP
80 END
```

RUN

NUMBER	SQ. OF NUMBER	TENS' DIGIT	UNITS DIGIT
4	16	1	6
6	36	3	6
14	196	9	6
16	256	5	6
24	576	7	6
26	676	7	6
34	1156	5	6
36	1296	9	6
44	1936	3	6
46	2116	1	6
54	2916	1	6
56	3136	3	6
64	4096	9	6
66	4356	5	6
74	5476	7	6
76	5776	7	6
84	7056	5	6
86	7396	9	6
94	8836	3	6
96	9216	1	6

STOP

PAGE 98

```
10 DIM D(3,3)
12 PRINT"IS THIS A 3RD OR 4TH ORDER DETERMINANT ? TYPE IN 3 OR 4."
13 MAT D=ZER
15 INPUT N
16 LET N=N-1
17 LET L=0
18 IF N>2 THEN 25
19 INPUT D(0,0),D(0,1),D(0,2)
20 INPUT D(1,0),D(1,1),D(1,2)
21 INPUT D(2,0),D(2,1),D(2,2)
23 GO TO 29
25 INPUT D(0,0),D(0,1),D(0,2),D(0,3)
26 INPUT D(1,0),D(1,1),D(1,2),D(1,3)
27 INPUT D(2,0),D(2,1),D(2,2),D(2,3)
28 INPUT D(3,0),D(3,1),D(3,2),D(3,3)
29 PRINT
30 PRINT
31 MAT PRINT D
32 FOR K=L+1 TO N
34 IF D(L,L)=0 THEN 92
35 LET R=D(L,K)/D(L,L)
40 FOR J=L TO N
45 LET D(J,K)=D(J,K)-R*D(J,L)
50 NEXT J
55 NEXT K
60 LET L=L+1
65 IF L<>N THEN 32
70 IF N>2 THEN 80
75 LET D(3,3)=1
80 LET T=D(0,0)*D(1,1)*D(2,2)*D(3,3)
82 PRINT
83 PRINT
85 PRINT" THE VALUE OF THE DETERMINANT IS--"T
90 GO TO 12
92 PRINT"THIS FORMAT INVOLVES A DIVISION BY ZERO"
93 PRINT"EXCHANGE ANY 2 ROWS OR COLUMNS IN YOUR PROBLEM"
94 GO TO 12
95 END
```

```
IS THIS A 3RD OR 4TH ORDER DETERMINANT ? TYPE IN 3 OR 4.
3
3,12,6
4,6,28
1,2,4


3            12           6            0
4            6            28           0
1            2            4            0
0            0            0            0


 THE VALUE OF THE DETERMINANT IS-- 60
IS THIS A 3RD OR 4TH ORDER DETERMINANT ? TYPE IN 3 OR 4.
4
3,2,-8,6
1,2,3,4
5,24,13,34
-6,7,14,1


3            2            -8           6
1            2            3            4
5            24           13           34
-6           7            14           1


 THE VALUE OF THE DETERMINANT IS---504
IS THIS A 3RD OR 4TH ORDER DETERMINANT ? TYPE IN 3 OR 4.
```

PAGE 99

```
10 PRINT"SIDE A","SIDE B","SIDE C","AREA","PERIMETER"
15 LET A=1
18 LET B=A+1
24 LET C=SQR(A*A+B*B)
28 LET W=INT(C)
32 IF W<>C THEN 70
40 LET G=A*B/2
45 LET P=2*(A+B+C)
50 IF G<>P THEN 70
52 LET P=P/2
55 PRINT
60 PRINT A,B,C,G,P
65 PRINT
70 LET B=B+1
75 IF B<100 THEN 24
80 LET A=A+1
85 IF A<100 THEN 18
90 STOP
95 END
```

```
SIDE A    SIDE B    SIDE C    AREA    PERIMETER

9         40        41        180     90


10        24        26        120     60


12        16        20        96      48

STOP
```

PAGE 100

```
10 PRINT"NUMBER","CALCULATED CUBE ROOT"
11 PRINT
14 LET N=2
16 LET F=.000005
20 LET A=(N+1)/2
24 LET P=N/(A*A)+2*A
26 IF P=3*A THEN 70
28 LET G=ABS(P-3*A)
30 IF G<F THEN 70
40 LET A=(N/(A*A)+2*A)/3
50 GO TO 24
70 PRINT
72 PRINT N,A
75 LET N=N+2
80 IF N<100 THEN 24
85 STOP
90 END
```

```
NUMBER          CALCULATED CUBE ROOT


2               1.25992186

4               1.58740105

6               1.81712083

8               2.00000002

10              2.15443469

12              2.28942849

14              2.41014226

16              2.5198421

18              2.62074139

20              2.71441762

22              2.80203933

24              2.88449914

26              2.9624976

28              3.03659012

30              3.10723339

32              3.17480279
```

PAGE 102

```
10 DIM C(3,4)
11 MAT C=ZER
12 LET T=-1
15 PRINT"INPUT 3 ROWS OF 4 NUMBERS EACH"
18 PRINT
20 INPUT C(0,0),C(0,1),C(0,2),C(0,3)
21 INPUT C(1,0),C(1,1),C(1,2),C(1,3)
22 INPUT C(2,0),C(2,1),C(2,2),C(2,3)
25 LET W=0
26 FOR K=0 TO 3
27 FOR J=0 TO 2
28 LET C(3,K)=C(3,K)+C(J,K)
29 NEXT J
30 NEXT K
32 FOR J=0 TO 3
34 FOR K=0 TO 3
36 LET C(J,4)=C(J,4)+C(J,K)
38 NEXT K
40 NEXT J
41 IF W<>0 THEN 80
42 IF T>0 THEN 85
43 IF T<0 THEN 47
44 PRINT
45 PRINT"THE EXPECTED FACTS ARE: "
46 GO TO 49
47 PRINT
48 PRINT"THE OBSERVED FACTS ARE: "
49 PRINT
50 PRINT"CATEGORY A","CATEGORY B",
"CATEGORY C","CATEGORY D","TOTALS"
51 PRINT
52 LET T=T+1
53 IF T<1 THEN 80
55 LET R=0
56 FOR J=0 TO 2
58 FOR K=0 TO 3
60 LET P=C(3,K)/C(3,4)*C(J,4)
61 LET R=R+((P-C(J,K))↑2)/P
62 LET C(J,K)=P
63 NEXT K
64 NEXT J
65 FOR J=0 TO 2
66 LET C(J,4)=0
68 NEXT J
70 FOR K=0 TO 4
72 LET C(3,K)=0
74 NEXT K
75 LET W=1
78 GO TO 26
80 MAT PRINT C
82 GO TO 42
85 PRINT
86 PRINT
87 PRINT"THE VALUE OF CHI SQUARE IS  "R
88 GO TO 11
90 END
```

```
INPUT 3 ROWS OF 4 NUMBERS EACH

26,88,56,66
32,112,308,400
78,94,12,48
```

THE OBSERVED FACTS ARE:

CATEGORY A	CATEGORY B	CATEGORY C	CATEGORY D	TOTALS
26	88	56	66	236
32	112	308	400	852
78	94	12	48	232
136	294	376	514	1320

THE EXPECTED FACTS ARE:

CATEGORY A	CATEGORY B	CATEGORY C	CATEGORY D	TOTALS
24.3151515	52.5636364	67.2242424	91.8969697	236
87.7818182	189.763636	242.690909	331.763636	852
23.9030303	51.6727273	66.0848485	90.3393939	232
136	294	376	514	1320

```
THE VALUE OF CHI SQUARE IS   353.31272
INPUT 3 ROWS OF 4 NUMBERS EACH
```

PAGE 103

```
10 LET L=10
12 DIM B(4)
14 PRINT
15 PRINT"SUM=13","SUM=14","SUM=15","SUM=16","SUM=17"
20 LET N=0
22 MAT B=ZER
25 LET T=-12
28 RANDOM
30 LET D=INT(10*RND(X))
35 IF D>5 THEN 30
40 LET T=T+D
45 IF T<=0 THEN 30
48 LET T=T-1
50 LET B(T)=B(T)+1
55 LET N=N+1
60 IF N<1000 THEN 25
65 PRINT
66 PRINT B(0),B(1),
B(2),B(3),B(4)
70 LET L=L-1
75 IF L>0 THEN 20
80 STOP
85 END
```

SUM=13	SUM=14	SUM=15	SUM=16	SUM=17
244	453	126	177	0
522	191	267	20	0
365	336	173	73	53
245	191	383	112	69
506	152	238	65	39
447	157	185	143	68
379	411	129	68	13
364	314	70	118	134
528	152	219	100	1
340	294	175	151	40

STOP

PAGE 104

```
10 DIM P(1000)
12 PRINT
14 PRINT"THE FOLLOWING CELLS WERE LEFT UNLOCKED: "
15 PRINT
20 MAT P=CON
24 LET L=2
30 LET M=L
35 FOR J=L TO 1000 STEP M
40 LET P(J)=P(J)+1
45 NEXT J
50 LET L=L+1
55 IF L<1000 THEN 30
58 LET K=1
60 FOR J=1 TO 1000
65 LET W=P(J)/2
70 LET R=INT(W)
75 IF W=R THEN 82
80 PRINT
81 PRINT J
82 NEXT J
85 STOP
90 END
```

THE FOLLOWING CELLS WERE LEFT UNLOCKED:

1	81	289	625
4	100	324	676
9	121	361	729
16	144	400	784
25	169	441	841
36	196	484	900
49	225	529	961
64	256	576	1000

PAGE 105

```
10 DIM R(3,4)
12 MAT R=ZER
14 PRINT
16 PRINT"WHAT SIZE RUG DO YOU NEED? "
18 INPUT L,M
20 IF L> 9 THEN 28
22 LET R(3,0)=9-L
24 LET R(3,1)=M
28 IF M>9 THEN 35
30 LET R(2,0)=9-M
32 LET R(2,1)=L
35 IF L>12 THEN 55
38 LET R(1,0)=12-L
40 LET R(1,1)=M
44 IF M>12 THEN 63
48 LET R(0,0)=12-M
50 LET R(0,1)=L
52 GO TO 63
55 IF M<= 12 THEN 48
60 PRINT
61 PRINT"SIZE IS TOO LARGE FOR WIDTH OF ROLLS"
62 GO TO 16
63 PRINT"PIECE LEFT FROM ROLL ","13.95 RUG","16.95 RUG","19.95 RUG"
64 PRINT
65 GOSUB 80
66 LET G=12
67 FOR J=0 TO 3
68 IF R(J,2)=0 THEN 78
69 IF J< 2 THEN 71
70 LET G=9
71 IF R(J,0)=0 THEN 76
73 PRINT"FROM"G" FT.ROLL"R(J,0)" BY "R(J,1),R(J,2),R(J,3),R(J,4)
75 GO TO 77
76 PRINT"NO PIECE LEFT IN "G"  FT.ROLL",R(J,2),R(J,3),R(J,4)
77 PRINT
78 NEXT J
79 GO TO 12
80 FOR J=0 TO 3
81 IF R(J,1)=0 THEN 94
82 LET P=4.65
83 IF J>1 THEN 86
84 LET N=4.00
85 GO TO 87
86 LET N=3.00
87 FOR K=2 TO 4
88 LET R(J,K)=N*R(J,1)*P
90 LET P=P+1
91 NEXT K
92 IF R(J,0)<>0 THEN 94
93 LET R(J,1)=0
94 NEXT J
95 RETURN
99 END
```

```
WHAT SIZE RUG DO YOU NEED?
9,12
PIECE LEFT FROM ROLL          13.95 RUG      16.95 RUG      19.95 RUG

NO PIECE LEFT IN  12  FT.ROLL  167.4          203.4          239.4

FROM 12 FT.ROLL 3 BY  12       223.2          271.2          319.2

NO PIECE LEFT IN  9  FT.ROLL   167.4          203.4          239.4


WHAT SIZE RUG DO YOU NEED?
6,8
PIECE LEFT FROM ROLL          13.95 RUG      16.95 RUG      19.95 RUG

FROM 12 FT.ROLL 4 BY  6        111.6          135.6          159.6

FROM 12 FT.ROLL 6 BY  8        148.8          180.8          212.8

FROM 9 FT.ROLL 1 BY  6         83.7           101.7          119.7

FROM 9 FT.ROLL 3 BY  8         111.6          135.6          159.6
```

PAGE 106

```
10 DIM G(99)
12 PRINT"CANNONS ON THE 100 HILLS ARE AS FOLLOWS: "
13 MAT G=ZER
14 PRINT
15 RANDOM
16 FOR J=0 TO 98
20 LET R=INT(1000*RND(X))
24 LET G(J)=R
26 NEXT J
28 LET G(99)=0
30 LET N=0
35 FOR J=0 TO 98
38 LET L=0
40 FOR K=J+1 TO 99
45 IF G(J)<G(K) THEN 60
50 LET L=L+1
60 NEXT K
65 IF G(J)=L THEN 80
70 LET G(J)=L
75 LET N=N+1
80 NEXT J
85 IF N<>0 THEN 30
94 PRINT
95 PRINT
96 MAT G=DIM(19,4)
97 MAT PRINT G
98 STOP
99 END
```

```
CANNONS ON THE 100 HILLS ARE AS FOLLOWS:

99     79     59     39     19
98     78     58     38     18
97     77     57     37     17
96     76     56     36     16
95     75     55     35     15
94     74     54     34     14
93     73     53     33     13
92     72     52     32     12
91     71     51     31     11
90     70     50     30     10
89     69     49     29     9
88     68     48     28     8
87     67     47     27     7
86     66     46     26     6
85     65     45     25     5
84     64     44     24     4
83     63     43     23     3
82     62     42     22     2
81     61     41     21     1
80     60     40     20     0
STOP
```

PAGE 107

```
10 PRINT"VALUE OF N","2 TO NTH","2 TO (N-1)TH","2 TO NTH-1","PERF.NO."
12 LET N=0
14 LET J=5
15 IF N<>2 THEN 18
16 LET N=N+1
17 GO TO 19
18 LET N=N+2
19 LET G=N-1
20 LET B=2↑N
22 LET C=2↑G
25 LET P=N
30 GOSUB 55
31 IF X=0 THEN 15
34 LET P=B-1
36 GOSUB 55
37 IF X=0 THEN 15
45 LET R=P*C
46 PRINT
47 PRINT N,B,C,P,R
48 LET J=J-1
50 IF J>0 THEN 15
52 STOP
55 LET D=2
58 IF D*D>P THEN 75
60 LET W=P/D
62 LET R=INT(W)
64 IF W=R THEN 72
66 LET D=D+1
68 GO TO 58
72 LET X=0
74 GO TO 78
75 LET X=1
78 RETURN
80 END
```

VALUE OF N	2 TO NTH	2 TO (N-1)TH	2 TO NTH-1	PERF.NO.
2	4	2	3	6
3	8	4	7	28
5	32	16	31	496
7	128	64	127	8128
13	8192	4096	8191	33550336

STOP

PAGE 109

```
10 PRINT"NUMBER","REVERSE","PRODUCT","SQUARE ROOT"
12 LET N=111
14 LET N=N+1
20 IF N<1000 THEN 30
25 STOP
30 LET H=INT(N/100)
34 LET R=N-100*H
38 LET T=INT(R/10)
40 LET U=R-10*T
45 IF H*T= 0 THEN 14
50 LET M=100*U+10*T+H
55 IF N>=M THEN 14
60 LET P=M*N
65 LET X=SQR(M*N)
68 LET W=INT(X)
70 IF W<>X THEN 14
75 LET X=SQR(P)
76 PRINT
78 PRINT N,M,P,X
80 GO TO 14
85 END
```

NUMBER	REVERSE	PRODUCT	SQUARE ROOT
144	441	63504	252
169	961	162409	403
288	882	254016	504
528	825	435600	660
768	867	665856	816

STOP

PAGE 110

```
8 DIM F(9,4)
9 LET N=0
10 PRINT"FACTORIAL REPRESENTATIONS OF:20,40,60 . . .1000, ARE:"
11 PRINT
15 MAT F=ZER
20 FOR J=0 TO 9
24 LET K=0
28 LET L=100000
30 LET D=2
35 LET N=N+20
38 LET T=N
40 LET G=INT(T/D)
45 LET R=T-G*D
48 LET T=G
50 LET F(J,K)=F(J,K)+L*R
55 IF G=0 THEN 68
60 LET D=D+1
66 LET L=L/10
67 GO TO 40
68 LET K=K+1
70 IF K<5 THEN 28
71 PRINT F(J,0),F(J,1),F(J,2),F(J,3),F(J,4)
72 PRINT
80 NEXT J
90 STOP
95 END
```

FACTORIAL REPRESENTATIONS OF:20,40,60 . . .1000, ARE:

13000	22100	2200	11300	20400
10	13010	22110	2210	11310
20410	20	13020	22120	2220
11320	20420	30	13030	22130
2230	11330	20430	40	13040
22140	2240	11340	20440	50
13050	22150	2250	11350	20450
1	13001	22101	2201	11301
20401	11	13011	22111	2211
11311	20411	21	13021	22121

STOP

PAGE 108

```
10 PRINT"X VALUE","CALC.E TO X",
"BU. T-IN FUNC.","DIFFERENCE"
12 LET X=0
15 LET G=1+3*X*X/28 +X↑4/1680
18 LET H=X/2+X↑3/84
20 LET Y=(G+H)/(G-H)
25 LET W=EXP(X)
30 LET D=ABS(Y-W)
32 PRINT
35 PRINT X,Y,W,D
40 LET X=X+.15
50 IF X<=3 THEN 15
55 STOP
60 END
```

X VALUE	CALC.E TO X	BUILT-IN FUNC.	DIFFERENCE
0	1	1	0
0.15	1.16183424	1.16183424	5.820766E-11
0.3	1.34985881	1.34985881	2.910383E-11
0.45	1.56831219	1.56831219	0
0.6	1.8221188	1.8221188	7.566996E-10
0.75	2.11700001	2.11700002	6.344635E-09
0.9	2.45960307	2.45960311	3.841706E-08
1.05	2.85765094	2.85765112	1.802691E-07
1.2	3.32011622	3.32011692	7.031485E-07
1.35	3.85742315	3.85742553	2.385001E-06
1.5	4.48168183	4.48168907	7.241033E-06
1.65	5.20695972	5.20697983	2.010912E-05
1.8	6.04959557	6.04964746	5.189294E-05

PAGE 112

```
9 PRINT"INSIDE","ON CIRCLE","OUTSIDE","IN/TOTAL","APPROX.PI"
10 LET K=200
11 PRINT
12 LET L=0
13 LET E=0
14 LET M=0
15 LET N=0
18 RANDOM
20 LET A=RND(X)
24 LET B=RND(X)
30 LET C=SQR(A*A+B*B)
32 IF C=1 THEN 48
34 IF C<1 THEN 42
38 LET M=M+1
40 GO TO 50
42 LET L=L+1
44 GO TO 50
48 LET E=E+1
50 LET N=N+1
52 IF N<K THEN 20
55 PRINT
56 LET T=(L+E)/K
57 LET P=4*T
58 PRINT L,E,M,T,P
60 LET K=K+200
65 IF K<=2000 THEN 18
70 STOP
75 END
```

INSIDE	ON CIRCLE	OUTSIDE	IN/TOTAL	APPROX.PI
154	0	46	0.77	3.08
305	0	95	0.7625	3.05
470	0	130	0.783333	3.13333333
629	0	171	0.78625	3.145
790	0	210	0.79	3.16
943	0	257	0.785833	3.14333333
1106	0	294	0.79	3.16
1265	0	335	0.790625	3.1625
1421	0	379	0.789444	3.15777778
1578	0	422	0.789	3.156

STOP

PAGE 113

```
10 DIM C(3,4),Y(3,4)
14 LET T=0
16 MAT Y=ZER
20 FOR L=1 TO 10
22 IF T=0 THEN 30
23 PRINT
24 PRINT "TYPE IN A NUMBER"
25 PRINT
26 INPUT G
28 GO TO 34
30 LET G=INT(100*RND(X))
34 IF G>30 THEN 22
35 IF G<11 THEN 22
38 LET J=INT((G-11)/5)
40 LET K=(G-11)-5*J
44 LET Y(J,K)=L
48 NEXT L
50 LET S=0
54 IF T=0 THEN 80
56 FOR J=0 TO 3
57 FOR K=0 TO 4
58 LET S=S+ABS(C(J,K)-Y(J,K))
59 NEXT K
60 NEXT J
61 PRINT
62 PRINT"YOUR SELECTION OF NUMBERS WAS AS FOLLOWS: "
63 PRINT
64 MAT PRINT Y
65 PRINT
66 PRINT
67 PRINT
68 PRINT"THE COMPUTER'S SELECTION OF RANDOM NUMBERS WAS: "
69 PRINT
70 MAT PRINT C
71 PRINT
72 PRINT
73 PRINT"THE WORST COMPARISON SCORE IS 110,THE BEST IS 0"
74 PRINT"YOUR COMPARISON SCORE WAS ----   "S
75 STOP
80 MAT C=Y
81 PRINT
82 PRINT"PICK ANY NUMBER FROM 11 THRU 30 "
84 LET T=1
88 GO TO 16
90 END
```

```
PICK ANY NUMBER FROM 11 THRU 30

TYPE IN A NUMBER
12
TYPE IN A NUMBER
17
TYPE IN A NUMBER
24
TYPE IN A NUMBER
16
TYPE IN A NUMBER
27

TYPE IN A NUMBER
18
TYPE IN A NUMBER
19
TYPE IN A NUMBER
13
TYPE IN A NUMBER
26
TYPE IN A NUMBER
25
```

```
YOUR SELECTION OF NUMBERS WAS AS FOLLOWS:

0        1        8        0        0
4        2        6        7        0
0        0        0        3        10
9        5        0        0        0


THE COMPUTER'S SELECTION OF RANDOM NUMBERS WAS:

0        0        0        0        1
7        3        0        9        5
0        4        2        0        10
6        0        0        0        0


THE WORST COMPARISON SCORE IS 110,THE BEST IS 0
YOUR COMPARISON SCORE WAS ----    44
STOP
```

PAGE 114

```
10 DIM T(9,4),B(4)
12 LET L=0
13 LET A=0
14 LET C=0
15 LET K=0
16 LET N=0
20 FOR J=A TO 9
22 FOR K=C TO 4
24 LET N=N+1
28 LET T(J,K)=N*(N+1)/2
30 LET W=SQR(T(J,K))
34 LET R=INT(W)
38 IF R<>W THEN 50
40 LET B(L)=T(J,K)
45 LET L=L+1
50 NEXT K
55 NEXT J
56 IF N>50 THEN 66
58 PRINT
60 PRINT"THE FIRST 50
TRIANGULAR NUMBERS ARE AS FOLLOWS: "
61 PRINT
62 MAT PRINT T
63 PRINT
64 PRINT
65 PRINT
66 IFL>4 THEN 80
70 LET A=9
74 LET C=4
78 GO TO 20
80 PRINT
82 PRINT"FIRST 5 NUMBERS THAT
ARE BOTH TRIANGULAR AND SQUARE ARE: "
83 PRINT
85 MAT PRINT B
90 STOP
95 END
```

```
THE FIRST 50 TRIANGULAR NUMBERS ARE AS FOLLOWS:

1       3       6       10      15
21      28      36      45      55
66      78      91      105     120
136     153     171     190     210
231     253     276     300     325
351     378     406     435     465
496     528     561     595     630
666     703     741     780     820
861     903     946     990     1035
1081    1128    1176    1225    1275


FIRST 5 NUMBERS THAT ARE BOTH TRIANGULAR AND SQUARE ARE:    1
                                                            36
                                                            1225
                                                            41616
                                                            1413721
STOP
```

PAGE 116

```
10 DIM D(19),B(9)
12 LET T=20
14 PRINT"TYPE IN FIRST NUMBER AND NO.OF ITEMS PER SEQUENCE"
15 PRINT
16 INPUT F,N
18 LET A=T/N
19 LET W=INT(A)
20 IF A=W THEN 24
21 PRINT
22 PRINT"NO.OF ITEMS MUST BE EXACT DIVISOR OF "T
23 GO TO 14
24 LET L=F+N-1
26 LET M=0
28 FOR J=0 TO T-1 STEP N
30 FOR K=F TO L
32 LET D(M)=K
34 LET M=M+1
35 NEXT K
36 NEXT J
38 PRINT
40 PRINT"CUT DECK WHERE ? HOW MANY FROM THE BOTTOM ?"
41 PRINT
42 PRINT"TYPE IN ANY VALUE FROM 2 THRU  "T/2
43 PRINT
44 INPUT C
45 IF C<=1 THEN 42
46 IF C>T/2 THEN 42
47 PRINT
48 PRINT"CUTTING "C" FROM BOTTOM AND REVERSING NUMBERS GIVES:"
49 PRINT
50 FOR J=0 TO C-1
51 PRINT
52 PRINT D(T-1-J)
54 LET B(J)=D(T-1-J)
56 NEXT J
58 LET M=0
60 LET P=0
61 PRINT
62 PRINT"WHERE DO YOU WANT ME TO INSERT THESE ?"
63 LET H=0
64 PRINT"TYPE IN THE INSERTION SPOT FOR "B(M)" ABOVE"
65 PRINT
66 INPUT G
68 IF P<=G THEN 74
69 PRINT
70 PRINT"INSERTION NUMBERS MUST INCREASE,TRY AGAIN"
71 PRINT
72 GO TO 64
74 IF G<=(T-C) THEN 80
75 PRINT
76 PRINT"INSERTION NUMBERS CAN NOT BE MORE THAN "T-C
77 PRINT
78 GO TO 64
80 LET P=G
82 LET G=G+H
88 FOR J=0 TO T-G-1
90 LET K=T-J-1
92 LET D(K)=D(K-1)
93 NEXT J
95 LET D(K-1)=B(M)
96 IF M=C-1 THEN 100
97 LET M=M+1
98 LET H=H+1
99 GO TO 64
100 PRINT
101 PRINT"THE SHUFFLED DECK LISTED IN GROUPS OF
"N" EACH ARE:"
102 PRINT
103 FOR J=0 TO T-1
104 PRINT D(J)
105 LET W=(J+1)/N
106 LET R=INT(W)
107 IF R<>W THEN 112
108 PRINT
110 PRINT
112 NEXT J
114 GO TO 14
115 END
```

```
TYPE IN FIRST NUMBER AND NO.OF ITEMS PER SEQUENCE

55,4

CUT DECK WHERE ? HOW MANY FROM THE BOTTOM ?

TYPE IN ANY VALUE FROM 2 THRU   10

 5

CUTTING  5 FROM BOTTOM AND REVERSING NUMBERS GIVES:

    WHERE DO YOU WANT ME TO INSERT THESE ?
    TYPE IN THE INSERTION SPOT FOR  58

THE SHUFFLED DECK LISTED IN GROUPS OF  4 EACH ARE:

55
56
58
57
```

PAGE 117

```
10 PRINT"SIDE A","SIDE B","SIDE C","AREA OF TRIANGLE"
11 PRINT
12 LET A=0
14 LET A=A+1
16 IF A<999 THEN 20
18 STOP
20 LET B=A+1
24 LET C=B+1
26 IF A+B=C THEN 14
28 LET S=(A+B+C)/2
32 LET K=SQR(S*(S-A)*(S-B)*(S-C))
36 LET R=INT(K)
40 IF R<>K THEN 14
49 PRINT
50 PRINT A,B,C,K
55 GO TO 14
60 END
```

```
SIDE A          SIDE B          SIDE C          AREA OF TRIANGLE

3               4               5               6

13              14              15              84

51              52              53              1170

193             194             195             16296

723             724             725             226974
STOP
```

PAGE 118

```
10 DIM T(9,4),B(3)
12 MAT T=ZER
14 LET S=0
16 MAT B=ZER
18 RANDOM
20 FOR M=0 TO 3
24 LET R=INT(100*RND(X))
26 IF R<=10 THEN 24
28 IF R>=61 THEN 24
30 LET J=INT((R-11)/5)
32 LET K=(R-11)-5*J
38 LET T(J,K)=T(J,K)+1
39 LET B(M)=10*J+K
41 NEXT M
42 LET S=S+4
46 FOR L=0 TO 2
47 IF B(L)<=B(L+1) THEN 52
48 LET G=B(L)
49 LET B(L)=B(L+1)
50 LET B(L+1)=G
51 GO TO 46
52 IF B(L)=B(L+1) THEN 20
54 NEXT L
55 FOR L=0 TO 1
56 LET G=INT(B(L)/10)
57 IF G+1<>INT(B(L+2)/10) THEN 20
58 LET G=B(L)-10*G
59 LET W=INT(B(L+2)/10)
60 IF G<>B(L+2)-10*W THEN 20
61 NEXT L
62 IF W<>INT(B(2)/10) THEN 20
64 FOR L=0 TO 3
65 LET J=INT(B(L)/10)
66 LET K=B(L)-10*J
68 LET T(J,K)=9999
70 NEXT L
73 PRINT
74 PRINT"SHELLS HITTING EACH SPOT AND 4 IMPACT SPOTS(9999)"
75 PRINT
78 MAT PRINT T
79 PRINT
80 PRINT
82 PRINT"A TOTAL OF "S" SHOTS WERE FIRED BEFORE HITTING 4 SPOTS"
84 STOP
90 END
```

```
SHELLS HITTING EACH SPOT AND 4 IMPACT SPOTS(9999)

81          101         113         85          89
9999        88          9999        95          85
9999        89          9999        79          85
95          78          87          98          113
91          98          88          83          106
99          84          107         90          100
81          93          80          91          76
88          75          73          85          80
82          104         89          105         91
91          100         84          87          99


A TOTAL OF  4520 SHOTS WERE FIRED BEFORE HITTING 4 SPOTS
STOP
```

PAGE 119

```
10 PRINT"SIDE A","NO. OF TRIANGLES","SUM OF ALL AREAS"
11 PRINT
14 FOR A=3 TO 98
15 LET V=0
16 LET L=0
18 FOR B=A+1 TO 99
20 FOR C=B TO 99
24 IF C>=(A+B) THEN 70
28 LET S=(A+B+C)/2
30 LET K=SQR(S*(S-A)*(S-B)*(S-C)
35 IF K=0 THEN 70
40 LET W=INT(K)
45 IF W<>K THEN 70
50 LET V=V+K
60 LET L=L+1
70 NEXT C
72 NEXT B
75 PRINT A,L," ",V
80 NEXT A
85 STOP
90 END
```

```
SIDE A NO. OF TRIANGLES  SUM OF ALL AREAS

3        2               42
4        2               114
5        3               228
6        3               228
7        3               336
8        3               240
9        6               1062
10       5               720
11       4               924
12       6               1050
13       8               1974
14       4               1092
15       9               2436
16       6               1704
17       8               2796
18       5               1980
19       2               570
```

PAGE 120

```
10 PRINT "FIRST NO.",
"SECOND NO.","PRODUCT"
12 LET N=0
14 LET N=N+1
15 IF N=10 THEN 14
16 IF N<100 THEN 20
18 STOP
20 LET M=1
24 LET M=M+1
28 IF M>=100 THEN 14
35 LET P=M*N
38 IF P<100 THEN 24
40 LET A=INT(P/100)
45 LET B=INT(M/10)
50 IF A<>B THEN 24
55 LET A=P-100*A
60 LET B=M-10*B
65 IF A<>B THEN 24
70 PRINT
75 PRINT N,M,P
80 GO TO 24
85 END
```

```
RUN

FIRST NO.       SECOND NO.  PRODUCT

 6              18          108

 7              15          105

 9              45          405
STOP
```

PAGE 121

```
10 DIM P(100)
12 LET H=2
14 LET K=H
16 LET T=K-1
18 FOR J=1 TO 100
20 LET P(J)=J
22 NEXT J
26 FOR J=K TO 100 STEP K
30 LET P(J)=0
32 NEXT J
40 FOR J=2 TO 100
42 IF P(J)<>0 THEN 52
44 IF P(J+1)=0 THEN 60
46 FOR L=J TO 99
48 LET P(L)=P(L+1)
50 NEXT L
52 NEXT J
60 LET S=1
62 FOR J=2 TO 100
64 LET S=S+P(J)
66 LET P(J)=S
68 NEXT J
70 LET T=T-1
72 IF T=0 THEN 80
75 LET K=K-1
78 GO TO 26
80 PRINT
81 LET R=H-1
82 PRINT"TEN SAFETY BOXES
CONTAIN FOLLOWING NO.OF DOLLARS FOR MAN "K
84 PRINT
85 PRINT P(1),P(2),P(3),P(4),P(5)
86 PRINT
87 PRINT P(6),P(7),P(8),P(9),P(10)
90 LET H=H+1
92 IF H<9 THEN 14
95 STOP
99 END
```

```
TEN SAFETY BOXES CONTAIN FOLLOWING NO.OF DOLLARS FOR MAN  1

1             4             9             16            25

36            49            64            81            100

TEN SAFETY BOXES CONTAIN FOLLOWING NO.OF DOLLARS FOR MAN  2

1             8             27            64            125

216           343           512           729           1000

TEN SAFETY BOXES CONTAIN FOLLOWING NO.OF DOLLARS FOR MAN  3

1             16            81            256           625

1296          2401          4096          6561          10000
```

PAGE 123

```
10 PRINT"JOB LENGTH","MAN 1","MAN 2","MAN 3","AMOUNT PAID"
12 LET H=0
14 LET H=H+10
16 IF H<=100 THEN 20
18 STOP
20 LET L=0
24 LET N=H/2 -1
30 FOR A=1 TO H
35 FOR B=A+1 TO N
40 LET C=H-(A+B)
45 LET P=A*B*C
50 IF P<=L THEN 60
52 LET L=P
53 LET X=A
54 LET Y=B
55 LET Z=C
60 NEXT B
62 NEXT A
65 PRINT
66 PRINT H,X,Y,Z,L
70 GO TO 14
75 END
```

JOB LENGTH	MAN 1	MAN 2	MAN 3	AMOUNT PAID
10	3	4	3	36
20	6	7	7	294
30	9	10	11	990
40	13	14	13	2366
50	16	17	17	4624
60	19	20	21	7980
70	23	24	23	12696
80	26	27	27	18954
90	29	30	31	26970
100	33	34	33	37026

STOP

PAGE 124

```
9 DIM B(4)
10 PRINT"FACTORIAL","2 OCCURS",
"3 OCCURS","5 OCCURS","10 OCCURS"
11 PRINT
12 LET N=100
14 LET B(0)=N
18 LET P=1
20 FOR J=1 TO 3
21 LET M=N
22 LET S=0
24 LET P=P+1
26 LET G=INT(M/P)
28 LET S=S+M-P*G
30 IF G=0 THEN 40
35 LET M=G
38 GO TO 26
40 LET B(J)=(N-S)/(P-1)
42 IF P<3 THEN 55
44 LET P=P+1
48 IF P>5 THEN 60
55 NEXT J
60 IF B(1)<B(3) THEN 70
65 LET B(4)=B(3)
68 GO TO 72
70 LET B(4)=B(1)
72 PRINT
74 PRINT B(0),B(1),B(2),B(3),B(4)
76 LET N=N+100
80 IF N<2000 THEN 14
85 STOP
90 END
```

FACTORIAL	2 OCCURS	3 OCCURS	5 OCCURS	10 OCCURS
100	97	48	24	24
200	197	97	49	49
300	296	148	74	74
400	397	196	99	99
500	494	247	124	124
600	596	297	148	148
700	694	345	174	174
800	797	396	199	199
900	896	448	224	224
1000	994	498	249	249

PAGE 125

```
8 DIM T(15)
9 PRINT
10 PRINT"WRITE ANY NUMBER FROM
3 TO 9 DIGITS ON A PIECE OF PAPER"
11 PRINT"WHEN READY,
12 INPUT W
13 LET S=0
14 LET E=0
15 LET H=-1
16 MAT T=ZER
17 PRINT"HOW MANY DIGITS
ARE THERE IN YOUR NUMBER ? TYPE IN ANSWER"
TYPE A ZERO AND THEN A CARRIAGE RETURN"
18 PRINT
19 INPUT N
20 LET G=N/2
21 IF G<>INT(N/2) THEN 23
22 LET E=1
23 FOR J=0 TO N-2
24 LET K=J+1
25 PRINT
26 PRINT"WHAT IS SUM OF DIGIT "K"
AND DIGIT "K+1" ?"
27 PRINT
28 INPUT T(J)
29 NEXT J
30 PRINT"WHAT IS SUM OF DIGIT "E+1"
AND LAST DIGIT ?"
31 PRINT
32 INPUT T(K)
36 FOR J=E TO N-1
38 LET H=-1*H
40 LET S=S+T(J)*H
41 NEXT J
42 LET S=S/2
43 LET T(K+1)=S
44 LET G=1
45 LET S=0
46 FOR J=0 TO N-1
50 LET L=N-J-1
52 LET T(L)=T(L)-T(L+1)
53 LET S=S+T(L)*G
54 LET G=10*G
56 NEXT J
58 PRINT
60 PRINT"YOUR NUMBER IS THE FOLLOWING-----"S
62 GO TO 9
65 END
```

```
WRITE ANY NUMBER FROM 3 TO 9 DIGITS ON A PIECE OF PAPER
WHEN READY, TYPE A ZERO AND THEN A CARRIAGE RETURN
0
HOW MANY DIGITS ARE THERE IN YOUR NUMBER ? TYPE IN ANSWER

6
WHAT IS SUM OF DIGIT  1 AND DIGIT  2 ?
8
WHAT IS SUM OF DIGIT  2 AND DIGIT  3 ?

9
WHAT IS SUM OF DIGIT  3 AND DIGIT  4 ?
17
WHAT IS SUM OF DIGIT  4 AND DIGIT  5 ?

18
WHAT IS SUM OF DIGIT  5 AND DIGIT  6 ?

18
WHAT IS SUM OF DIGIT  2 AND LAST DIGIT ?

10

YOUR NUMBER IS THE FOLLOWING----- 718999
```

PAGE 126

```
10 PRINT"NO.OF THROWS","WINS FOR A",
"WINS FOR B","PCT A","PCT B"
12 LET [illegible]=0
13 LET [illegible]=0
14 LET [illegible]=0
15 LET H=-1
16 LET [illegible]=1
18 LET H=-1*H
20 LET [illegible]=INT(10*RND(X))
21 LET [illegible]=INT(10*RND(X))
24 IF X*Y=0 THEN 20
25 IF X>[illegible] THEN 20
26 IF Y>6 THEN 20
28 LET Z=X+Y
30 IF T=1 THEN 40
32 IF Z=P THEN 44
34 IF Z=7 THEN 60
36 RANDOM
38 GO TO 20
40 IF Z<>7 THEN 50
44 IF H<0 THEN 48
46 LET A=A+1
47 GO TO 68
48 LET B=B+1
49 GO TO 68
50 IF Z=11 THEN 44
51 LET T=2
52 IF Z<4 THEN 60
53 IF Z=12 THEN 60
55 LET P=Z
59 GO TO 20
60 IF H>=0 THEN 66
62 LET A=A+1
64 GO TO 68
66 LET B=B+1
68 LET N=N+1
70 IF N<1001 THEN 75
72 STOP
75 LET W=INT(N/100)
78 LET G=N/100
80 IF W<>G THEN 88
82 LET R=INT(100*A/(A+B))
84 LET S=INT(100*B/(A+B))
85 PRINT
86 PRINT N,A,B,R,S
88 IF T=2 THEN 16
89 GO TO 20
90 END
```

```
NO.OF THROWS   WINS FOR A   WINS FOR B   PCT A   PCT B
100            53           47           53      47
200            113          87           56      43
300            153          147          51      49
400            211          189          52      47
500            250          250          50      50
600            299          301          49      50
700            342          358          48      51
800            401          399          50      49
900            438          462          48      51
1000           487          513          48      51
STOP
```

PAGE 128

```
10 DIM R(39),T(39)
14 LET V=0
16 FOR J=0 TO 39
18 LET R(J)=INT(10000*RND(X))
19 NEXT J
20 LET K=0
21 LET L=0
24 FOR J=0 TO 39
26 IF R(J)=1 THEN 60
28 LET H=R(J)
30 FOR M=0 TO V
32 LET Z=INT(H/10)
34 LET G=H-10*Z
36 LET H=Z
38 NEXT M
40 IF G<>L THEN 60
42 LET T(K)=R(J)
48 LET R(J)=1
52 LET K=K+1
60 NEXT J
64 LET L=L+1
66 IF L<10 THEN 24
68 PRINT
69 MAT T=DIM(7,4)
70 PRINT
71 MAT PRINT T
72 MAT T=DIM(39)
74 MAT R=T
76 LET V=V+1
80 IF V<4 THEN 20
85 STOP
90 END
```

```
5750 5412 7374 846  3608
4630 1762 8955 6126 9058
6610 412  2265 2686 2508
8750 5112 9315 5796 509
2090 8333 5795 7436 4759
9980 5244 9135 7827 1629
3341 5574 3616 2358 39
1562 984  6996 3588 5429

3608 3616 7436 2358 9980
2508 6126 39   9058 984
509  7827 3341 4759 2686
6610 1629 5244 1562 3588
5412 5429 846  1762 2090
412  4630 5750 2265 5795
5112 8333 8750 5574 6996
9315 9135 8955 7374 5796

39   9315 7436 3616 5795
9058 8333 2508 1629 5796
2090 3341 509  4630 7827
5112 2358 1562 2686 846
6126 7374 5574 5750 8955
9135 5412 3588 8750 9980
5244 412  3608 4759 984
2265 5429 6610 1762 6996

39   2090 3616 5750 7827
412  2265 4630 5795 8333
509  2358 4759 5796 8750
846  2508 5112 6126 8955
984  2686 5244 6610 9058
1562 3341 5412 6996 9135
1629 3588 5429 7374 9315
1762 3608 5574 7436 9980
```

PAGE 130

```
10 DIM S(99),T(99)
12 FOR J=0 TO 99
14 LET R=INT(1000*RND)
16 LET S(J)=R
18 NEXT J
20 MAT S=DIM(19,4)
21 PRINT
22 PRINT
24 MAT PRINT S
25 MAT S=DIM(99)
28 LET B=1
29 MAT T=CON
30 FOR J=1 TO 99
32 FOR K=0 TO J-1
34 IF S(J)<=S(K) THEN 44
35 IF T(J)>T(K) THEN 38
36 LET T(J)=T(K)+1
38 IF T(J)<=B THEN 44
40 LET B=T(J)
42 LET G=J
44 NEXT K
46 NEXT J
48 PRINT
49 PRINT
50 PRINT"THE LARGEST
SUBSEQUENCE CONTAINS "B" TERMS"
52 PRINT
53 PRINT"ONE SUCH SUBSEQUENCE HAS THE FOLLOWING TERMS---"
54 PRINT
56 LET W=T(G)
57 PRINT S(G)
58 LET W=W-1
60 IF W=0 THEN 68
62 LET G=G-1
64 IF T(G)=W THEN 57
66 GO TO 62
68 STOP
70 END
```

```
361 612 192 897     969
156 209 342 685     642
575 268 259 234     61
699 782 769 86      40
463 41  571 807     492
50  511 466 27      677
524 162 172 487     940
557 360 694 62      790
661 905 230 81      434
541 931 584 858     28
334 579 426 211     417
875 913 920 800     449
235 98  875 614     992
475 250 561 344     508
84  3   234 755     27
895 579 985 960     799
833 737 808 95      487
176 743 866 264     260
358 998 753 879     93
226 542 267 766     666
```

```
THE LARGEST SUBSEQUENCE CONTAINS  16 TERMS

ONE SUCH SUBSEQUENCE HAS THE FOLLOWING TERMS---

992
969
960
897
866
808
769
743
737
579
360
268
209
176
84
50
STOP
```

PAGE 131

```
10 PRINT"ANGLE","NO.OF MILS","NO.OF RADIANS","ARC LENGTH"
12 LET A=0
14 LET M=A*1600/90
16 LET R=.00098175*M
20 LET S=M/1000
25 PRINT A,M,R,S
30 LET A=A+5
35 IF A<=90 THEN 14
40 STOP
45 END
```

ANGLE	NO.OF MILS	NO.OF RADIANS	ARC LENGTH
0	0	0	0
5	88.8888889	8.726667E-02	8.888889E-02
10	177.777778	0.174533	0.177778
15	266.666667	0.2618	0.266667
20	355.555556	0.349067	0.355556
25	444.444444	0.436333	0.444444
30	533.333333	0.5236	0.533333
35	622.222222	0.610867	0.622222
40	711.111111	0.698133	0.711111
45	800	0.7854	0.8
50	888.888889	0.872667	0.888889
55	977.777778	0.959933	0.977778
60	1066.66667	1.0472	1.06666667
65	1155.55556	1.13446667	1.15555556
70	1244.44444	1.22173333	1.24444444
75	1333.33333	1.309	1.33333333
80	1422.22222	1.39626667	1.42222222
85	1511.11111	1.48353333	1.51111111
90	1600	1.5708	1.6

STOP

PAGE 132

```
10 DIM T(2)
12 PRINT"ANGLE A","ANGLE B",
"ANGLE C","FUNCTION"
13 PRINT
14 LET R=.017453292
15 LET C=90
16 LET A=1
18 LET B=180-(A+C)
19 IF B>90 THEN 44
20 LET T(0)=R*A
22 LET T(1)=R*B
24 LET T(2)=R*C
26 LET G=0
28 FOR J=0 TO 2
29 LET X=COS(T(J))
30 LET W=SQR(1+8*X*X)
31 IF J<>0 THEN 34
32 LET G=G+W/SIN(T(2))
33 GO TO 36
34 LET G=G+W/SIN(T(J-1))
36 NEXT J
40 PRINT A,B,C,G
44 LET A=A+10
48 IF A<46 THEN 18
50 LET C=C-10
55 IF C>0 THEN 16
60 STOP
65 END
```

ANGLE A	ANGLE B	ANGLE C	FUNCTION
1	89	90	61.3682039
11	79	90	9.92514418
21	69	90	7.86794244
31	59	90	7.21992413
41	49	90	6.89527361
11	89	80	9.35808059
21	79	80	7.17296148
31	69	80	6.62099986
41	59	80	6.38666013
21	89	70	7.19016261
31	79	70	6.41458204
41	69	70	6.16921928
31	89	60	6.70456881
41	79	60	6.21847015
41	89	50	6.67856214

STOP

PAGE 133

```
10 DIM C(5)
11 PRINT"TYPE IN VALUES OF CONSTANTS: C(0),
C(1),C(2),C(3),C(4),C(5)"
TYPE IN VALUES OF CONSTANTS: C(0),C(1),C(2),C(3),C(4),C(5)


1,2,3,4,5,6

THE POLYNOMIAL FUNCTION YOU ARE SOLVING IS-----


Y= 1+ 2*X+ 3*X↑2+ 4*X↑3+ 5*X↑4+ 6*X↑5

NOW TYPE IN THE VALUE OF X

3

WHEN X= 3 THE VALUE OF THE FUNCTION,Y, IS 2005
DO YOU WANT TO TRY ANOTHER VALUE FOR X ?

IF YES, TYPE IN 1.  IF NO, TYPE IN 2
12 PRINT
13 PRINT
14 INPUT C(0),C(1),C(2),C(3),C(4),C(5)
15 PRINT
18 PRINT"THE POLYNOMIAL FUNCTION YOU ARE SOLVING IS-----"
19 PRINT
20 PRINT
22 PRINT"Y="C(0)"+"C(1)"*X+"C(2)"*X↑2+"C(3)"*X↑3+"C(4)"*X↑4+"C(5)"*X↑5"
23 PRINT
24 PRINT"NOW TYPE IN THE VALUE OF X "
25 PRINT
26 INPUT X
27 PRINT
28 LET Y=0
29 FOR J=0 TO 5
30 IF X<>0 THEN 33
31 LET Y=Y+C(0)
32 GO TO 35
33 LET Y=Y+C(J)*X↑J
34 NEXT J
35 PRINT"WHEN X= "X" THE VALUE OF THE FUNCTION,Y, IS "Y
36 PRINT"DO YOU WANT TO TRY ANOTHER VALUE FOR X ?"
37 PRINT
38 PRINT"IF YES, TYPE IN 1.  IF NO, TYPE IN 2 "
39 PRINT
40 INPUT A
42 IF A=1 THEN 24
44 GO TO 11
50 END
```

PAGE 134

```
8 PRINT"KING A","KING B","KING C","EMPEROR","PCT FOR A"
9 PRINT
10 LET A=1
12 LET B=A+1
13 LET C=B+1
14 LET X=1
16 IF(A*A-X)*(B*B-X)<>C*C-X THEN 24
18 LET W=A+B+C+X
19 LET P=100*A/W
20 PRINT
22 PRINT A,B,C,X,P
24 LET X=X+1
28 IF X<100 THEN ;6
30 LET A=A+1
35 IF A<100 THEN 12
40 STOP
45 END
```

KING A	KING B	KING C	EMPEROR	PCT FOR A
1	2	3	5	9.09090909
2	3	4	2	18.1818182
2	3	4	10	10.5263158
3	4	5	7	15.7894737
3	4	5	17	10.3448276
4	5	6	14	13.7931034
4	5	6	26	9.75609756
5	6	7	23	12.195122
5	6	7	37	9.09090909

PAGE 135

```
10 PRINT"NO.OF GAMES","NO.OF WINS","NO.OF LOSSES"
12 PRINT
13 LET N=0
14 LET C=0
15 LET Y=0
16 LET A=INT(100*RND(X))
17 LET B=INT(100*RND(X))
18 IF A>52 THEN 16
19 IF B>52 THEN 16
20 IF A*B=0 THEN 16
22 IF A>13 THEN 28
24 LET Y=Y+1
26 GO TO 32
28 IF B<14 THEN 24
30 LET C=C+1
32 LET N=N+1
34 LET W=INT(N/100)
36 IF W<>N/100 THEN 40
38 PRINT
39 PRINT N,Y,C
40 IF N<=1000 THEN 16
45 STOP
50 END
```

NO.OF GAMES	NO.OF WINS	NO.OF LOSSES
100	44	56
200	79	121
300	118	182
400	160	240
500	206	294
600	258	342
700	294	406
800	331	469
900	377	523
1000	420	580

STOP

PAGE 136

```
10 PRINT"1000 DIGIT","100 DIGIT","10 DIGIT","UNITS","EXPONENT"
12 FOR X=0 TO 9
16 FOR H=0 TO 9
18 FOR T=0 TO 9
20 FOR U=0 TO 9
25 LET G=1000*X+100*H+10*T+U
30 FOR M=2 TO 4
32 LET F=X↑M+H↑M+T↑M+U↑M
35 IF F<>G THEN 45
40 PRINT
42 PRINT X,H,T,U,M
45 NEXT M
50 NEXT U
54 NEXT T
58 NEXT H
60 NEXT X
70 STOP
75 END
```

1000 DIGIT	100 DIGIT	10 DIGIT	UNITS	EXPONENT
0	0	0	0	2
0	0	0	0	3
0	0	0	0	4
0	0	0	1	2
0	0	0	1	3
0	0	0	1	4
0	1	5	3	3
0	3	7	0	3
0	3	7	1	3
0	4	0	7	3
1	6	3	4	4
8	2	0	8	4
9	4	7	4	4

STOP

PAGE 138

```
10 DIM C(29,4)
12 PRINT"SCORE X","SCORE Y",
"RANK X","RANK Y","SQ.OF DIFF."
13 PRINT
14 LET N=9
16 FOR J=0 TO N
18 LET C(J,0)=INT(100*RND(X))
20 LET C(J,1)=INT(100*RND(X))
21 IF C(J,0)*C(J,1)=0 THEN 18
22 NEXT J
24 LET K=0
28 FOR J=0 TO N
30 LET E=0
31 LET G=0
32 LET H=C(J,K)
33 LET C(J,K)=0
34 FOR M=0 TO N
36 IF H<=C(M,K) THEN 40
38 LET G=G+1
39 GO TO 45
40 IF H<>C(M,K) THEN 45
42 LET E=E+1
45 NEXT M
48 LET C(J,K)=H
50 LET C(J,K+2)=N+2-(G+E/2)
55 NEXT J
60 IF K>=1 THEN 70
65 LET K=1
68 GO TO 28
70 LET R=0
72 FOR J=0 TO N
74 LET C(J,4)=(C(J,2)-
76 LET R=R+C(J,4)
78 NEXT J
80 LET D=6*R/(N*(N*N-1))
82 LET R=1-D
84 FOR J=0 TO N
86 PRINT
88 PRINT C(J,0),C(J,1),
C(J,2),C(J,3),C(J,4)
90 NEXT J
92 PRINT
93 PRINT
94 PRINT"THE RANK CORRELATION
COEFFICIENT IS EQUAL TO "R
96 LET N=N+10
97 IF N<=30 THEN 16
98 STOP
99 END
```

```
RUN
SCORE X  SCORE Y  RANK X  RANK Y  SQ.OF DIFF.


 36       15       6       9       9
 57       69       3       3       0
 46       5        5       10      25
 52       55       4       4       0
 66       54       2       5       9
 33       87       8       2       36
 23       47       9       6       9
 8        89       10      1       81
 83       17       1       8       49
 35       22       7       7       0



THE RANK CORRELATION COEFFICIENT
IS EQUAL TO -0.816667
61                 20   8     20   144
26                 78   12    6    36
4                  51   20    14   36
16                 36   18    16   4
90                 93   2     2    0
57                 91   9.5   4    30.25
9                  25   19    19   0
73                 74   7     8    1
99                 54   1     13   144
19                 34   16    17   1
25                 76   13    7    36
57                 46   9.5   15   30.25
17                 69   17    9    64
23                 58   14.5  11   12.25
42                 92   11    3    64
87                 56   4     12   64
23                 98   14.5  1    182.25
80                 86   5     5    0
75                 26   6     18   144
89                 68   3     10   49



THE RANK CORRELATION COEFFICIENT IS EQUAL TO  8.596491E-02
```

PAGE 140

```
10 DIM D(59),P(3)
12 LET N=60
14 FOR J=0 TO N/2-1 STEP 5
16 PRINT
17 PRINT"TYPE IN 5 NUMBERS OF 2 DIGITS EACH; SEPARATED BY COMMAS"
18 PRINT
20 INPUT D(J),D(J+1),D(J+2),D(J+3),D(J+4)
24 FOR K=J TO J+4
26 LET D(K)=10*D(K)
28 LET D(K+30)=10*INT(100*RND(Z))+1
30 NEXT K
32 NEXT J
36 FOR J=0 TO N-2
38 IF D(J)>=D(J+1) THEN 50
40 LET G=D(J)
42 LET D(J)=D(J+1)
44 LET D(J+1)=G
45 GO TO 36
50 NEXT J
51 MAT P=ZER
52 LET R=1
54 LET H=0
56 FOR J=0 TO N-2
58 LET U=D(J)-10*INT(D(J)/10)
60 LET V=D(J+1)-10*INT(D(J+1)/10)
64 IF U<>V THEN 69
66 LET H=H+1
67 IF J=N-2 THEN 70
68 GO TO 80
69 LET R=R+1
70 IF H>3 THEN 78
72 LET P(H)=P(H)+1
73 GO TO 79
78 LET P(3)=P(3)+1
79 LET H=0
80 NEXT J
82 PRINT
83 PRINT"1 RUNS","2 RUNS","3 RUNS","OVER 3 "
84 PRINT
85 PRINT P(0),P(1),P(2),P(3)
86 LET N=N/2
88 LET M=N+1
90 LET S=(N*N-N)/(2*N-1)
91 LET W=SQR(S)
92 LET L=INT(M-1.96*W)
93 LET U=INT(M+1.96*W)
94 PRINT
95 PRINT"CHANCES ARE ONLY ABOUT 3 OUT OF 100 THE TWO SETS OF"
96 PRINT"SCORES CAME FROM THE SAME DISTRIBUTION IF THE NUMBER"
97 PRINT"OF RUNS IS AS LOW OR LOWER THAN "L" OR AS HIGH AS "U
98 PRINT
99 PRINT
100 PRINT"IN THIS CASE, THE NUMBER OF RUNS WAS  "R
101 STOP
102 END
```

```
TYPE IN 5 NUMBERS OF 2 DIGITS EACH; SEPARATED BY COMMAS

23,13,44,55,63

TYPE IN 5 NUMBERS OF 2 DIGITS EACH; SEPARATED BY COMMAS

65,23,14,56,77

TYPE IN 5 NUMBERS OF 2 DIGITS EACH; SEPARATED BY COMMAS

34,35,65,78,90

TYPE IN 5 NUMBERS OF 2 DIGITS EACH; SEPARATED BY COMMAS

31,21,55,68,96

TYPE IN 5 NUMBERS OF 2 DIGITS EACH; SEPARATED BY COMMAS

70,60,55,64,31

TYPE IN 5 NUMBERS OF 2 DIGITS EACH; SEPARATED BY COMMAS

90,87,65,44,21

1 RUNS          2 RUNS          3 RUNS          OVER 3

 12              11              4               3

CHANCES ARE ONLY ABOUT 3 OUT OF 100 THE TWO SETS OF
SCORES CAME FROM THE SAME DISTRIBUTION IF THE NUMBER
OF RUNS IS AS LOW OR LOWER THAN  23 OR AS HIGH AS  38
```

PAGE 142

```
8 PRINT
10 PRINT"TYPE IN: PAYMT,P,INT.RATE,R,NO.YRS.,N,PR.VALUE,V,SUM,S"
12 PRINT"PUT ZEROS FOR THOSE YOU WANT TO FIND.ANY 2(BUT R)CAN BE ZERO"
14 PRINT
16 PRINT
20 INPUT P,R,N,V,S
24 IF R=0 THEN 85
25 LET G=(1+R)↑N
26 IF P=0 THEN 66
30 IF N=0 THEN 46
32 LET V=P*(G-1)/(R*G)
34 LET S=V*G
36 LET V=INT(100*(V+.005))/100
37 LET S=INT(100*(S+.005))/100
38 PRINT
40 PRINT"PAYMENTS","INT.RATE","NO.YRS.","PR.VALUE","SUM"
41 PRINT
42 PRINT P,R,N,V,S
44 GO TO 8
46 IF V=0 THEN 58
48 LET N=LOG(P/(P-V*R))/LOG(1+R)
50 LET N=INT(100*(N+.005))/100
51 LET S=V*(1+R)↑N
52 GO TO 37
58 LET N=LOG((R*S+P)/P)/LOG(1+R)
60 LET N=INT(100*(N+.005))/100
62 LET V=S/(1+R)↑N
63 LET V=INT(100*(V+.005))/100
64 GO TO 38
66 IF N=0 THEN 80
68 IF V=0 THEN 74
69 LET P=V*R*G/(G-1)
70 LET P=INT(100*(P+.005))/100
71 LET S=V*G
72 GO TO 37
74 LET P=R*S/(G-1)
76 LET P=INT(100*(P+.005))/100
78 GO TO 62
80 LET N=LOG(S/V)/LOG(1+R)
81 LET N=INT(100*(N+.005))/100
82 LET P=R*S/((1+R)↑N-1)
83 LET P=INT(100*(P+.005))/100
84 GO TO 38
85 PRINT"THIS SOLUTION REQUIRES THE INT.RATE TO BE KNOWN-START OVER."
86 GO TO 8
90 END
```

```
RUN

TYPE IN: PAYMT,P,INT.RATE,R,NO.YRS.,N,PR.VALUE,V,SUM,S
PUT ZEROS FOR THOSE YOU WANT TO FIND.ANY 2(BUT R)CAN BE ZERO

50,.03,16,0,0
PAYMENTS      INT.RATE      NO.YRS.       PR.VALUE      SUM
50            0.03          16            628.06        1007.84

TYPE IN: PAYMT,P,INT.RATE,R,NO.YRS.,N,PR.VALUE,V,SUM,S
PUT ZEROS FOR THOSE YOU WANT TO FIND.ANY 2(BUT R)CAN BE ZERO

0,.045,0,3902.38,9411.42
PAYMENTS      INT.RATE      NO.YRS.       PR.VALUE      SUM
300           4.5E-02       20            3902.38       9411.42

TYPE IN: PAYMT,P,INT.RATE,R,NO.YRS.,N,PR.VALUE,V,SUM,S
PUT ZEROS FOR THOSE YOU WANT TO FIND.ANY 2(BUT R)CAN BE ZERO

300,.045,0,0,9411.42
PAYMENTS      INT.RATE      NO.YRS.       PR.VALUE      SUM
300           4.5E-02       20            3902.38       9411.42
```

PAGE 144

```
9 PRINT
10 PRINT"TYPE IN PYMT,P,INT.RATE,R,NO.YEARS,N,PRES.VALUE,V,SUM,S"
11 PRINT
12 INPUT P,R,N,V,S
14 IF R=0 THEN 18
16 PRINT"INT.RATE,R,MUST BE ZERO IN THIS APPLICATION,START OVER"
17 GO TO 10
18 IF N<>0 THEN 34
20 LET R=P*(1/V-1/S)
22 LET N=LOG(S/V)/LOG(R+1)
24 PRINT
26 PRINT"PAYMENT","INT.RATE","NO.OF YRS.","PRES.VALUE","SUM"
27 PRINT
30 PRINT P,R,N,V,S
32 GO TO 9
34 IF P<>0 THEN 42
36 LET U=1/N*LOG(S/V)
38 LET R=EXP(U)-1
39 LET P=R*S/((1+R)↑N-1)
40 GO TO 24
42 IF S=0 THEN 48
43 LET R=2*(S/P-N)/(N*(N-1))
44 LET G=S/P-N
46 GO TO 52
48 LET G=V/P
50 LET R=P/V
52 LET E=.0000005
53 LET L=0
54 LET H=0
56 LET F=0
58 LET X=N
60 FOR J=1 TO N-1
61 LET D=J+1
62 LET Y=N-J
63 LETX=X*Y*R/D
64 LET F=F+X
65 NEXT J
66 IF S<>0 THEN 68
67 LET F=1/R*(1-1/(1+R*(N+F)))
68 LET W=ABS(F-G)
69 IF W<E THEN 94
70 IF S=0 THEN 80
71 IF F>G THEN 76
72 LET L=R
73 LET R=R+(H-L)/2
74 GO TO 56
76 LET H=R
78 LET R=R-(H-L)/2
79 GO TO 56
80 IF F>G THEN 88
82 LET H=R
84 LET R=R-(H-L)/2
86 GO TO 56
88 LET L=R
90 LET R=R+(H-L)/2
92 GO TO 56
94 IF S=0 THEN 97
95 LET V=S/(1+R)↑N
96 GO TO 24
97 LET S=V*(1+R)↑N
98 GO TO 24
99 END
```

```
TYPE IN PYMT,P,INT.RATE,R,NO.YEARS,N,PRES.VALUE,V,SUM,S
478.14,0,20,6219.59,0
PAYMENT       INT.RATE          NO.OF YRS.    PRES.VALUE    SUM
478.14        4.500046E-02      20            6219.59       15000.0038

TYPE IN PYMT,P,INT.RATE,R,NO.YEARS,N,PRES.VALUE,V,SUM,S
850.62,0,13,0,14500
PAYMENT       INT.RATE          NO.OF YRS.    PRES.VALUE    SUM
850.62        4.395052E-02      13            8289.51473    14500

TYPE IN PYMT,P,INT.RATE,R,NO.YEARS,N,PRES.VALUE,V,SUM,S
850,0,15,8560.29,0
PAYMENT       INT.RATE          NO.OF YRS.    PRES.VALUE    SUM
850           5.450132E-02      15            8560.29       18975.5936

TYPE IN PYMT,P,INT.RATE,R,NO.YEARS,N,PRES.VALUE,V,SUM,S
850,0,0,8560.29,18975.59
PAYMENT       INT.RATE          NO.OF YRS.    PRES.VALUE    SUM
850           5.450131E-02      14.9999976    8560.29       18975.59
```

PAGE 145

```
10 PRINT"TYPE IN PYMT,P,INT.RATE,R,NO.YRS.,N,PR.VALUE,V,AND SUM,S"
12 PRINT"PUT ZEROS FOR THOSE YOU WANT TO FIND. ANY 2 CAN BE ZERO"
13 PRINT
14 PRINT
16 INPUT P,R,N,V,S
18 IF R=0 THEN 46
20 LET G=(1+R)↑N
22 IF P=0 THEN 36
24 IF N=0 THEN 28
25 LET V=P*(G-1)/(R*G)
26 LET S=V*G
27 GO TO 91
28 IF V=0 THEN 32
29 LET N=LOG(P/(P-V*R))/LOG(1+R)
30 LET S=V*(1+R)↑N
31 GO TO 91
32 LET N=LOG((R*S+P)/P)/LOG(1+R)
33 LET V=S/(1+R)↑N
34 GO TO 91
36 IF N=0 THEN 42
37 IF V=0 THEN 40
38 LET P=V*R*G/(G-1)
39 GO TO 26
40 LET P=R*S/(G-1)
41 GO TO 33
42 LET N=LOG(S/V)/LOG(1+R)
43 LET P=R*S/((1+R)↑N-1)
44 GO TO 91
46 IF N<>0 THEN 52
48 LET R=P*(1/V-1/S)
49 LET N=LOG(S/V)/LOG(1+R)
50 GO TO 91
52 IF P<>0 THEN 56
53 LET U=1/N*LOG(S/V)
54 LET R=EXP(U)-1
55 GO TO 43
56 IF S=0 THEN 60
57 LET R=2*(S/P-N)/(N*(N-1))
58 LET G=S/P-N
59 GO TO 62
60 LET G=V/P
61 LET R=P/V
62 LET E=.0000005
63 LET L=0
64 LET H=0
65 LET F=0
66 LET X=N
68 FOR J=1 TO N-1
70 LET D=J+1
71 LET Y=N-J
72 LET X=X*Y*R/D
73 LET F=F+X
74 NEXT J
75 IF S<>0 THEN 77
76 LET F=1/R*(1-1/(1+R*(N+F)))
77 LET W=ABS(F-G)
78 IF W<E THEN 89
79 IF S=0 THEN 87
80 IF F>G THEN 84
81 LET L=R
82 LET R=R+(H-L)/2
83 GO TO 65
84 LET H=R
85 LET R=R-(H-L)/2
86 GO TO 65
87 IF F>G THEN 81
88 GO TO 84
89 IF S=0 THEN 30
90 GO TO 33
91 PRINT
92 PRINT"PAYMENTS","INT.RATE","NO.YRS.","PR.VALUE","SUM"
93 PRINT
94 LET P=INT(100*(P+.005))/100
95 LET R=INT(10000*(R+.00005))/10000
96 LET N=INT(100*(N+.005))/100
97 LET V=INT(100*(V+.005))/100
98 LET S=INT(100*(S+.005))/100
99 PRINT P,R,N,V,S
100 GO TO 8
101 END
```

```
TYPE IN PYMT,P,INT.RATE,R,NO.YRS.,N,PR.VALUE,V,AND SUM,S
PUT ZEROS FOR THOSE YOU WANT TO FIND. ANY 2 CAN BE ZERO


0,0,23,965.69,2380.16

PAYMENTS      INT.RATE      NO.YRS.      PR.VALUE      SUM

 65            0.04          23           965.69        2380.16


TYPE IN PYMT,P,INT.RATE,R,NO.YRS.,N,PR.VALUE,V,AND SUM,S
PUT ZEROS FOR THOSE YOU WANT TO FIND. ANY 2 CAN BE ZERO
```

PAGE 146

```
10 DIM T(99)
12 LET N=20
14 MAT T=CON
15 LET S=0
16 LET X=0
18 LET K=0
20 LET K=K+1
22 LET Y=K
24 LET G=5*K*K-1
28 FOR J=0 TO G
30 LET L=INT(100*RND)
32 IF L>=N THEN 30
34 IF T(L)=0 THEN 50
36 LET T(L)=0
40 LET X=X+1
48 LET Y=Y-1
50 NEXT J
51 LET S=S+G+1
52 IF Y<=0 THEN20
54 PRINT
56 PRINT "ACTUAL NO.","CALC. NO.","NO.OF SAMPLES"
58 PRINT
60 PRINT N,X,S
65 LET N=N+20
70 IF N<=100 THEN 14
75 STOP
80 END
```

```
ACTUAL NO.     CALC. NO.     NO.OF SAMPLES

 20             20            150

ACTUAL NO.     CALC. NO.     NO.OF SAMPLES

 40             40            275

ACTUAL NO.     CALC. NO.     NO.OF SAMPLES

 60             60            275

ACTUAL NO.     CALC. NO.     NO.OF SAMPLES

 80             79            455
```

PAGE 147

```
12 PRINT
13 PRINT"TYPE IN SIZE OF MORTGAGE,INTEREST RATE,AND NO.OF YEARS"
14 PRINT
15 INPUT V,R,N
16 PRINT
17 PRINT"PYMT.NO.","PRIN.AT START","INT.PYMT.","PRIN.PYMT.","NEW PRIN"
18 PRINT
19 LET G=(1+R/12)↑(12*N)
20 LET P=(R*V*G)/(G-1)
21 LET P=P/12
22 LET P=INT(100*(P+.005))/100
24 LET H=0
25 LET K=0
26 LET W=0
28 LET P=P+H
29 LET E=V
30 LET A=0
31 LET S=0
32 LET T=0
33 LET A=A+1
34 LET B=E
36 LET C=B*R/12
37 LET C=INT(100*(C+.005))/100
38 LET S=S+C
40 IF B<P THEN 44
41 LET D=P-C
42 LET D=INT(100*(D+.005))/100
43 GO TO 47
44 LET D=B
45 LET W=1
47 LET T=T+D
48 LET E=B-D
49 LET E=INT(100*(E+.005))/100
50 IF H<>0 THEN 62
51 IF A=1 THEN 58
52 IF A<>12*N THEN 57
53 IF E=0 THEN 58
54 LET D=D+E
55 LET T=T+E
56 LET E=0
57 IF A/12<>INT(A/12) THEN 62
58 PRINT
59 PRINT A,B,C,D,E
62 IF W<>0 THEN 68
64 IF A<12*N THEN 33
68 IF H=0 THEN 74
69 LET K=K+H
70 LET X=F-(S+T)
71 LET J=K
72 GO TO 86
74 LET F=S+T
75 LET X=F
76 LET J=V
77 PRINT
78 PRINT
79 PRINT
80 LET Q=INT(10000*R)/100
81 PRINT" ","SUMMARY OF MORTGAGE PAYMENTS"
82 PRINT"MORTGAGE="V"  INT.RATE="Q"  NO.YRS.="N"  PYMT.PER MO.="P
83 PRINT
84 PRINT"MORTGAGE","NO.PYMTS","PRIN.PYMTS.","INT.PYMTS.","TOTAL PYMTS"
85 PRINT
86 PRINT J,A,T,S,X
87 IF H=0 THEN 91
88 LET H=10
89 IF K<100 THEN 26
90 GO TO 12
91 PRINT
92 PRINT
93 PRINT
94 PRINT"SUMMARY OF POSSIBLE SAVINGS BY MAKING EXTRA MONTHLY PAYMENTS"
95 PRINT
96 PRINT"EXTRA PER MO.","NO.PYMTS","PRIN.PYMT.","INT.PYMT.","SAVINGS"
97 PRINT
98 GO TO 88
99 END
```

PAGE 150

```
10 DIM P(5,3)
11 MAT P=ZER
12 FOR J=0 TO 5
14 LET P(J,0)=J+1
16 LET T=0
20 FOR L=1 TO 100
21 LET S=0
22 LET M=0
24 LET R=INT(10*RND(X))
26 IF R>6 THEN 24
28 IF R=0 THEN 24
30 IF R<>6 THEN 34
32 LET S=S+1
34 LET M=M+1
36 IF M<6 THEN 24
38 IF S<>(J+1) THEN 40
39 LET T=T+1
40 NEXT L
42 LET P(J,1)=T
44 LET W=J+1
46 LET C=0
47 LET B=1
48 FOR A=1 TO W
50 LET B=A*B
52 NEXT A
54 LET W=6-W
56 IF C<>0 THEN 62
58 LET C=B
60 GO TO 47
62 LET D=B*C
64 LET P(J,2)=720*5↑(5-J)/(D*46656)
65 LET P(J,2)=INT(100*(P(J,2)+.005))
66 LET P(J,3)=ABS(P(J,1)-P(J,2))
68 NEXT J
70 PRINT
71 PRINT"NO.OF 6'S","IN 100 TRIES","BY RULE","ABS.DIFF."
72 PRINT
73 MAT PRINT P
74 STOP
75 END
```

NO.OF 6'S	IN 100 TRIES	BY RULE	ABS.DIFF.
1	46	40	6
2	23	20	3
3	8	5	3
4	1	1	0
5	1	0	1
6	0	0	0

STOP

SUMMARY OF MORTGAGE PAYMENTS

MORTGAGE= 32000 INT.RATE= 6.75 NO.YRS.= 25 PYMT.PER MO.= 221.09

MORTGAGE	NO.PYMTS	PRIN.PYMTS.	INT.PYMTS.	TOTAL PYMTS
32000	300	32000	34328.03	66328.03

SUMMARY OF POSSIBLE SAVINGS BY MAKING EXTRA MONTHLY PAYMENTS

EXTRA PER MO.	NO.PYMTS	PRIN.PYMT.	INT.PYMT.	SAVINGS
10	270	32000	30177.07	4150.96
20	245	32000	27005.28	7322.75
30	225	32000	24485.77	9842.25999
40	209	32000	22427.18	11900.85
50	195	32000	20708.15	13619.88
60	183	32000	19247.81	15080.22
70	172	32000	17990.08	16337.95
80	163	32000	16893.74	17434.29
90	155	32000	15928.78	18399.25
100	147	32000	15072.53	19255.5

PAGE 152

```
6 LET U=0
7 LET X=0
8 LET Y=0
9 LET Z=0
10 DIM S(29,4)
11 PRINT
12 PRINT"TYPE IN DEBT,SIZE OF BONDS,INT.RATE,AND YRS.TO RETIREMENT"
13 INPUT D,B,R,N
14 PRINT
15 PRINT"YEAR","VALUE","INTEREST","PAYMENT","AMT.RETIRED"
20 MAT S=ZER
24 LET G=1/(1+R)↑N
26 LET P=R*D/(1-G)
28 LET P=INT(100*(P+.005))/100
30 LET K=0
32 LET V=0
34 FOR J=0 TO N-1
36 LET L=J+1
38 LET S(J,K)=L
40 LET S(J,K+1)=D-V
41 LET U=U+S(J,K+1)
42 LET S(J,K+2)=R*S(J,K+1)
43 LET X=X+S(J;K+2)
44 LET H=P-R*S(J,K+1)
46 LET W=H/B
48 LET W=INT(W+.5)
50 LET S(J,K+4)=W*B
51 LET Z=Z+S(J,K+4)
52 LET S(J,K+3)=S(J,K+4)+S(J,K+2)
53 LET Y=Y+S(J,K+3)
54 LET V=V+S(J,K+4)
55 NEXT J
56 IF Z=D THEN 61
57 LET S(N-1,4)=S(N-1,4)+D-Z
58 LET S(N-1,3)=S(N-1,3)+D-Z
59 LET Y=Y+D-Z
60 LET Z=D
61 LET J=0
62 LET K=0
63 IF S(J,0)=0 THEN 69
64 PRINT
65 PRINT S(J,K),S(J,K+1),S(J,K+2),S(J,K+3),S(J,K+4)
66 LET J=J+1
68 GO TO 63
69 PRINT " ","------","------","------","------"
70 PRINT"   TOTALS",U,X,Y,Z
72 GO TO 6
74 END
```

```
TYPE IN DEBT,SIZE OF BONDS,INT.RATE,AND YRS.TO RETIREMENT
100000,1000,.065,10

YEAR          VALUE         INTEREST      PAYMENT       AMT.RETIRED

1             100000        6500          13500         7000

2             93000         6045          14045         8000

3             85000         5525          13525         8000

4             77000         5005          14005         9000

5             68000         4420          13420         9000

6             59000         3835          13835         10000

7             49000         3185          14185         11000

8             38000         2470          13470         11000

9             27000         1755          13755         12000

10            15000         975           15975         15000
              ------        ------        ------        ------
   TOTALS     611000        39715         139715        100000
TYPE IN DEBT,SIZE OF BONDS,INT.RATE,AND YRS.TO RETIREMENT
```

PAGE 154

```
8 DIM D(4),F(9)
9 MAT D=ZER
10 LET D(4)=1
11 LET F(0)=1
12 LET F(1)=1
13 LET F(2)=2
14 LET F(3)=6
15 LET F(4)=24
16 LET F(5)=120
17 LET F(6)=720
18 LET F(7)=5040
19 LET F(8)=40320
20 LET F(9)=362880
21 PRINT"NUMBER IS"," ","SUM OF FACTORIALS OF ITS DIGITS IS"
22 PRINT
24 LET S=D(4)+10*D(3)+100*D(2)+1000*D(1)+10000*D(0)
26 LET S1=0
27 LET W=0
28 FOR J=0 TO 4
29 IF W<>0 THEN 32
30 IF D(J)=0 THEN 38
31 LET W=1
32 LET V=D(J)
33 IF V=9 THEN 50
34 IF V<>8 THEN 36
35 IF S<40000 THEN 50
36 LET S1=S1+F(V)
38 NEXT J
40 IF S<>S1 THEN 50
42 PRINT
44 PRINT S," "," ",S1
50 LET D(4)=D(4)+1
52 FOR J=0 TO 4
54 IF D(J)=0 THEN 64
56 IF D(J)<10 THEN 64
58 LET D(J)=D(J)-10
60 LET D(J-1)=D(J-1)+1
62 GO TO 52
64 NEXT J
66 IF D(0)<5 THEN 24
70 STOP
75 END
```

```
NUMBER IS                             SUM OF FACTORIALS OF ITS DIGITS IS

1                                     1

2                                     2

145                                   145

40585                                 40585
STOP
```

PAGE 155

```
10 DIM M(99,4),L(4)
15 FOR J=0 TO 99
18 READ M(J,0)
20 IF J=0 THEN 30
24 LET M(J-1,1)=M(J-1,0)-M(J,0)
30 NEXT J
32 LET M(99,1)=M(99,0)
40 PRINT"           PEOPLE LIVING AND DYING EACH YEAR OUT OF 1,023,102"
41 PRINT" ","(FROM THE 1941 CSO 2.5% MORTALITY TABLE)"
42 PRINT
43 PRINT" "," "," ","CHANCES OF LIVING TO YEAR:"
44 PRINT"AGE","NO.LIVING","NO.DYING","  2000","  2025"
45 PRINT"---","---------","--------","  ----","  ----"
46 LET A=1
48 LET X=2
50 LET L(0)=A
51 LET L(1)=M(A,0)
52 LET L(2)=M(A,1)
53 IF A+32<=99 THEN 56
54 LET L(3)=0
55 GO TO 58
56 LET G=M(A+32,0)/M(A,0)
57 LET L(3)=INT(100*(G+.005))
58 IF A+57 <=99 THEN 61
59 LET L(4)=0
60 GO TO 63
61 LET G=M(A+57,0)/M(A,0)
62 LET L(4)=INT(100*(G+.005))
63 PRINT
64 PRINT L(0),L(1),L(2),L(3)"/100",L(4)"/100"
65 LET A=A+X
67 IF A<5 THEN 50
69 LET X=5
70 IF A<95 THEN 50
72 LET X=4
74 IF A<100 THEN 50
75 STOP
78 DATA 1023102,1000000,994230,990114,986767
79 DATA 983817,981102,978541,976124,973869
80 DATA 971804,969890,968038,966179,964266
81 DATA 962270,960201,958098,955942,953743
82 DATA 951483,949171,946789,944337,941806
83 DATA 939197,936492,933692,930788,927763
84 DATA 924609,921317,917880,914282,910515
85 DATA 906554,902393,898007,893382,888504
86 DATA 883342,877883,872098,865967,859464
87 DATA 852554,845214,837413,829114,820292
88 DATA 810900,800910,790282,778981,766967
89 DATA 754191,740631,726241,710990,694843
90 DATA 677771,659749,640761,620782,599824
91 DATA 577882,554 75,531133,506403,480850
92 DATA 454548,427593,400112,372240,344136
93 DATA 315982,287973,260322,233251,206989
94 DATA 181765,157799,135297,114440,95378
95 DATA 78221,63086,49838,38593,29215
96 DATA 21577,15514,10833,7327,4787
97 DATA 3011,1818,1005,454,125
99 END
```

PEOPLE LIVING AND DYING EACH YEAR OUT OF 1,023,102
(FROM THE 1941 CSO 2.5% MORTALITY TABLE)

			CHANCES OF LIVING TO YEAR:	
AGE	NO.LIVING	NO.DYING	2000	2025
1	1000000	5770	91/100	71/100
3	990114	3347	92/100	68/100
5	983817	2715	91/100	65/100
10	971804	1914	90/100	55/100
15	962270	2069	87/100	42/100
20	951483	2312	83/100	27/100
25	939197	2705	77/100	14/100
30	924609	3292	69/100	5/100
35	906554	4161	59/100	1/100
40	883342	5459	45/100	0/100
45	852554	7340	31/100	0/100
50	810900	9990	17/100	0/100
55	754191	13560	7/100	0/100
60	677771	18022	2/100	0/100

PAGE 158

```
10 DIM M(99,1),L(8,3)
15 FOR J=0 TO 99
18 READ M(J,0)
20 IF J=0 THEN 30
24 LET M(J-1,1)=M(J-1,0)-M(J,0)
30 NEXT J
32 LET M(99,1)=M(99,0)
34 PRINT
35 PRINT
36 PRINT "TYPE IN YOUR PRESENT AGE IN YEARS"
37 PRINT
38 INPUT A
39 LET D=1970
40 FOR J=0 TO 8
41 LET N=D-1969
42 LET L(J,0)=D
43 LET L(J,2)=D
44 IF(D-1969+A)>99 THEN 53
45 LET D=D+10
47 LET L(J,1)=M(A+N,0)/M(A)
48 LET L(J,1)=INT(100*(L(J,1)+.005))
49 IF L(J,1)<=99 THEN 52
50 LET L(J,1)=99
51 GO TO 54
52 IF L(J,1)>=1 THEN 54
53 LET L(J,1)=1
54 LET L(J,3)=100-L(J,1)
55 NEXT J
56 PRINT
57 PRINT" ","YOUR CHANCES OF LIVING","YOUR CHANCES OF DYING"
58 PRINT" ","UNTIL","ARE","BEFORE","ARE"
59 PRINT" ","------","------","------","------"
60 FOR J=0 TO 8
62 PRINT
64 PRINT" ",L(J,0),L(J,1)"/100",L(J,2),L(J,3)"/100"
65 IF L(J,1)=1 THEN 34
66 NEXT J
70 GO TO 34
78 DATA 1023102,1000000,994230,990114,986767
79 DATA 983817,981102,978541,976124,973869
80 DATA 971804,969890,968038,966179,964266
81 DATA 962270,960201,958098,955942,953743
82 DATA 951483,949171,946789,944337,941806
83 DATA 939197,936492,933692,930788,927763
84 DATA 924609,921317,917880,914282,910515
85 DATA 906554,902393,898007,893382,888504
86 DATA 883342,877883,872098,865967,859464
87 DATA 852554,845214,837413,829114,820292
88 DATA 810900,800910,790282,778981,766967
89 DATA 754191,740631,726241,710990,694843
90 DATA 677771,659749,640761,620782,599824
91 DATA 577882,554975,531133,506403,480850
92 DATA 454548,427593,400112,372240,344136
93 DATA 315982,287973,260322,233251,206989
94 DATA 181765,157799,135297,114440,95378
95 DATA 78221,63036,49838,38593,29215
96 DATA 21577,15514,10833,7327,4787
97 DATA 3011,1818,1005,454,125
99 END
```

```
TYPE IN YOUR PRESENT AGE IN YEARS

26

              YOUR CHANCES OF LIVING        YOUR CHANCES OF DYING
              UNTIL          ARE            BEFORE         ARE
              ------         ------         ------         ------

              1970           99/100         1970           1/100

              1980           95/100         1980           5/100

              1990           89/100         1990           11/100

              2000           76/100         2000           24/100

              2010           54/100         2010           46/100

              2020           25/100         2020           75/100

              2030           4/100          2030           96/100

              2040           1/100          2040           99/100


TYPE IN YOUR PRESENT AGE IN YEARS
```

PAGE 160

```
10 DIM C(104)
12 MAT C=ZER
13 LET J=0
14 PRINT
15 PRINT"THIS PROGRAM FINDS THE MEAN AND MEDIAN OF UP TO 100 SCORES"
16 PRINT"YOU CAN ENTER ANY NUMBER OF SCORES UP TO 100"
17 PRINT
18 LET X=0
19 LET N=0
20 PRINT
22 PRINT"TYPE IN 5 SCORES PER LINE SEPARATED BY COMMAS. AFTER THE"
23 PRINT"LAST SCORE,TYPE 9999 AND FILL OUT REST OF LINE WITH ZEROS"
24 INPUT C(J),C(J+1),C(J+2),C(J+3),C(J+4)
26 FOR J=X TO X+4
28 IF C(J)=9999 THEN 40
30 LET N=N+1
31 NEXT J
32 LET X=X+5
33 LET J=X
34 PRINT
35 PRINT"O.K. PUT IN 5 MORE"
36 GO TO 24
40 LET A=INT(N/5)
41 LET C(J)=0
42 LET B=N-5*A
43 LET V=5*A
46 LET M=0
48 FOR J=0 TO N-1
50 IF C(J)>=C(J+1) THEN 58
52 LET L=C(J)
53 LET C(J)=C(J+1)
54 LET C(J+1)=L
55 GO TO 46
58 LET M=M+C(J)
60 NEXT J
62 LET G=(N+1)/2
64 LET W=INT(G)
66 IF W=G THEN 72
68 LET M1=(C(W)+C(W-1))/2
70 GO TO 74
72 LET M1=C(W-1)
74 LET M=M/N
75 PRINT
76 PRINT
77 PRINT"THE SCORES USED IN THIS PROBLEM ARE AS FOLLOWS:"
78 PRINT
79 FOR J=0 TO V-1 STEP 5
80 PRINT C(J),C(J+1),C(J+2),C(J+3),C(J+4)
81 PRINT
82 NEXT J
83 IF B=0 THEN 92
84 GO TO(85,87,89,91)B
85 PRINT C(V)
86 GO TO 92
87 PRINT C(V),C(V+1)
88 GO TO 92
89 PRINT C(V),C(V+1),C(V+2)
90 GO TO 92
91 PRINT C(V),C(V+1),C(V+2),C(V+3)
92 PRINT
93 PRINT
94 PRINT"NO.OF SCORES","THE MEAN IS","THE MEDIAN IS"
95 PRINT
96 PRINT N,M,M1
97 STOP
98 END
```

```
THIS PROGRAM FINDS THE MEAN AND MEDIAN OF UP TO 100 SCORES
YOU CAN ENTER ANY NUMBER OF SCORES UP TO 100

TYPE IN 5 SCORES PER LINE SEPARATED BY COMMAS. AFTER THE
LAST SCORE,TYPE 9999 AND FILL OUT REST OF LINE WITH ZEROS
34,67,53,98,112

O.K. PUT IN 5 MORE
98.6,345,112.67,77,80

O.K. PUT IN 5 MORE
718.567,345.96,987.77,2,55.888

O.K. PUT IN 5 MORE
6.79,566,9999,0,0

THE SCORES USED IN THIS PROBLEM ARE AS FOLLOWS:

987.77         718.567        566            345.96         345

112.67         112            98.6           98             80

77             67             55.888         53             34

6.79           2

NO.OF SCORES   THE MEAN IS    THE MEDIAN IS

17             221.190882     98
```

PAGE 161

```
10 DIM D(99,3)
11 LET N=0
12 MAT D=ZER
14 PRINT"THIS PROGRAM FINDS Z SCORES AND PERCENTILE RANKS"
15 PRINT"OF UP TO 100 SCORES"
16 PRINT
17 PRINT"TYPE IN 1 STUDENT NUMBER AND SCORE SEPARATED BY A COMMA"
18 PRINT"AFTER THE LAST SCORE, TYPE THE LINE: 9999,9999"
19 PRINT
20 PRINT
22 LET V=0
24 LET W=0
28 FOR J=0 TO 99
32 INPUT D(J,0),D(J,1)
36 IF D(J,0)=9999 THEN 47
38 LET N=N+1
40 LET V=V+D(J,1)
42 LET W=W+D(J,1)*D(J,1)
44 NEXT J
45 GO TO 50
47 LET D(J,0)=0
48 LET D(J,1)=0
50 LET M=V/N
52 LET S=SQR(N*W-V*V)/N
53 PRINT
54 PRINT"NO. OF SCORES IS "N" AVER.SCORE IS "M" AND SIGMAS IS "S
55 PRINT
58 FOR J=0 TO N-1
60 LET D(J,2)=(D(J,1)-M)/S
61 LET D(J,2)=INT(1000*(D(J,2)+.0005))/1000
62 LET X=D(J,2)
64 LET G=X-X↑3/6+X↑5/40-X↑7/336+X↑9/3456-X↑11/42240
66 LET D(J,3)=G/SQR(2*3.14159)
68 LET D(J,3)=INT(1000*(D(J,3)+.0005))/10 + 50
70 NEXT J
72 PRINT
73 PRINT"STUDENT NO.","RAW SCORE","Z SCORE","% ILE RANK"
75 FOR J=0 TO 99
76 IF D(J,0)=0 THEN 82
77 PRINT
78 PRINT D(J,0),D(J,1),D(J,2),D(J,3)
80 NEXT J
82 STOP
85 END
```

```
NO. OF SCORES IS  30 AVER.SCORE IS  63.7 AND SIGMAS IS  15.3712936
```

STUDENT NO.	RAW SCORE	Z SCORE	% ILE RANK
1	34	-1.931	3.1
2	56	-0.5	31
3	67	0.215	58.5
4	42	-1.411	8
5	87	1.516	93.5
6	78	0.93	82.4
7	65	0.085	53.4
8	63	-0.045	48.3
9	46	-1.15	12.6
10	77	0.865	80.6
11	89	1.646	95
12	50	-0.89	18.8
13	45	-1.216	11.3
14	75	0.735	76.9
15	62	-0.11	45.7
16	61	-0.175	43.2
17	64	0.02	50.8
18	70	0.41	65.9
19	74	0.67	74.9
20	79	0.995	84

PAGE 165

```
10 DIM C(99,2),L(4)
11 LET N=0
12 MAT C=ZER
13 MAT L=ZER
15 PRINT"THIS PROGRAM FINDS THE PEARSON LINEAR CORRELATION,R,BETWEEN"
16 PRINT"TWO SETS OF SCORES-X SCORES AND Y SCORES-FOR UP TO 100 SETS"
17 PRINT
18 PRINT
19 PRINT"TYPE IN STUDENT NUMBER FOLLOWED BY TWO SCORES. SEPARATE"
20 PRINT"THE THREE BY COMMAS. AFTER LAST ENTRY,TYPE: 9999,0,0"
21 PRINT"IF YOU GOOF ON AN ENTRY,ENTER IT ANYWAY, SINCE YOU CAN"
22 PRINT"MAKE CORRECTIONS AFTER THE LAST LINE HAS BEEN TYPED IN"
23 PRINT
24 FOR J=0 TO 99
26 INPUT C(J,0),C(J,1),C(J,2)
28 IF C(J,0)= 9999 THEN 34
29 LET N=N+1
30 NEXT J
32 GO TO 36
34 LET C(J,0)=0
35 PRINT
36 PRINT"TO CORRECT A PREVIOUS INPUT LINE,TYPE: LINE NUMBER, THEN"
37 PRINT"THE THREE CORRECT INPUTS. IF YOU MADE NO ERRORS, OR AFTER"
38 PRINT"YOU HAVE ENTERED THE LAST CORRECTION,TYPE IN 5555,0,0,0"
39 PRINT
40 INPUT A,B,C,D
42 IF A=5555 THEN 48
44 LET C(A-1,0)=B
45 LET C(A-1,1)=C
46 LET C(A-1,2)=D
47 GO TO 40
48 PRINT
49 PRINT
50 PRINT"STUDENT NO.","X SCORES","Y SCORES"
51 PRINT
52 FOR J=0 TO N-1
54 LET L(0)=L(0)+C(J,1)
55 LET L(1)=L(1)+C(J,2)
56 LET L(2)=L(2)+C(J,1)*C(J,2)
57 LET L(3)=L(3)+C(J,1)*C(J,1)
58 LET L(4)=L(4)+C(J,2)*C(J,2)
60 PRINT C(J,0),C(J,1),C(J,2)
62 NEXT J
64 PRINT" ","--------","--------"
65 PRINT"TOTALS",L(0),L(1)
66 PRINT
67 PRINT
68 PRINT
70 PRINT"NO.OF SCORES","AVER.OF X'S","AVER.OF Y'S","SIGMA X","SIGMA Y"
72 LET S1=SQR(N*L(3)-L(0)*L(0))/N
73 LET T1=INT(100*(S1+.005))/100
75 LET S2=SQR(N*L(4)-L(1)*L(1))/N
76 LET T2=INT(100*(S2+.005))/100
78 LET M1=INT(100*(L(0)/N+.005))/100
80 LET M2=INT(100*(L(1)/N+.005))/100
82 PRINT
83 PRINT N,M1,M2,T1,T2
85 LET R=(N*L(2)-L(0)*L(1))/(N*N*S1*S2)
87 LET R=INT(100*(R+.005))/100
88 PRINT
89 PRINT
90 PRINT"CORRELATION,R,BETWEEN X AND Y SCORES IS "R
92 PRINT
95 STOP
99 END
```

```
THIS PROGRAM FINDS THE PEARSON LINEAR CORRELATION,R,BETWEEN
TWO SETS OF SCORES-X SCORES AND Y SCORES-FOR UP TO 100 SETS
TYPE IN STUDENT NUMBER FOLLOWED BY TWO SCORES. SEPARATE
THE THREE BY COMMAS. AFTER LAST ENTRY,TYPE: 9999,0,0
IF YOU GOOF ON AN ENTRY,ENTER IT ANYWAY, SINCE YOU CAN
MAKE CORRECTIONS AFTER THE LAST LINE HAS BEEN TYPED IN

1331,35,67     1351,88,75
1332,46,75     1352,64,69
1333,55,85     1353,58,45
1334,64,82     1354,71,52
1335,58,92     1355,46,65
1336,62,53     9999,0,0
1337,75,83
1338,85,90
1339,87,71
1340,44,76
1341,72,65
1342,83,73
1343,47,74
1344,84,96
1345,49,82
1346,58,76
1347,63,57
1348,80,93
1349,57,76
1350,56,66

TO CORRECT A PREVIOUS INPUT LINE,TYPE: LINE NUMBER, THEN
THE THREE CORRECT INPUTS. IF YOU MADE NO ERRORS, OR AFTER
YOU HAVE ENTERED THE LAST CORRECTION,TYPE IN 5555,0,0,0
5555,0,0,0

STUDENT NO.   X SCORES   Y SCORES

1331          35         67
1332          46         75
1333          55         85
1334          64         82
1335          58         92
1336          62         53
1337          75         83
1338          85         90
1339          87         71
1340          44         76
1341          72         65
1342          83         73
1343          47         74
1344          84         96
1345          49         82
1346          58         76
1347          63         57
1348          80         93
1349          57         76
1350          56         66
1351          88         75
1352          64         69
1353          58         45
1354          71         52
1355          46         65
              --------   --------
TOTALS        1587       1838

NO.OF SCORES   AVER.OF X'S   AVER.OF Y'S   SIGMA X   SIGMA Y

25             63.48         73.52         14.83     12.85

CORRELATION,R,BETWEEN X AND Y SCORES IS  0.24
```